The Eternal Bliss Machine

The Eternal Bliss Machine

America's Way of Wedding

by

Marcia Seligson

WILLIAM MORROW & COMPANY, INC.
New York   1973

Seligson, Marcia.
    The eternal bliss machine.

    1. Marriage customs and rites—United States.
I. Title.
GT2703.S44   392'.5'0973   72-126
ISBN 0-688-00158-0
2 3 4 5 77 76 75 74 73

This is for my father

Acknowledgments

My eternally blissful thanks—for their devotion, support, sanity, laughter and love—to Nancy Hardin, Judy and Abe Ginnes, Tom Pollock, Avery and Judy Corman, Danny Goldman, Don Congdon, Judith and Mort Gerberg, Marc Jaffe, Sherry Arden and Larry Hughes.

Most of all, to my heaven-sent editor and friend, without whose unflagging genius and $30,000 wedding I'd still be in the chorus line—Joni Evans.

Contents

Introduction

I first discovered that there is something hilarious about weddings when I was a bridesmaid at Dee Dee Epstein's, during the summer of my nineteenth year. She was the first of our crowd to get married and it was my debut as a bridesmaid, so excitement ran absolutely amuck for months and months prior to the Big Day. (So, I should add, did jealousy and hatred for our bosom pal Dee Dee, who was not only getting married and being unspeakably smug about it but was also having a colossal super-extravaganza circus of a wedding—The Dream of Dreams.)

I have never forgotten one moment of Dee Dee's wedding, and its indelible imprint on my brain is probably the single factor responsible for this book. It took place at an ocean-front beach club on Long Island, near the surburban town where I grew up. A vulgar nook, it had somehow succeeded in convincing the world that, by virtue of its six (yes, six) swimming pools, it was the apex of CLASS. What I remember most vividly about the El Patio Beach Club is that no matter how far out into the ocean you swam, you could always hear cha-cha music. It was the perfect spot for Dee Dee's wedding.

Five hundred revelers crammed the El Patio that hot Sunday in June. Upon entering, each had been handed a newspaper entitled *The Epstein-Horowitz Gazette*—a ten-page printed journal recounting the lives of Dee Dee Epstein and Malcolm Horowitz, our groom. Malcolm's first twenty years—which, as I recall, did not make the spiciest of biographies—included an adorable shot taken at his bar mitzvah and a laudatory quote from his high school Spanish teacher; about our bride we learned that there were those who believed she would become a renowned concert pianist—up until the age of sixteen, when she got sick of having no fingernails and gave up the whole thing.

The climax of the bacchanal was the arrival of the wedding cake—a fourteen-foot mountain of stark white goo. Against the cake was placed a ladder which Dee Dee daintily climbed, brandishing a long silver knife. At the peak, she dramatically slashed into the sugar hulk, thereby releasing a battalion of anxiety-ridden white doves.

Six months later Phyllis Nussbaum (who was marrying Harvey Cohen) successfully one-upped Dee Dee—with an eight-foot-long replica of a cruise ship made out of chopped liver, green olives for the portholes and pimientos spread along the bow spelling out *S.S. Cohen.* Then, before the ten-course dinner, we gathered to watch home movies of the couple's respective childhoods, complete with chubby eleven-year-old Phyllis (she dieted herself to sylphdom before her wedding, regained every ounce plus instantaneously thereafter) doing the fabulous J-stroke that won her the All-Round Canoeing medal at Camp Evergreen Acres.

Because of my own background, I believed—prior to writing this book—that only Jewish weddings were funny and grotesque and wildly absurd. But in the last two years I've traveled all over this country and attended 45,000 weddings (or so it seems), and clearly I was wrong. Whatever it is about weddings that makes people go a little bananas—construct ships out of chopped liver or dye mashed potatoes pink to match the bridesmaids' dresses—it transcends ethnic division and crosses state lines.

Being a reporter at a wedding is a little like being a reporter at an orgy—you don't know quite where you fit in.

Sometimes, depending on the ambiance and my own zest, I would participate—drink champagne, mambo with grand-daddy, glut myself on the goodies. At other times I remained A Reporter—cordial, questioning, slightly aloof and probably rather menacing. Occasionally I felt moved, frequently I found myself giggling and sometimes I was repelled.

All to be expected, I guess. The only emotional response that truly surprised me about myself happened while I was standing in the rain on the White House grounds watching little Tricia march down the aisle on the arm of her beaming father, and suddenly, astoundingly, I felt a small tear form in the eye. But that's the thing about weddings. They're very tricky.

The Eternal Bliss Machine

1. The American Way

The wedding, they say, is a dodo bird. Extinct.

They say that America's children are abandoning established American values with the speed and ferocity of a cat bolting from the garden hose. Marriage, we are told, is in its terminal stages, gasping for its dying breath as the new breed of youth shuns wedlock for cohabiting, or one-to-oneness for the communal clan. Those few who are still choosing to get married, everybody insists, are certainly not doing it the way their parents or even older sisters and brothers did—that is, in the traditional, conventional fashion of flowing white lace, "Oh, Promise Me" and a week in Bermuda. Garish, extravagant wingdings of the doves-soaring-from-cakes school are dead; bridal showers, engagement diamonds, trousseaus, a frippery of the past; the "Dearly-beloved-we-are-gathered-together" litany, meaningless, obsolete. That's what everybody says about weddings in America.

They are dead wrong.

Consider these facts:

> ——In 1971, there were 2,196,000 marriages in America, 648,000 more than in 1961. In those ten years the steady increase paralleled the population growth, that is, 1 percent of the population got married every year.
>
> ——Seven out of eight first-time couples are married in a church or synagogue.

——Seven out of eight first-time brides receive an engagement ring.

——In 1971, 80 percent of all first-time weddings were formal; in 1967, that figure was 73 percent.

——In 1971, 96 percent of marrying couples held a reception; in 1967, 85 percent.

——84.5 percent of first-time brides wear a formal bridal gown.

——The wedding industry represents $7 billion a year to the American economy.

Said "wedding industry"—that is, those products and services involved with the first marriage itself and with the formation of a new family household—boasts a staggering bank of statistics to prove its glowing health. Two billion dollars last year spent on wedding receptions; 40 percent of the total jewelry industry; $1 out of every $8 spent on home furnishings and appliances, $640,000,000 in honeymoon travel—all are being joyously shelled out by America's youth. We have come to believe that *most* of this youth now embraces a substantial chunk of counter-culture ideology beginning with hair and ending with rejection of the classic American dreams. We've known that they are avid consumers (not yet immune to that invincible strain of national virus), but we thought their purchases confined to rock albums and marijuana. We would assume—if the rumors be true about youthful shunning of the acquisitiveness of their elders—that if and when married they would build their own furniture or do the orange-crate routine. We are, then, startled to learn that 84 percent of all American newlyweds begin their life together as the proud owners of a basic set of establishment fine china dinnerware. That is, incidentally, 17 percent more than ten years ago.

Making generalizations about American youth has of late become a thorny dilemma. Woodstock makes headlines, as do campus demonstrations, marijuana busts, freaky outfits,

Mick Jagger and the wedding on a Big Sur cliff where the bride and groom arrived on horseback—nude—and all the guests peeled off their jeans and tie-dyed shirts in a whooping tribal celebratory dance. One makes vast assumptions based on *Time* magazine covers and the seven o'clock news, but the question always remains: How many? How many kids are dropping out, dropping acid, dropping their drawers at their weddings? Many, many fewer, I believe, than we think.

Hair, not too many years ago, was considered an apt yardstick for measuring a stranger; you knew a guy's politics by its length. But our culture has a way of absorbing external aberrations without a ripple disturbing the fabric, and now one can attend a Rotary Club convention and be hand-shook to death by hirsute hail-fellows. Clothes, too, no longer peg the man, as our Hollywood moguls and sky-blue-blooded aristocrats today parade about town in hand-sewn couturier dungarees. And scruffy rock stars drive gleaming Bentleys. So where are we, who's who and what's really going on "Out There"?

Occasional whiffs of evidence surface to countermand the headlines. A Louis Harris poll of American high school and college students in *Life* last year unearthed some surprising opinions from youth—surprising in their "straightness" for a generation that is often presumed to be spending much of its waking life prone. "Is it perfectly all right to enjoy sex for its own sake?" posed one question. Forty-four percent of college kids said "No." "Should any girl who wants an abortion be allowed to have one?" "No" from 45 percent. One-half replied "No" to the question, "Will sexual experience before marriage contribute to happiness later?" And— what to me seemed the most astonishing revelation—52 percent of the respondents answered "Yes" to "Do young men still consider virginity until marriage important in a woman?"

Along the same lines, *Playboy* conducted a college survey

in 1971 and discovered that 44 percent of the women questioned were virgins.

That is not to say that *nothing* has changed; it is, rather, a claim that the transformations in lifestyle and values among America's youth are not yet as widespread or as dramatic as one frequently assumes. It is also a claim that, whatever shifts and transfigurations and somersaults *are* occurring in this country, whatever fortresses may be crumbling or future shocks rumbling through the land's crust, there is at least one stronghold in which tradition will rule —almost, statistically, every time. The American Way of Wedding.

The fact is that we Americans are getting married almost precisely as we did a hundred years ago. We are adorning ourselves in long white romantic gowns, going to church or a hotel or country club, repeating established vows that we have heard at other folks' weddings for years, sipping champagne, cutting cake, dancing, tossing the bouquet, posing for pictures, fleeing through a shower of rice as we head for our Caribbean honeymoon—repeating, that is, all the clichés. We have invariably spent more than we can afford and we will certainly tell ourselves it was the most beautiful wedding in history. Although there is no such thing as "the typical American wedding"—as many styles of weddings exist as the styles of citizens giving them—every single one possesses the same ritualistic ingredients, the same replay of ancient custom and primeval symbolism, the same predictable plot and standard players. A wedding is, after all, a wedding.

But that very fact—the suspenseless, every-wedding-is-just-like-every-other-wedding truth—bespeaks some fundamental human need. A minister in Atlanta says: "People simply *crave* weddings—the guests as well as the families. Although they are all the same, in a sense, they are all profoundly different, and somehow crucial to us."

Like a newborn baby. We automatically find it irresistible and unique despite its resemblance to all the babies surrounding it. Babies and weddings both seem to tap in us a wellspring of emotion that is as ever-present as it is indefinable and ultimately mysterious. Both are, surely, metaphors for the beginning of new life, emblems of perpetual hope and continuity. In the case of a wedding, all connections to reality are suspended as the radiant bride floats down the flower-decked aisle and we feel ourselves choke up (by my informal tally, 80 percent of all wedding guests choke up). It simply does not matter who she is, whether we know her well or even like her much. Our knowledge of the perils of marriage, the zooming divorce rate, the possibilities of emotional bloodbath—none of it has any place at a wedding. The wedding is wired in to other needs that are monumental and timeless.

One of those innate psychic hungers is for ritual—prescribed and repeated systems of observance, "a sense of formal, sanctified public ceremonial" (as defined in an essay in *Time* magazine). Boy Scout parades are rituals, as are political conventions, Christmas cards, football games, funerals. (Even, in some circles, orgies.) Ritual provides our lives with a point of stability, an equilibrium and consistency, a bridge with the past. A family that says grace every single night before beginning the meal is expressing, in that act, not only their religious sentiments but a reassurance of the regularity of family life. Institutionalized validation.

"Rituals are society's unwritten permission for civilized man to express primitive emotions: fear, sexuality, grief," continues *Time*. They invite people "to be more human in public—more themselves—than they dare to be in private." We carry on, ritualistically, like distempered puppies on New Year's Eve and dance like Zorba the Greek at weddings. And we mark the flow of time with rituals: national holidays, of course, but then, as the author of *Future Shock* points out, there is "the opening of Congress every January; the appearance of new car models in the fall; seasonal variations in fashion; the April 15 deadline for filing income tax."

As American life gets more fragmented, our drive to

create new ceremonial observances and to strengthen the old becomes heightened. Especially fierce is our hookup to the most primitive of all rituals—the rites of passage.

Every culture, in every time throughout history, has commemorated the transition of a human being from one state in life to another. Birth, the emergence into manhood, graduation from school at various levels, birthdays, marriage, death—each of these outstanding steps is acknowledged by a ceremony of some sort, always public, the guests in effect becoming witnesses to the statement of life's ongoingness, of the natural order of history. To insure the special significance of the rite of passage, its apartness from any other event of the day, these rituals usually require pageantry, costumed adornment, and are accompanied by gift-bearing and feasting. We wear black to funerals, bring presents to christenings and birthday parties, get loaded at wakes, eat ourselves sick at bar mitzvahs. Birth, marriage and death, to be sure, are the most elemental and major steps, and as there is only one of those ritual commemorations for which we are *actually*, fully present, the wedding becomes, for mankind, its most vital rite of passage. And for this reason it is anchored at the very core of civilization.

For the rites of passage the ceremony itself is organic to the society for which the individual is being groomed, in his journey from one state to the next. In African hunting societies, for example, a boy at puberty is thrown naked into the jungle and required to kill a lion. His value as a man will be judged by how successful he can be in meeting the demands of his culture. In America, newlyweds are being prepared for their roles in a consumer society, so it is surely appropriate that all of the dynamics of wedding hoo-hah testify to these commercial, mercantile terms. Gifts are purchased not only by the "witnesses" but by bride for groom, groom for bride, bride for attendants, attendants for bride. Prenuptial parties, bachelor dinners, showers. The ever-mushrooming splash and flash circusness of the wedding itself. The American wedding is a ritual event of ferocious, gluttonous consuming, a debauch of intensified buying, never again to be repeated in the life of an American couple.

And it is, historically, a public, not private, event. "The wedding is a doorway to new status. It is the announcement of a new relationship between two persons, a relationship in which society, as well as the two individuals themselves, is interested," writes the author of *Marriage for Moderns*. Society's interest exists to protect established moral standards, to legitimize children and to safeguard property rights, and "for this reason there are a ceremony, records, a public expression of willingness on the part of the couple, witnesses, sanction of the state and frequently of the church. . . ." The church, they say, is interested in weddings because God apparently is in favor of marriage.

What, then, does it all mean to the individuals concerned —the girl, the boy and the families? To ask this question of the people involved, folks who are dedicating more money, time, energy and emotion to this one day, indeed these few hours, than to any previous or future activity in their lives— is to receive a series of answers that are but variations on the same theme: THE WEDDING IS THE MOST IMPORTANT DAY IN LIFE.

—"The most beautiful thing about my wedding was the look on my dad's face. He felt this was the height of achievement of his whole life."

—"I had always dreamed about being a beautiful bride for as long as I could remember. I just loved every single minute of it, and even though it was ridiculously expensive and there were months of aggravation, I would go through it again in a minute."

—"It will give me something perfect to look back on for my whole life."

—"I eloped, and I made myself a promise that my daughter would have a lavish, absolutely gorgeous wedding. I planned it from the day she was born."

Life's One Perfect Day, The Ultimate Moment, The Fulfillment of Dreams, The Measure of Achievement. Very heavy baggage, it would seem, to carry to a wingding with a little booze, a couple of deviled eggs, a white dress and a rumba or two. But that in no way is what the wedding embodies for the participants.

To the bride's family, those who actually create the wedding, it becomes a symbol of the fulfillment of their roles as parents. Mama, the nurturer, devotes her life toward preparing her daughter to follow in her footsteps—wifehood, motherhood. On the wedding day the proof is right out front that she has succeeded in her big job. A classic illustration of maternal power is the California woman who was so thrilled with her daughter's sweet-sixteen party at the posh Bel-Air Hotel that, right then and there, she made a reservation for five years hence—the girl's twenty-first birthday—for her wedding. Those five years were spent making certain it all came about as programmed. Sure enough. . . .

Daddy, too, has satisfied *his* ordained role as the provider by being able to splurge on such a splendid razzle-dazzle. And the heroine of this family drama, the bride, is exhibiting to the world that she turned out all right, was transformed overnight from frog to princess, from flawed adolescent to flawless woman, and now she's doing what she's supposed to do. Everybody fulfills his destiny at The Wedding.

The American family assumes its responsibility for certain steps in the evolution of its child. It will provide her with toys, clothing, piano lessons if she has a wink of talent, braces if her teeth so demand, summer camp, as much education as she can absorb. The final and climactic of her birthrights is the wedding. It is the grand, required send-off gift; after that she's on somebody else's shoulders. (The most touching moment of any wedding is when Daddy dances with his daughter in a sort of oedipal instant replay.) But she should never forget she had such swell parents who gave her this magic day; and they should always remember how they did right by little Nell.

According to Barbara Donovan, the editor of *Bride's Magazine*, "The American girl is married long before she is even in high school. Her images of her wedding day begin when she's *practically* an infant." As evidence, take The Bride Game—a board game like Monopoly or Sorry, but this highly popular item is for girls aged eight to fourteen. On the box is a picture of a bride decked out in long white veil, bouquet—except she looks to be about eleven years old. "The object of the game," asserts the instructions, "is to be the first girl to get her complete matching wedding party along with the necessary accessories for the wedding ceremony." She gets wedding cake cards, bridal bouquet cards, ring cards, something-old-something-new cards, and she moves with dice rolls from bridal salon to pastry shop to jewelry store—to the aisle. The winner of The Bride Game is the first tot to reach the spot marked "Ceremony." Eight years old and she already *knows,* by God, that she must acquire her diamond and her garter and all her THINGS before she can get to the altar. She also knows that *she* is the superstar of the wedding, the sole subject of all the attention and adoration. There is not, in The Bride Game, a solitary man, nary a mention of the groom.

Ladies in ancient Greece computed their age from the day of their marriage, not from birth. Our view of the wedding day as the true beginning of a woman's existence is only slightly more insidious. About two years after I graduated from college, I visited a school pal in her New York bachelor-girl's apartment, which she shared with two other young single women. There was scarcely a stick of furniture, not a painting or plant to perk up the barrenness. I asked her why and she replied: "Oh, I'm not going to fix up an apartment until my *REAL* life!" I knew immediately what she meant and I never forgot the remark. Nor what it revealed about how women experience their lives, what they diminish in importance, what they exalt.

It's the old Cinderella mythology. While little boys are dreaming heroic dreams of conquering worlds, little girls are yearning for transformation—becoming beautiful, becoming a woman, becoming a mommy. As marriage is the single event which will presumably guarantee that metamorphosis, it is, naturally, the day for which her entire life has been in preparation. She is, today, the fairy princess, queen for a day, Eliza Doolittle at the ball, Miss America floating down the ramp, becrowned and ethereal. For a man, marriage is but a continuation of growth and change; for her it is the *REAL* beginning. The prince is, classically, passive and fairly indifferent toward an occasion that does not represent to him what it does to his lady; he goes through with it because she wants it, the families want it, society wants it, and it is payment of his last dues as a "child."

"A man looks pretty small at a wedding, George," says a character in *Our Town.* "All those good women standing shoulder to shoulder, making sure that the knot's tied in a mighty public way." The groom is cut out of the maneuvers of the wedding game, just as is the bride's father whose traditional role is to pay the bills and get wistfully drunk. The groom, as it turns out, does not even partake in the processional to the altar, but sort of sneaks in, inconspicuously, through a side door and is—somehow—just THERE.

The industry both causes and mirrors the insignificance of the male. Where, for instance, is *Modern Groom Magazine?* The bridal apparel industry (how come no "groomal apparel" industry?) has special corporations for bridesmaids' garb, mother-of-the-bride dresses, even flower girl doodads. The men—even though there are as many male attendants as female—must rent, borrow, steal their outfits—who cares anyway, who even notices them? Their job is basically to escort the women, to be appendages to the princess and her ladies-in-waiting.

The American Way of Wedding is a glaring reflection of the American way of life. Primarily, it is a metaphor for our two paramount, lifelong concerns as a people—Love and Money.

Does anybody doubt the immeasurable strain of romanticism lurking in the American head? It tends to lie dormant;

we hardly realize—in the steely face of our computer technology—what marshmallows we are in our souls. But then,
periodically, we are confronted with cultural phenomena
the message of which is undisguised and unavoidable. Rod
McKuen, the crown-prince mush huckster of all time, sells
seven million books of poetry, even more record albums,
standing-room-only concerts, and all that he's hawking is
loneliness and misery and MUSH. Erich Segal pens an éclair
about wondrous love and exquisite dying and never once in
your life having to say you're sorry, and lo and behold . . .
one of the hugest-selling books, biggest-grossing movies in
history. And then there is that Seagull, Jonathan Livingston.
Lurking right behind the computer is the worship of the
Hallmark Card, the adoration of the soap opera, the glorifi-
cation of The Wedding.

"Oh, to be a June Bride. You've dreamed of it since you
were a little girl. You've seen yourself wrapped in clouds
of white gliding up a rose-strewn aisle toward an altar bathed
in summer sunlight." This molasses from an old issue of
a bridal magazine says it all. The American wedding is
nothing if not profoundly romantic, pure magical fantasy.
And, whatever the simplicity or exorbitance—it is theater.
A dramatic ritual of romance in which the same "plot" is
enacted each and every time, the same "characters" in their
inevitable "costumes" appear and only the "sets" change,
depending on the style of the pageant. It can be a musical
comedy, a Wagnerian opera, a rodeo, or a carnival or a
vaudeville or burlesque. The same elements emerge. The
rehearsal, in which everybody practices his defined role (let's
see: now the bride hands her bouquet to the maid of honor
to hold; now the maid of honor lifts the bride's veil; now she
switches the bride's train around while the couple kisses).
The "director" arranges the elaborate staging, insists on the
split-second timing and the impeccable coordination of detail.
Star, costars (Mama is the second lead and on occasion has
been known to attempt the old upstaging routine on her
precious offspring) and bit players. Opening night, stage

fright and an audience. The unfolding and outcome are, as we've said, without suspense, but, on the other hand, so is *Gone with the Wind* the fourteenth time you've seen it and still Rhett's final exit evokes from us the same teary sentimental response every single time. And the wedding quells the same hunger as all theater—it spirits us away from daily life with its banalities and drabness and downright reality for one golden, unblemished moment in time.

In order to perpetuate our romantic passion for love and weddings, the industry has solely dedicated itself to the first-time bride. Although 25 percent of our marriages consist of people making their second or third trips, they are utterly ignored by the forces of the bridal business. In part, the dismissal is realistic—old hands tend not to throw immense wedding spectaculars or purchase entirely brand-new rigs of furniture. But what concerns us here is illusion, not reality. The bride-figure can feed our *Love Story* fevers only by her symbolic innocence, her non-tarnishment, her utterly pure belief in the perfection of love and marriage. A bride who has been through the *Sturm und Drang* of divorce is—well—stained. She simply is not, cannot be, Ali MacGraw. The demon Reality is the number one killer of romance, so let's simply obliterate the demon and get back to that divine wedding with The Vision in white organza.

And then, since weddings have something to do with marriage, what does this idealization of the romantic say about our conceptions of marriage? For one thing, it encourages the "and-they-lived-happily-ever-after" myth that ends every proper fairy tale. It talks to our American optimism, our ever-blazing hopes for eternal love and happiness, hopes without which most weddings would not take place. And a strange equation is made: the more perfect and glorious the wedding, the more perfect and glorious will be the marriage. The Madison Avenue/Hollywood technique of delusion governs—use the right deodorant or mouthwash or eye-liner and life will be rosy-peachy. Cause and effect, logic created where there is no logic.

Traditional vows speak of "till-death-us-do-part" and other expectations of lifelong, unchanging togetherness bliss that today's growing army of marriage counselors claim are greatly responsible for the divorce rate. So, if it is true that marital failure is linked to the unrealistic expectations with which one enters marriage, then how grossly the American wedding must contribute to the 40 percent of American marriages that ultimately end up down the drink.

How can *anything* that follows, after all, measure up to such a high—especially for our bride? When again will she get to play movie star on Academy Award night? When will she ever again be the focus of such mass worshipful acclaim, so many gifts? When will she ever be able to indulge herself in such an orgy of shopping? What sort of act can follow the climbing of a ladder to scale the heights of one's very own fourteen-foot wedding cake?

One girl, having been married in a Phoenix hotel gala that cost $20,000 and required eight months of intense preparation, and was not entirely dissimilar to opening night at the Ringling Brothers, told me she plunged into the blackest depression of her life after two months of marriage. "I prolonged the wedding as long as I could," she admitted. "I spent three weeks writing my thank-you notes and returning gifts and talking about the wedding with all my girlfriends. But then, it was really finished. And so was I."

Americans spend fortunes on weddings, borrow thousands from banks, hock the family jewels, sacrifice next summer's vacation. They arrange productions so lavish, so imaginative, so SHOW BIZ as to put Darryl Zanuck out of work. Thousands of people, in fact, spend more on getting their children married than on their education. Okay, we understand why The Wedding as ritual is a central part of the culture. But why the chopped liver cruise ships, the kitsch, the hilarious/ grotesque extravaganza? If a wedding is a wedding—and they all are made up of the same components, fill the same personal needs—then why does a nice girl from a nice family having a nice wedding at the Waldorf-Astoria Hotel in

Manhattan hire a live horse to dance the "Blue Danube Waltz" with its trainer? (The horse, incidentally, added several other unexpected touches to the evening.) Why does a simple middle-class family in Woodstock, Illinois, build a special knotty-pine wedding chapel—with stereo, mind you—in their backyard, tearing it down immediately after the wedding?

It's all about MAKING IT. Making it, that is, in the American sense of being able to acquire GOODS, showing off POSSESSIONS, upward mobility on the THING scale, asserting your escalating status to your friends with SYMBOLS. The concept, of course, is strictly middle-class American, where the structure is always fluid, the challenge is to rise and rise, and the possibilities are seemingly limitless. (The upper and lower classes have a fixed place resting on their birth that is not generally mobile and is denied by the middle class.) Margaret Mead writes of middle-class existence: ". . . the expectation that life is a sort of race, a challenge to one's thrift and one's industry, a race in which one can only win if he displays the necessary aspirations and the necessary skill. Life depends, not upon birth and status, not upon breeding or beauty, but upon effort; effort that will be rewarded in riches, in material goods which are the signs that the effort was made, that one has in the language of childhood been 'good.' "

The wedding—simply because it *is* such a splurge by its very definition, such an emotional happening, such a terrific reason for all sorts of outpourings—is a quintessential vehicle for letting-it-all-hang-out materialism. The ostentation overkill present in so very many weddings is obvious only to the outsider. To the host, it is his validation as a man, a father. And the realization of The American Dream.

Certainly, more pure motives exist for the gigantic wedding jamboree. We tend today to be cut off from our roots, disconnected from community life. The nuclear family—to coin popular sociological phraseology—has replaced the extended family or clan environment, and we are isolated, lonely. There are few enough occasions left in life for communal gathering, the wedding and the funeral being the primary two, and it is only the wedding that permits opportunity for rejoicing and feasting with folks we care about.

I've said that there is no such animal as "The Typical American Wedding," and that is an interesting fact about American life. In so many areas the subcultures that make up our populace are becoming increasingly homogenized, the barriers disappearing. Neighborhoods are not so strictly "black" or "white" or "Greek" anymore; corporate life is no longer quite so WASP, cops not so Irish, all psychoanalysts are not Jewish or gangsters Italian. But weddings are different. Anchored in historical group traditions, plus reflecting the subtle and not-so-subtle position and values of the group on the American ladder, American weddings are a true smorgasbord. Middle-class Jews do it differently than middle-class Italians; weddings in South Carolina are not much like weddings in Iowa. Hotel fiestas bear little resemblance to those at the local Kiwanis Club.

And nobody—but NOBODY—tosses a wedding blowout barbecue like the folks in Texas, Nosirreebob.

The claim has also been made that very little has changed, that even the hippest hippies tend to crawl back to the bourgeois womb for their nuptials. But let's acknowledge the few alterations. Wedding garb is much perkier than it used to be, for one. Not particularly for the bride, who after all carries that symbolic legacy up the aisle with her, but for the supporting players, the attendants—male and female—who frequently wear high-fashion duds these days. The population at weddings is also shifting to more of the couple's friends and fewer of the branch managers from the Wichita office of Daddy's company. There's a decline in the number of prenuptial parties and bridal showers; on the other hand, more money is being spent on the gifts. There's the existence of the "New Wedding," which, although still a speck under the microscope today, will distinctly influence the future.

But the sweeping majority of clergy throughout the country (recall that seven out of eight first marriages take place in church or synagogue) give testimony to the fact that the writing of one's own ceremony, desires for Dylanesque music, indeed *any* swervings from the established conventions, is surprisingly rare. A *Bride's Magazine* survey indicated that only 25 percent of the couples interviewed requested any modifications in standard ceremony, and those were primarily musical.

Barbara Donovan, at *Bride's,* receives occasional letters from young women on the theme. "We want to do something different for our ceremony," they claim, "something personally meaningful to us. Could you write it for us?" From fear of seeming foolish, of bucking the powerful waters of tradition, of trusting their own individual expression, of hurting their families, of defying ancient myth, even these kids—kids who have at least pondered something besides their costumes and the menu—retreat ultimately to the "Dearly beloved" script.

I have sat in on pre-wedding conferences—summit meetings between the families and the florist, say—where the interminable discussion of detail, the fixation on the most minute of decisions (should the peonies at the altar be in white vases or clear vases?) became so fiery, so obsessive, so charged with emotion that one would have assumed—had you dropped in midstream—that the subject at hand was nothing smaller than the fate of the planet. You see, in the American wedding rite the one area least cared about, most dismissed, is the marriage vow. And what does that icy footnote say about our vision of matrimony and our ladder of values?

The wedding, to us, is really a panacea, a mini-microcosm of all of the dreams and goals and fantasies and promises that American life has to offer. When it's over, five hours later, there's the debris, the soggy egg salad, the droopy peonies, the cigarettes shredding in the champagne glasses, and the bills. Somehow it's all worth it. And so it goes on.

And on.

2. In the Beginning...

. . . And on. Marriage. One of humankind's most ancient and persistent institutions. And the wedding one of its primeval and surprisingly unchanged rites of passage. Almost all of the customs operative today are merely echoes of the past—everything from the presence of flowers and a veil, to the old shoes and rice, to the bridesmaids and processional. At one time every last ingredient bore a very specific and vitally significant meaning. Today, although the original substance is lost to us, we incorporate them into our weddings because—well, just because. Because they're traditional and ritualistic and we mortals crave tradition and ritual. And because—as the man said about the mountain peak—they're THERE.

Anthropologists have argued for centuries about the origins of marriage, whether in fact it was sexual instinct that bound men and women together, or survival considerations, or economic factors, or an emotional craving for protection and permanency. One popular view—and that espoused by the most renowned marriage and wedding rite historian, Edward Westermarck—is that wedlock originally came about as a result of the helplessness of the newborn child, *its* need for family nurture and protection. Thus, in contrast to common belief, Westermarck claims that "marriage is rooted in the family rather than the family in marriage."

Among early peoples, *everybody* married, bachelorhood being considered a crime against nature. As the main issue was children, *not* to bear offspring was to be denied entrance into the Gates of Paradise—a notion persisting today in many cultures. An unmarried man, says Westermarck, "is looked down upon as an almost useless member of the community and . . . there is no greater reproach for a high-class Hindu than to have a daughter unmarried at the age of puberty. A family with such a daughter is supposed to labour under the displeasure of the gods. . . ." (Punishment for such a crime, by the way, means retroactive damnation for three generations of already-dead ancestors.)

Of the three forms of pairing—monogamy, polygamy (a man with many wives) and polyandry (a woman with many husbands)—monogamy has been historically the most perseverant, although probably not by natural impulse so much as practical motivations—the economic hardship of having several mates, say, or the confusion implicit in group grope or the unavailability of a squadron of partners.

And until very recently matrimony has taken place, especially for girls, at a very young age, often at the onset of puberty. (A Lady Mary Villiers, we are told, was a widow at the age of nine.) People didn't live very long, for one thing. Then, as we shall see, marriage was primarily a buy-and-sell arrangement perpetrated by the girl's family for profit, the bride being the commodity for sale, and a young lamb—strong, a virgin, easily shaped to the master's will—could bring the better monetary deal.

The earliest known form was Marriage by Capture, in which a man invaded another tribe and kidnapped a woman whom he judged to be potentially a good slave and hardy worker. She was, in effect, booty, prey to be conquered—testimony to his valor and muscle—a trophy. Although this barbarism became obsolete with the birth of Christianity, it remained legal in England until the thirteenth century and occurred periodically among southern Slavs until the 1800's. (Westermarck says that the Yahgans and the Onas of Tierra del Fuego are still doing it today.)

The interesting footnote to Marriage by Capture is how many of the classic elements of our current weddings are but ghosts from that antiquity. The captor, for instance, always took with him several husky colleagues to aid in the seizure and escape; the defenseless victim surrounded herself with girlfriends to attempt to stave off the kidnapping. As true wedding ceremonies later evolved, these figures became the best man, the ushers and the bridesmaids. The earliest wedding gifts were those tokens the conquering hero would bestow upon the bride's enraged father as appeasement. The business of tying old shoes to the back of newlyweds' getaway cars carries multiple meaning, but one surely harkens back to the skirmishes between enemy camps as groom stalked bride and heavy shoes were hurled after him. The getaway became the honeymoon.

The most common and longest-lasting system was the Marriage by Purchase. Still in active evidence today throughout the globe, this method both reflected and perpetuated the growing strength of patriarchy, in which the male of the family had supreme power and control, a woman had no more legal status or free will than a child and could be bargained for, sold and traded like the prize sow. A marriage helped to make the patriarchal father an even more powerful influence in his community, as it was planned in order to heighten his economic station and as an alliance between important families. The bride thus became the mercantile pawn and the matrimony a sort of rural corporate merger. In theory, the father was losing valuable labor by his daughter's exit and thus he must be well compensated; and, too, she—and the offspring that she would bear—would be her husband's most valuable "possession," so he should be willing to pay for her in the same way that he would pay for a sturdy new plow.

The word "wedding," in fact, refers to the "wed"—the "bride-price." That is, that amount of money, goods or property paid to the lass's father for her purchase. The level of negotiations would depend on the wealth of the families and the qualities of the girl—her beauty, strength and abilities. As she was considered more salable if pure, chastity became a big virtue. (In parts of Morocco, today, a workingman pays $70 to $100 for a virgin, only $30 for a widow or divorcée.) Proof of virginity became a necessary part of the wedding ceremonial—inspection of the bridal sheets the morning after or, as in Greece, the bride's stained nightgown left hanging in the window for days.

The bride, naturally, had no voice whatsoever in the choice of husband or in the arrangements of the transaction. Neither does a goat when it is being sold to the farmer next door. And once she was married she had no more influence or autonomy as a wife than she did as a child. Even the liberty of deciding divorce was confined to men, who could legally abandon their wives for being barren or for being rotten cooks—or for virtually any other failing in servitude.

The husband paid the bride-price to his future father-in-law; the bride came to the marriage with a dowry, a gesture of repayment to the groom. What was exchanged depended on what was valuable and available. In New Guinea, for instance, the groom bought his lady with pigs, fruit, shells, beads, and she in turn brought bananas, earthenware pots and bird-of-paradise plumes. Money, of course, has been an ever-popular bartering ram. But whatever the terms, our bride received nothing. Daddy got the bride-price; hubby got her dowry and complete control over her person. And, like the probing of a horse's teeth to judge its worth, the groom could examine the goods beforehand to decide whether it was adequate and—if not—cancel the whole deal. Even in later eras, when marriages for love were being made, lots of haggling took place over the components of the dowry, and receipts were exchanged immediately following the ceremony.

In societies where chastity was not a particular virtue (some Algerian tribes, or among the aborigines of Nicaragua), the young girl was expected to earn her dowry by prostitution.

"Giving the bride away" earmarked the transfer of owner-ship from father to husband (in Russia the father would beat his daughter gently with a new whip and then turn it over to the groom); dowry was translated to "trousseau"; the best man was frequently a go-between, both in the financial negotiations and in the relationship, such as it was, of the twosome, who were usually not permitted to communicate prior to the wedding.

An offshoot of the purchase system was one in which the man, in exchange for receiving a wife, worked for the girl's family. The period of servitude may have lasted anywhere from one year to fifteen, during which time he might or might not have had access to her. Sometimes this custom was organic to the culture but more frequently came about when the suitor was too poor to buy his woman outright. Rather like washing the restaurant's dishes when one cannot fork up for the bill. It also served as a period of probation—a means of testing his ability to work hard and his general accept-ability as a son-in-law.

During the entire time span from the primitive Marriage by Capture to the late Middle Ages, religion played little part in the wedding ritual. As an alliance between families, with no ostensibly loftier spiritual vision than political op-portunism or pure economics, a wedding was a family and community folk fest, an extraordinarily joyous frolic, but not the slightest bit solemn or linked to religious sentiment. It began generally as a "processional" of the entire village or tribe, led by the bride's father, making its merry way to the groom's habitat where the lass was turned over to her new master. *That* transfer alone comprised the legal wedding rite. Feasting, music and dance followed, often for days. (The Vikings, in fact, celebrated each wedding for a continuous month.) But nowhere a hint of God's presence or the benefit of clergy.

The early Christian fathers, you see, were opposed to the whole idea of marriage, preaching that celibacy was surely man's highest striving. They considered virginity in itself a pious and noble end, for both men and women, an exalted renunciation of the goal of procreation. Affairs of the spirit were distinctly more important, for one reason; for another, the end of the world was clearly imminent, so it was futile to think about propagating the species. The churchmen also despised women because of the sexual pleasure and temptations they invited, and looked at intercourse—even within marriage—as a truly dirty deed.

St. Paul, who himself remained a bachelor, mollified the standard ecclesiastical contempt for matrimony by declaring: "It is good for a man not to touch a woman. Nevertheless, to avoid fornication, let every man have his own wife, and let every woman have her own husband . . . for it is better to marry than to burn." (I Corinthians 7:1–2; 9.)

And then, as the church assumed more power in general, it attempted to invade the human universes previously left private—like marriage. As word began to spread that God's blessing was a good thing for wedlock—although any marriage was certainly lawful without it—couples, as part of the ritual, would go to the church for benediction *after* they were wed.

By the thirteenth century, weddings had fallen under religious control and the church then insisted on the mutual consent of the newlyweds as a condition. Marriages, in practice, were still arranged by the families, still affairs of the purse, as most children did not possess the willfulness to rebel against the entrenched custom and the all-domineering father (the priest actually just acted as replacement for father in the service of turning the bride over to her lord). Nonetheless, the rule of mutual consent was, in philosophy, a gigantic step forward in marital history.

The Council of Trent in 1563 declared that any marriage not performed by a priest was null and void, and it was then not until the eighteenth century—with the French Revolution and moves for independence in the American colonies—that the pendulum swung back and matrimony once again became thought of as a private and civil venture.

It was also not until the eighteenth-century Enlightenment that the odd concept of romantic marriage caught flame. Lovers' passion had naturally always existed but had had nothing at all to do with the business of wedlock. It was only with the slight psychological elevation of woman's status that conjugal affection could begin to substitute for sheer enslavement. To date, Marriage for Love has been the shortest evolutionary stage of conjugal history.

Most of today's wedding customs predate the intrusion of the church; they are moored, rather, in magic and superstition and paganism. But the most common means of celebrating the marriage throughout history has been by feasting, the custom of eating together having always symbolized the public bringing together of families, affirmation of the strongest kinships.

Surrounding the actual wedding were the preparatory and final rituals, betrothal, in some cultures, being as vital a commemoration, as splendid a feast, as the wedding itself, signifying as it did the settling of the financial terms of the union. (Westermarck has said that the whole purpose of the wedding, in fact, "is to give publicity to the union . . . to distinguish a recognized marriage from an illicit connection.") The time span between betrothal and wedding ranged from a few hours to years: Jews, in the Middle Ages, held both rites on the same day, to avoid the peril of sexual yearnings; other groups would plight their offsprings' troths at birth and the twosome would not be allowed to look upon one another until the wedding day itself.

Then, as marriage always implies sexual intercourse and procreation, the wedding night was as much public participation as the events preceding. Guests would follow the couple into the bedroom, the male attendants undressing the groom and tussling to capture the bride's garter; the parents would make elaborate fertility toasts over the bed, and cowbells, having been surreptitiously affixed to the mattress, would make joyful noise unto the activities that followed. It was not unusual for the "witnesses" to hang about outside until the first consummation was completed and the husband gave some public sign of its satisfactoriness.

Every ingredient within the marriage rite, born of primitive magical belief, symbolizes one of, or several of, four ideas: fertility, female submission, separation from one family and union with another, or the protection from evil. There is much overlapping and much anthropological nitpicking about which element falls within which category, whether—for example—the Russian father's beating of his daughter primarily signifies male mastery over women or is, in fact, an act to expel the evil spirits from the bride's body. All in all, one senses that ancient peoples were so cradled in superstition that each act probably bears many meanings simultaneously—rather like carrying a rabbit's foot AND not walking underneath a ladder, the theory being that one can never be too careful about luck.

Badges of fertility, to insure both consummation and reproduction, are woven through the wedding. The presence of food and flowers are clear symbols of fruitfulness and the continuance of life. In France, wheat is showered over the newlyweds; in America it is rice and in Greece nuts and dates. All are gestures of the bride's contact with seed-bearing plants. Slices of wedding cake are given to guests to take home to guarantee their own fecundity. And fragile objects are broken to indicate the breaking of the bride's hymen: in parts of England a plate containing salt is smashed over the groom's head, and Jews traditionally stomp on a glass.

The woman's submission to her husband has been established since the dawn of marital history, and some of our most durable wedding traditions find their sources in this state of affairs. The wedding ring, for example, was originally—in the time of Marriage by Capture—a rope tied around the woman's waist or wrist and ankles, to subdue her. Later on it became the initial token of purchase as the groom presented a ring at betrothal time, a pledge to the bride's father of their fiscal bargain. The girl wore this insignia of bondage on her left hand specifically because the right hand was thought to represent power and authority, the left oppression and weakness. The fourth finger was chosen as it was believed that a vein led directly from there to the heart—one of the few *romantic* notions, curiously enough, in the whole wedding story.

The most conspicuous emblem of maidenly chastity and subservience is the veil. After the bride was bargained for and the terms set, she was then veiled, as an announcement to the world that she was "sold" and that no man but her master could gaze on her.

In parts of the globe the rites of male domination are even more dramatic: a Moroccan groom beats his woman three times between the shoulders with the handle of his dagger, and in Croatia men used to box their brides'. ears at the ceremony.

Rites of passage always entail a separation from the past and a connecting to the future. In this instance the couple is being severed from their families and joined to one another. The holding of hands during the ceremony (in some countries the hands are literally tied together) manifests their union, as do the traditions of eating from the same plate—or feeding one another a bit of wedding cake—or drinking from the same glass. Union is another symbolic function of the wedding ring.

Among primitive people, the dread of evil spirits pervaded each society with a profound force that constituted much of its dynamic. All ritual—whether joyous or mournful, so long as it was significant—remembered the omnipresent need to appease, or drive away, or trick the malevolent influences that were supposed to be always hovering about. Young brides and grooms were believed to be the most vulnerable and endangered, due to their innocence and happiness, and the history of wedding rites is permeated with symbolic means for protecting against the unseen powers. In Russia, for ex-

ample, the doors, windows and chimney were shut tight for
the ceremony; shooting off guns was a common practice in
central Europe; Arabic grooms would lay a sword on the
bridal bed and a pistol under the pillow prior to the wedding.
It was also believed that the presence of great quantities of
food would pacify or seduce the demons. Another reason for
the "old shoe" is that malignant spirits are supposedly afraid
of leather.

One means to safeguard the couple was by deception—the
wearing of masks or disguises. In Moorish weddings the bride
and groom were painted all over with henna, as to be virtually unrecognizable; bridesmaids and groomsmen originally
dressed precisely like the bride and groom in order to outfox
the spirits. And in Denmark the couple would wear old
clothes of the opposite sex—guaranteed to utterly baffle *everybody*. The veil, besides signifying male domination, was a
disguise. And today it is still considered bad luck for a bride
to participate in her own wedding rehearsal, an understudy
being used instead as yet another means of fooling the ominous evil eye.

The dangers were assumed to be lurking either above or
below the earth, so appropriate precautions were taken: carrying the bride over the threshold to protect her from the
ground monsters (also a mark of enslavement); carpeted aisles;
paths strewn with flowers; the Jewish "chuppa" (pronounced
"huppa"), or canopy, offering the couple sanctuary from evil
above.

The mythical idea is that only first-time brides and grooms
are considered to be in a state of peril as it is only they who
are passing into a new state of life and who are therefore
innocent. It is the ancient explanation of why only first marriages and not subsequent ones are attended by such elaborate
hoopla and are so full of crucial symbolization.

What cannot be ignored in this historical tapestry of marriage and the wedding, the theme that occurs and reoccurs

throughout the ritualistic reenactment of centuries-old customs and patterns, is the subjugation of women, the view of women as chattels, as non-people. It is as inextricably braided into the historical framework of marriage as a symphonic theme is inseparable from the body of the music, just to be repeated again and again in tiny variation.

The primitive male mind, anchored in endless terrors of the unknown, feared women perhaps above all else. All the aspects of femaleness—in their enigmatic differences from the male structure and function—became sources of dread. Menstrual blood intimated the woman was an instrument of the devil, inhabited by the evilest of essences. Pregnant women, too, were abnormal, arcane, and thus made to live apart from the family until their strange condition passed. The fact that dread of the woman was deeply mingled with desire only exaggerated the terrors. And these notions have knitted their way through time. The early Christian leaders, as said, believed celibacy to be the noblest mode of living. Consorting with women was—well, degrading. And even as recently as the late Middle Ages, the monks and priests denounced women as the vessels of evil.

Within the wedding ritual, the alleged impending perils from demonic forces are directly related to women—men are merely the helpless victims. In many cultures a period of abstinence from sex follows the wedding, under the belief that evil spirits can slip inside the woman's vagina during intercourse and she, in turn, will transmit them to her guileless husband. Purification ceremonies—dispelling the monsters through bathing or use of fire—were traditional in the past, and persist even today in America among the Orthodox Jews, whose brides are required to attend the "mikvah" (ritual bath) prior to the wedding.

There are but two ways to deal with the objects of our profoundest fears: we must destroy them or we must contain them so that they do not destroy us. Thus the fear of women has been masked by contempt, subjugation, containment.

Aristotle said: "The male is by nature fitter for command than the female, just as the elder and full-grown is superior to the younger and more immature," and the echoes of that need to diminish women by looking upon them as helpless and subordinate children wail loudly through the course of human history.

Despite the gigantic inequities operative today where women are concerned, it is not, I grant you, easy to regard Miss American Bride as oppressed. The wedding, of course, is a matriarchal totalitarian event, in which men have no more relevance than the elevator operator on a self-service elevator. The bride is the Virgin Fairy Princess Star; her groom is—okay, let's say it—mere woodwork, attracting less interest than the parsley surrounding the chicken breasts, far less attention than the bartender.

Rampant female chauvinism? It would certainly seem so, this exaltation of women, dismissal of men. But on closer examination the truth becomes clear. The bride is the central figure because the real change in status is hers. She changes her name to her husband's, prepares to have children, follows him wherever he goest because his work is assumed paramount. He continues his growthful journey through the real world as before, with the addition of a new appendage, a wife; she is transferred from economically dependent child to economically dependent "adult." The language says it succinctly: "Wife" originally meant "woman"; "husband" meant "master of the house." And this day is her one brief breakout between anonymities.

In the days of wife purchase, she was paraded through town en route from father's domicile to husband's, exhibited for the crowds much as the grand-prize refrigerator/freezer is wrapped in pink satin bows and shown off before the audience at the quiz show. Today she poses on pedestals, glides through misty clouds of mauve stage lighting, glorifies the cover of *Modern Bride,* becomes enshrined in chicken salad. But it's all the same thing.

The Virgin Princess is essentially no more real woman than is the degraded slave-wench; pedestal-sitting is as far removed from eyeball-to-eyeball equality as are the chains. Deifying women in the abstract has been a repeated historical pattern: Ancient goddesses were worshiped for fertility and sexual allurement, while ladies on the earth were dominated and demeaned; the age of chivalry and courtly love romanticized and idealized women, while still allowing them no rights, no autonomy. The process is simply called Dehumanization, and it is the same game whether she is being stared up at or looked down upon.

3. The Love Machinery

On this very day, experts estimate, 5641 American girls will become engaged to be married to a like number of American boys. Mere minutes after the "Okay, let's" or the "Well, if you insist" or the "YIPPEE THANK GOD AT LAST" is uttered by one of the parties, the love machinery goes into operation. All the cogs and wheels of American enterprise are greased, primed and mobilized into action as this new consumer entity—the About-to-Be-Newlyweds—is born. It will dump $7 billion into the economic pot between day of engagement and six-months wedding anniversary. Six hundred million of that will find its way to the engagement ring boys, $1 billion to the trousseau brokers (luggage, lingerie, apparel and cosmetics), $3.5 billion to the home furnishings and appliance merchants. The new entity will be enriched by $200 million worth of gifts.

Small wonder that the least ardent of the bride's wooers is the groom. She—much more so than he, in his secondary role in the wedding operetta—is the instrument of all-consuming consumerism, the figure almost totally responsible for this mountain of what the industry calls "bride-generated purchases." Only a portion ($2 billion) is related to wedding-day festivities, the rest to the before and the after. She suddenly becomes—this American child of 20.3 years, in all of her economic innocence and inexperience—an overnight FORCE. An instant giant in the marketplace. A purchasing power. And a target.

The machine fires into operation.

One father of the bride, a journalist writing of his daughter's wedding, reports that shortly after her engagement announcement appeared in the local newspapers, she counted seventy-five phone calls from photographers, eighteen from orchestras, twenty-three from engravers of wedding announcements, twelve from bakers of wedding cakes, nineteen from florists, eleven from jewelers, twenty-one from caterers, fourteen from hotels, two from lingerie dealers, thirty-two from honeymoon travel agents, nine from wedding gown salons, and "one from a men's tailor who, for some unaccountable reason, mistook her for the groom."

The groom, as a rule, receives calls only from the insurance peddlers (one of whom, when told the boy already had full coverage, asked for the names of any of his engaged friends). But, as recounted to me by a man married in the mid-1950's, flukes occur. His fiancée was besieged by the usual assortment of solicitations; he got nothing, except for one small notice that arrived in a plain brown envelope. It suggested, with great delicacy, that he, as an about-to-be-newlywed, purchase a substance called "Double X Ointment" —guaranteed to be delivered in an equally unobtrusive plain brown package. The magical balm was to be applied to his penis on the wedding night—to eliminate the slightest possibility of premature ejaculation.

If one were to follow a bride—hand-in-hand with her mother, tailed at ten paces by the groom—through the ritualistic parade from engagement to honeymoon, one would be struck by the ever-spiraling web of detail and expenditure and obsession in which the participants are caught. Engagement announcements, photographs, party; the ring; the wedding invitations; the wedding preparations; the trousseau; the bridal showers; the registering for gifts; the new home and massive catalog of accompanying purchases; the wedding itself; the honeymoon. And each category is inevitably and inextricably shackled to outpouring of money and acquisition of things. It is as if, in our culture, the wedding—the outstanding rite of passage—is concretized, validated, only by the number of treasures which one can carry into the new life.

A girl in my college dormitory got engaged and instantaneously assembled a three-ring looseleaf notebook which she called "My Marriage Book." Although it exactly resembled a standard classroom notebook, the dividing categories were not "French" or "Trigonometry" but, rather, "Stemware," "Linens," "Sterling Silver Flatware," and on and on. She carried this Bible with her *everywhere,* for eight months, neatly pasting in ads from magazines, inserting notes to herself on objects she would see on her interminable daily shopping trips and wanted to own, dashing off memos on alternative china patterns. "My Marriage Book." A rumor ultimately spread through the dorm that Annette actually slept with it under her pillow in case a vision of The Perfect Ice Bucket should come to her in a dream.

Part of the wedding choreography is the obsession to do it *right.* It is why dreary books on wedding etiquette proliferate, why the job of "wedding consultant" is such a juicy one, and why the bridal magazines invariably devote a section of every issue to the Umpteen Commandments of weddingdom (there are, not coincidentally, more ordinances governing weddings than any other zone of human behavior).

Having decided the where and when of the wedding arrangements, the next paramount step is the invitations—the dominion in which the *most* stringent regulations command. *Bride's Book of Etiquette* says: "There is no procedure connected with a wedding which is more bound by tradition and etiquette than the issuing of invitations and announcements. Ingenuity and individuality have no place here. The wording is set by the laws of etiquette, as are the stationery and the engraving." Not to mention the addressing, the folding, the sealing, the stamping and the timing of the mailing. With the commitment to print the family is, in a sense, making its first appearance on the wedding stage and the audience is making its first in the long series of critical evaluations. I recall, as a child, my mother receiving a wedding invitation and reflexively running her finger over the print to see if it was raised, thus indicating hand engraving—the costliest and classiest process. By that simple gesture she could get the initial clues of what kind of a shindig it would be, what price-level gift she should purchase and whether or not it was necessary to buy a new dress. (Today, with the miracles of modern science, hand engraving can be faked in a technique known as "raised printing," which is not only the cheapest, but virtually undetectable.)

Bess Harris, the invitations saleswoman with Cartier in New York for the last thirty years, is ramrod rigid in her bailiwick. Engagement announcements, she insists, are outré. ("It's bad etiquette. Only Jews and Italians do it.") If the wedding is in church, one must say, claims Miss Harris, so-and-so "requests the honour of your presence," but if in a hotel, it's "the pleasure of your company." She quakes at the mere mention of informality. "We're very firm about etiquette. An invitation with the Cartier imprint assumes perfection; that's why people come to us and they abide by what we tell them."

As American family life gets more complex, so accordingly do wedding invitations. Unbendable rules exist to cover the wording variances of an invitation being issued by the bride's divorced mother, or by the bride's divorced and remarried mother, or the bride's widowed mother, the bride's widowed and remarried mother, the groom's widowed father, the bride's widowed father and on and on and on. Then, too, there are military laws for the reception cards, the will-be-at-home cards, the church admission cards (to avoid crashers), pew cards and of course the occasional cancellation notices —which must certainly be as Emily Postian as anything else.

For very large weddings, Cartier peddles gift acknowledgment cards: "Miss So-and-so acknowledges the receipt of your wedding gift and will take pleasure in writing you herself in the near future."

Bess Harris is trapped in the eye of an invitation revolution that she clearly finds appalling. "Years ago we'd make you walk out of the store if you asked for a colored invitation. It was intolerable. Now people have become psychedelic and we're allowing the *most* ridiculous things. Blue printing instead of black." In a what-is-this-world-coming-to slump, she continues, unhappily: "It used to be that if the text was in bad taste, we wouldn't do it. If the girl's parents were divorced and both wanted to be on the invitation anyway—well, it's just dead wrong—but now we'll do it if the client fusses a lot. I don't approve at all."

Many folks consider the services of a calligrapher as essential to wedding bliss as the Cherries Jubilee. Calligraphy—fancy script handwriting—is an expiring art, currently performed by only a handful of octogenarians. They address envelopes, table cards ("You are seated at table number 6"), place cards and menu cards ("Broiled Pheasant, Souffléd Potatoes") in an elegant, old-worldly script that leads one to fantasies of a top-level scroll directed from the Archbishop of Canterbury to the King. It bespeaks Class.

Class, and the immersion in minutiae. One bride, having received the scripted envelopes from her calligrapher ($1 per address), traveled three hours from her upstate New York community into Manhattan to visit the main branch of the post office. Why? Because she wanted a very special stamp to befit the superb script and had to peer through books and books of possibilities until she finally settled on a blue-and-green peacock number, which then had to be ordered from Washington, D.C.

Love—to the jeweler—means $1 billion a year shelled out by the matrimonial set for articles falling into the "Jewelry Industry" playpen: that is, rings, silver, china and crystal. Of that sum, $750 million, in 1971, was spent for wedding and engagement rings, a soaring increase over the $600 million spent the previous year.

Startlingly clear proof, it seems, of how truly little is being dismantled of the American way of wedding is the statistic that 87 percent of all American brides receive engagement rings, and four out of five of those are diamonds. The diamond, in our society, possesses symbolic values and implications that are inescapable; it is, perhaps, the key status object in our treasury. More so than cars, homes, yachts, fur coats, a diamond is distinctly a sweeping extravagance—solely decorative, arrantly functionless. Not even, despite the mythology, a good investment. Elizabeth Taylor, the empress of consumption overkill, already owns everything in the world; as her ultimate vanity, the peak act of self-aggrandizement, she thus purchases the largest diamond boulder in existence, 69.42 carats, costing well over $1 million and which she is permitted to wear—according to insurance regulations ($66,000 a year in premiums)—only twenty times a year. The fact that the little shopgirl, whose life will never bear any glittering resemblance whatsoever to Elizabeth Taylor's, can also possess a diamond, albeit a microscopic cousin, is terrific status.

At the time in history when brides themselves were purchased, the engagement period was specifically meant for the exchange of tokens—the girl's father putting up security that the marriage would take place, the groom making a down payment of food, cattle or jewels. The diamond ring, as token, did not make its appearance until the fifteenth century when Archduke Maximilian of Austria—in a great frenzy to get married and rush back to the wars—presented Mary of Burgundy with the first of its kind. (Women, in general, were not permitted to wear jeweled rings.)

Even as diamonds came into engagement ring fashion, they were still rare and, therefore, the prerogative of the very rich. It was not until the mid-nineteenth century that huge quantities were discovered in South Africa and not until the

1900's that they were cut into tiny stones and mass-marketed. Today the average "little shopgirl" in America gets half a carat, at an average cost of $328.85.

The symbolism is infinitely heavier than the stone, associated not only with affluence but with permanent stability —as with the physical hardness and indestructibility of the diamond itself. "Diamonds Are Forever," the ad asserts. Forever love and marriage, forever security. "A kiss on the hand may be quite continental," sings Lorelei Lee, but we all *know* what a girl's to rely on in the crunch. A gleaming security blanket. A badge that, as one jeweler capsulized, "everybody respects because everybody knows what it means and what it's worth."

"The wedding," says Morton Sarett, president of the Jewelry Industry Council, "is the highest occasion in life, the ultimate event. It is understandable, then, that you would want to solemnize it with things of the highest value. You're not going to put a piece of paper around your finger." Sarett believes the tradition and psychic need for the diamond ring is so pervasively ingrained in our culture that promotion from the industry isn't really necessary. "It all perpetuates itself," he says. In addition, the diamond ring is, in all likelihood, the first piece of "real jewelry" that any young girl will own, so, along with every other motivation, the ring signifies her entrance into adulthood. Adulthood, by the American definition of owning things.

I spoke to one bride who sneered at the idea of an engagement ring, admitted to rebelling against the competitive aspect. "I always look at other girls' rings to see how big they are. I don't want people doing that to me." What's implied, of course, is not disdain but that she is afraid she can't compete, would have a ring gladly, but only if she could be sure it were the heftiest rock on the block.

In New York City I went to visit two corporations with grand claims: Zalè is, they say, the largest jeweler in the world; J. R. Wood and Sons (Art Carved Rings), the biggest in "the fancy wedding ring business." Wedding ring sales tally to approximately $107 million a year. For 90 percent of our newlyweds, that means two rings per couple (it's an old tradition in Europe, but did not spread in the United States until World War II, when men were separated for long periods from their wives). More than five thousand manufacturers exist throughout the country; the wedding band is so easy a creation that retail jewelers turn them out themselves in the back room.

In their building on Thirty-third Street, near the Hudson River, Zale purports to have more money stored, in jewelry, than any bank in the world. The only outfit that buys rough diamonds, cuts the stones themselves and then grinds out two thousand engagement rings every day, Zale also has a network of 950 retail stores around the country. J. R. Wood, by contrast, manufactures only wedding rings—700,000 a year —and since approximately three million a year are sold, they capture a solid wedge of the pie. Apparently, I am given to understand, more changes are being executed in the ring business than in any other wedding category. "Kids are more sophisticated today," says Allan Ginsberg, from Zale. "They don't come in anymore with their hats in hand, not knowing what they want, insecure. They're more discerning, and the biggest trend that I notice is the dying of the classic, klutzy bread-and-butter look." (That look, he explains, means the center diamond in the white gold setting.) Lyman Wood sees an upswing in zingier rings for second weddings. "And our second-marriage sales are zooming by the minute," he says.

Geographical differences in ring styling seem to be as vast as the distances. In the South and West, says Wood, yellow gold is favored over the more common white gold. In the South too, more tiny diamonds, more flash, more ornateness; in rural areas, where outdoor life predominates, rings are heavier, more durable. *The Wall Street Journal* quotes a Chicago jeweler as claiming a noticeable interest in jade, sapphire and emerald wedding rings. "Two years ago I wouldn't have carried such things in the store because they weren't in line with wedding etiquette. But today's young couples simply won't buy assembly-line platinum bands that look like washer rings." "Styling parallels fashion fads in general," says Allan Ginsberg. "Like the knitting craze in women's clothing, we are going for the roped, twisted effects in rings. Antiquing is big, just like the attraction for old clothes and period costumes. We follow style, we don't set it, we just respond to all the other movements in fashion around the country."

The offices of both Wood and Zale, incidentally, have the locks-and-guards security of a missile base. Before Lyman Wood will let me tour the joint, I must be thoroughly checked out, but once en route I easily understand the caution. I could not have imagined such a quantity of gold and diamonds, in all forms—lumps, chunks, dust, pebbles. The workers, as one would expect, handle the precious goodies with the nonchalance of men who spend their days injecting the clams into clam chowder.

Since 86 percent of all first-time brides—more than four out of five—read either or both of the bridal publications, *Modern Bride* and *Bride's,* and since both conduct frequent and exhaustive market research studies worthy of a nervous presidential candidate, one can assume that they know their girl. Inside and out. They know, for example, that 67 percent of their readers live at home until they get married, that three out of five have attended college, that 73 percent expect to work full time during the first year of marriage. They know, too, that she averages out to 20.3 years old, her guy is 21.8, and together they earn $7,900 a year. They know that most young women read bridal magazines before they are even engaged, and that prospective brides, on the average, will look at a particular page of interest exactly 12.1 times. Even further, they know precisely how many newlyweds will buy an electric blanket, what percentage of those will be king-size as opposed to queen-size, and how many total dollars will be spent on that blanket in each major city in America. It stands to reason, then, that one can discover a lot about who she is, this American bride of today, and what are her goals and values, by looking at what the experts feed her.

Bride's says their magazine deals with three areas: "(1) how to be sure the wedding and wedding trip will be perfect in every detail; (2) how to make her husband happy through knowledge of him and understanding of herself; (3) how to successfully plan and furnish a first home to suit both new members of the family as well as their guests." "Our target girl," says Barbara Donovan, "is between eighteen and twenty-four, getting married for the first time and changing her lifestyle and place of residence. All the information gathered between our magazine's covers is to help her make the transition between two very different lives. To that end, *Bride's* is basically a textbook."

"A bridal magazine has the relevance of a Sears Roebuck catalog," from the slightly more cynical George Morrissey, publisher of *Modern Bride*. "Our girl isn't special. She's any girl who is getting married in a formal ceremony and moving to a new home." What his girl is, certainly, is utterly unprepared to deal with the tidal wave of purchasing under which she is being swept, the buying bout that will surpass, statistically, any other period of her life. She is being thrust, as it were, right from the womb into the gross, churning American marketplace. Though she has undoubtedly been dreaming of and planning for this golden time since childhood, what on earth does she know of carats and baguettes and electric brooms and Alençon lace? Despite the Pill and TV, what does she know about the *real* issues— wall-to-wall carpeting?

That's what the magazines are for. *Modern Bride* boasts more advertising pages than any other consumer magazine in

America (not to mention the first contraceptive ads in a national publication). Hundreds of ads for bridal gowns, sterling silver, luggage, mattresses, tuxedos, honeymoon resorts, linoleum, sex manuals, eye makeup, china and vaginal douche powder. The feature subjects in every issue are standard: where to go on your honeymoon, with the standard Caribbean nooks touted and the same couples-smooching-under-the-palms photography; detachable booklets on wedding etiquette (to place under your pillow? carry in your handbag?); first-home furnishing and hostessing hints—everything from the basics of how-to-set-a-perfect-table to the basics of how-to-whip-up-a-perfect-paella; columns on beauty advice ("How do I make my feet look divine for my wedding?") and columns on etiquette ("Can my bridesmaids carry parasols as late as September 3?" The answer, by the way, is yes. Summer was not officially ended, that year, until September 4.) In *Bride's* especially, there is the *de rigueur* monthly article on sex, but the weight of the feature material is placed on bridal fashions.

After reading a truckload of *Bride's* and *Modern Bride,* I came away with a strong sense of our American bride being astonishingly ignorant about *most* adult concerns, in addition to the silver-china-vacuum cleaner issues. In an article in *Bride's* of June, 1972, entitled "Questions Brides Ask About Sex," the first query is "What will happen when my husband and I have sex?" And the author really-truly explains, à la my seventh-grade social hygiene class, about foreplay ("Usually lovemaking starts with the couple kissing, touching and stroking each other"). Shockingly elemental, in a magazine that advertises vaginal foam. On the other hand, the same author condones masturbation, even explaining the zippiest way to do it. In the very next month's issue appears a piece called "This Is the Way to Wash Your Clothes." The bride is—at least as the magazines perceive her—not only inexperienced in the realms that we would expect ("How You Go About Buying a House" seems like an obviously pertinent story), but fundamentally helpless.

She is also deeply romantic about her wedding, most particularly in how she wants to look for it. And she clearly believes that marriage is the most glorious and rapturous state on earth. Whether she is gliding down a flower-strewn aisle like an angel/movie star or whether she is cooking dinner on her brand shiny new electric frypan or making her new bed with her crisp new floral sheets, she is glowingly happy. All activities, when one is married, are divine. That is the key message.

George Morrissey says *Modern Bride* is identical now to what it was ten years ago. "Every issue is primarily the same; we haven't done anything different really since the inception except for more travel interest and the contraception ads. We don't assume a girl is a virgin until her wedding night anymore, but we *do* imply she'll be happier if she brings her total love to just one guy. We don't denigrate freedom; we just applaud chastity."

Barbara Donovan, by sharp contrast, sees subtle shifts in focus and attitude of her publication—the mirror of changes around us. *Bride's* was the first bridal magazine, born in 1934, published only on the east coast, and given away free to girls whose engagement announcements appeared in local newspapers. In these thirty-nine years it has gone from a quarterly to eight issues a year, from no charge to $1, from a shopping catalog for upper-class Gentile girls—with feature articles like "How to Handle Your Servants Once You're Married"—to a guide aimed at every American bride of what they call "the formal wedding mentality." She says: "We've gone from showing the spectrum of concrete objects to showing a spectrum of abstract thoughts. We say, 'You don't need to conform either to the submissive housewife role or the new liberated role. You can develop your own wife-style.' And we talk about the total range of wife-styles." ("Wife-style" is jargon invented at *Bride's*. The editors must be very proud of its cleverness, as they use it *relentlessly*.)

Witness some of the modifications Donovan speaks of:

In June, 1969, *Bride's* ran an article titled "What Sex

Means to a Man," which begins: "The first thing a wife must understand is that sex to her husband is an imperious and driving ruler." Men are the raging carnal beasts and ladies the cuddly pussycats. Three years later (in the August, 1971, issue), "How to Handle Sexual Hangups" describes a couple who had lived together before marriage, had even gone through an illegal abortion—a time-honored tradition to be sure, but generally not shouted about in a bridal book. A letter to the beauty-advice column in the same issue asks: "Since I've started taking birth control pills, my tummy protrudes. What can I do to hide the little bulge beneath my wedding dress?" The answer naturally, is about bulges, but the forthright implication and acceptance of premarital shenanigans is what's striking, and new.

On the other hand, *Bride's* is having an obvious psychic conflict. They are basically peddling schmaltz with a Lawrence Welk vengeance. They want to deal with reality, with the shifting of women's position, but, like *Cosmopolitan,* they're not sure if too much reality isn't bad for business. So they tend to get cute. A feature called "How to Solve Problems of Two Working Partners" is very WITH IT in tackling issues of liberation from the defined marital roles. But the solution is sugary, simplistic Pollyanna. Just-talk-about-it-and-it-will-go-away-because-you-love-each-other-to-death.

The ever-skyrocketing success figures of both *Bride's* and *Modern Bride* indicate the robust health of the industry; ad revenues and circulations increase every year. But their strength also provides a clue to the perpetuation of our romantic mythology about weddings and marriage, in which life is just a sterling silver bowl from Oneida, Ltd., overflowing with yummy Bing cherries from our adorable together jaunt to the supermarket.

At no other time in one's life does such an unrelenting purchasing marathon take place. The newlywed bride spends an average of $3500 to furnish and equip her first home—

more than any other homemaker in America. Extensive market research conducted by the bridal magazines indicates that she enters her married life with 120 major new products and plunks an annual $3½ billion into the strongboxes of the home furnishings and appliance makers. The figure has soared 45 percent since 1964.

An old elbow-in-the-ribs joke stated that all the newlyweds needed to set up housekeeping was a bed, yok yok. But like all jokes, it contained a microbe of reality. Today the couple begins with what it took their parents twenty years to collect. They buy by the roomful, it arrives by the vanload. Seventy-three percent expect to purchase a dishwasher, 91 percent a washing machine, 86 percent a sewing machine, 72 percent a color TV, 80 percent an electric wafflemaker, 64 percent an electric toothbrush.

(It should be pointed out that the subjects of these research studies are readers of *Bride's,* who—as a category—buy the magazine primarily as a shopping guide, so are perhaps more acquisitive than non-readers. However, four out of five American brides read it, so the figures are fairly generalized.)

Several factors influence the quantity of newlywed spending. One is, of course, that more marriages take place each year; another, that sofas are costlier today than in 1960. But subtler elements contribute too, like the extension of the average engagement period to eleven months—twice what it was ten years ago. A longer time to shop, hence more available funds. Then, most young marrieds now live in a two-paycheck situation, as 84 percent of *Bride's* readers are working full or part time when they wed and 94 percent anticipate working for a few years after marriage. (Today's couple is tending toward delaying children and having fewer than their predecessors.) Schemes for buying on credit are so numerous and accessible that the newlywed—like the rest of us—finds overextended purchasing irresistibly seductive.

Young couples are much more likely than older folk to spend every cent they have on furnishing a home and go into immediate debt. Owing money, procuring wares one cannot pay for, no longer carries the heinous puritan connotations it once did. We are led to believe in the moral rightness of instant gratification—I want what I want NOW. Charles Reich, in *The Greening of America,* talks about the power of advertising over the youthful consumer: "The American economy . . . has made a separate consumer market out of youth in order to sell more products; it has made youth widely aware of one another in order to stimulate sales by example; it has subjected youth to the stimuli of constant changes, possibilities, and opportunities. Here advertising is dealing with an unformed group in the society, and they are likely to be far more sensitive to the invitation to live *now* than their more settled elders. Thus, advertising is capable of creating a maximum of dissatisfaction, and a minimum willingness to accept the drudgery of life, in the volatile 'youth market.' They listen with a different ear, and it has made them promises that the rest of us have not heard."

Again, the bridal ads spell out the subtext and reinforce the theme. A beautiful *now* couple cuddles on the grass in front of their starkly dramatic new home on the dunes; the headline proclaims, "It wasn't designed with your grandmother in mind"; the ad is for Oxford Bone China. Another gorgeous and chic twosome is entertaining their equally spiffy friends in urban elegance. "Some people know how to live," captions this ad for Lenox China and Crystal. A rapturously romantic child-couple looks into each other's eyes while the ad copy, for Oneida stainless steel, says: "Some things you decide with your heart. The things that matter. Like your stainless."

The things that matter. Like your stainless. . . .

What she doesn't get under her own purchasing steam the bride will acquire through marital largesse. Two hundred million dollars' worth of wedding gifts are bought each year—and not merely one gift per couple, which would seem the reasonable state of business. The procedure begins, frequently, with an engagement gift, obligatory when one receives an engagement announcement or is invited to an engagement party. When I was a teen, betrothal celebration was mandatory, as blatantly feted as the wedding to follow. From all reports, this custom has died, or at least temporarily moved into hibernation. Even within an institution so glutted by extravagance, perhaps there is a fail-safe point. Or perhaps the excess has merely shifted channels—from the engagement to the bridal shower.

The custom was, historically, for the townspeople to contribute some practical object from their own households to aid the newlyweds in setting up housekeeping. In my youth, a lass was given an informal luncheon-shower; very ritualistic it was, with standard games invariably played. My favorite took place as the bride-to-be unwrapped her presents and one guest would "secretly" jot down everything she said, then read the remarks aloud as "This-is-what-Nancy-will-say-on-her-wedding-night." The comments were always, as they were supposed to be, of the "Oh, I can't get it out!" or the "OOOOO—it's so BIG!" ilk. It was very funny and titillating in the late '50's.

Of course, the high point of the day was the unwrapping of the treasures, which was basically the whole point of being there in the first place. If you were married, you looked back to your own engagement/wedding/shower spree with wistfulness, as nothing since had quite lived up to that euphoria. If you were single, you envied and became even more impatient than you already were to "get yours." Anyway, the gifts were simple and practical—cookbooks, a frying pan, a nightgown.

In recent years, what seems to have occurred is polarization. Some brides—the very rich, the very social *or* the very ethnic—have as many as eight showers tossed for them, and an offering as humble as a Teflon pan probably couldn't get you past the front door. I attended a shower for 120 ladies at the Bridgeport, Connecticut, American Legion Hall—a six-course dinner *avec* fifteen-piece orchestra. The engraved invitations just happened to mention the names of the bride's silver and china patterns and the stores where they could be purchased. The evening's jollies consisted of her opening each of the hundred-odd shower gifts that literally engulfed the stage, including two vacuum cleaners, a king-sized bed and THREE color TV sets. Undoubtedly an expression of the wedding psyche that believes the new household must be completely stocked at its inception. Instant fulfillment of needs. "The things that matter. Like your stainless." Insurance for the marriage.

Two hundred million dollars spent on wedding gifts each year, and the corpulence of that sum *must* be abetted by the genius who invented the Gift Registry. In a sense, it's an intrinsic American consumer device, a celebration of letting-it-all-hang-out Greed. What happens is that the bride—sometimes with groom, more frequently with Mama—goes to a department store or housewares shop, or several of each, in which she selects every goody she would like to own. Starting out with her silver patterns (sterling and "everyday"), china (fine and "everyday") and glassware, she then gets into linens and cookery and "accessories" (her crystal jam pot and silver vegetable warmer and electric wok). Then, with the abiding help of the store's bridal consultant, she registers the hundreds of nest-feathers on an interminable form sheet. She will inform every prospective donor at which stores she is registered and then they will know what to buy her. After Aunt Hazel purchases the jam pot, the store will check it off the registry sheet, so duplications cannot occur. It's a brilliant scheme for everybody—the store gets all that gift loot, Aunt Hazel doesn't have to devote days to picking out something she's basically sure the girl will loathe, and Our Bride gets everything she's ever in her life wanted.

I myself thought the practice of gift registry was dead. Of

all the wedding institutions, it seems the most outdated, the most out-of-sync with the lifestyle of youth. Who cares about sterling silver anymore? Bone china? Porcelain soup tureens? Artichoke plates? I agreed with *The New Yorker* writer who, in covering the wedding gift shopping scene, said: "It is not the business of youth—especially of today's youth—to gloat over silver and crystal. Why, then, do well-wishers continue to ply young couples with decanters and asparagus servers of Cartier and Tiffany and Baccarat and Buccellati, instead of with the meat grinders and manure spreaders of the Whole Earth Catalog?" Why indeed? Because the givers would rather risk the indifference of the recipients than to tread on whole earth, to buy something with which they are personally unfamiliar and heavily uncomfortable? Because they assume that asparagus servers will find a nook in every hippie's haven once he returns, inevitably, to the bourgeois fold?

Or because they know something that I didn't, namely that 86 percent of all readers surveyed by *Bride's* anticipated the acquisition of crystal stemware, 84 percent fine china dinnerware and 58 percent sterling silver flatware.

Six out of ten brides apparently still do register and experts say the figure would be exceedingly higher if every town had the facilities. J. L. Hudson's, in its nine Detroit and suburban stores, has sixty-one consultants and, using computers that update the forms three times weekly, registers 22,000 brides a year. A middle-class bride in St. Louis registered at four local emporiums and the bonanza started streaming in the instant invitations were received; two years later, as laughingly reported by the girl herself, over a hundred gifts lay, still in their original boxes, in her mother's basement.

One day I follow a young twosome, Linda and Jerry, as they go to register at Geary's in Beverly Hills. It is a large and fashionable store devoted exclusively to homemaking and it does the heaviest bridal registry volume in Los Angeles.

Linda and Jerry are both students at U.C.L.A., she an undergraduate studying psychology, he in law school. They have been peripherally involved in peace demonstrations and pot; he devotes time to the American Civil Liberties Union and she belongs to a woman's rap group; they do not view themselves either as "hippie" or "establishment" and they are getting married six months hence in a fancy frolic at the Century Plaza Hotel.

By the time we arrive at Geary's, they have already selected their sterling, china and glassware patterns. "It really took weeks of debate," says Linda. "It's a very big decision, you know. You only get these things once in your life and we both wanted to think about it a lot and talk it over with our parents." Their selections, rather to my surprise, are old-fashioned and highly ornate. And very expensive. "Royal Doulton's Buckingham Minton" china is rimmed in florid gold leaf; the "Windsor" silver pattern is baroque and leaden. Apparently this is typical. Only 10 percent of all sterling buyers choose contemporary designs.

We are greeted by Miss Windsor; she is, like all the saleswomen in Geary's, at once prim and mushy. Like the old-maid schoolteacher who sniffles as she reads "Ode to a Nightingale" to her class. It is her first day on the job and Linda and Jerry are her very first couple. "I'm a part of your new life," she coos. "Isn't that nice? This is a very lucky day."

They commence the registering, a procedure that will consume close to three hours, with the fine china dinnerware. Do they want settings for six, eight or twelve, Miss Windsor needs to know. Twelve, naturally. That's five basic pieces—dinner plate, dessert/salad, bread and butter, teacup and saucer. But nobody stops at the basic. There's your demitasse cup and saucer, your variety of platters, your gravy boat, covered vegetable dish and uncovered vegetable dish, sugar bowl and cream pitcher, coffeepot, something called a chop dish.

The first in a ceaseless series of frenzied debates concerns which soup bowl to get, and poor, frazzled Miss Windsor works herself into a mini-flipout about whether her charges should have the cream soup dish, the soup/cereal (which she asserts is "more versatile than the cream soup" but then changes her mind, which frazzles her even more) or maybe —what about this?—the fruit saucer, which seems to be good for soup, cereal AND fruit. They finally settle on something —I never do learn what—and press on. The tablecloths, twenty minutes on those. Napkins, place mats. Stemware— "Medici by Franciscan"—goblets, sherbet/champagne/fruit, wine. Everyday dishes—"Franciscan Gourmet"—and a replay of the soup-bowl crisis. It appears to me that Linda is checking off *everything* on the sheet. There seems to be no household treasure produced by man that she does not want to call her very own.

Meanwhile, the phone on Miss Windsor's desk rings incessantly with inquiries from gift donors. "Has Miss So-and-so gotten her mortar and pestle yet?" "What has she registered that costs under twenty-five dollars?" Evidently, as the wedding draws near, Geary's can get over twenty-five calls a day and it gets so that the saleswomen know the bride's cargo by heart.

Now to the silver: I am dazedly weary and Jerry is stupefyingly bored. Like a proper groom, he withdraws into some livelier private universe and the show now belongs to the two ladies who become more delirious by the moment. "Do we need a sterling silver pickle fork, honey?" Linda asks her groom politely. Honey doesn't hear the question. Linda checks it off. Cheese server? Cold meat fork? Pie knife, sugar tongs, jelly server? Natch. Check check check. More more more.

It is a ritual, this gift registry business, that seems to the observer enormously utilitarian and dizzyingly appalling at one and the same time. Who can argue that it's not better to receive merchandise that you really want than some unreturnable grotesquerie? You're going to get presents anyway, and you're setting up house, so why not spell out your desires, make clear your tastes? Why not, indeed.

It's just the mindless systematic avarice that makes one cringe so. Like eating chocolate after chocolate after chocolate far beyond the point where one can still taste anything at all. An Austrian crystal-and-silver wine dispenser for $125? Sure, why not? Check it off on the list. The ultimate shopping orgasm.

Finally we leave, spent, Miss Windsor's parting sentiment echoing behind us: "Remember my name. It's the same as your silver pattern. Windsor. It's providential. I just *know* you'll be happy."

Happiness, you see, is ordained by the objects we purchase, marital bliss ensured by the right choice of china pattern. That the quality of the marriage is, in some way, substantially connected to the 120 major new products obsessively accumulated by the newlyweds is clear. It is the fundamental message of the wedding industry.

4. The Ethnic Ethic: Keeping the Faith

At a veterans' hall in Pittsburgh a young Polish couple throws a wedding for 450 that lasts the entire weekend. The sausage and beer are continually replenished while folks go home, nap and return for more revelry. The orchestra plays marathon polkas for two days.

At another Polish bash on New York's Lower East Side the bride replaces her veil with a babushka, whirls around the floor with the male guests, each of whom pins a dollar on her dress. The groom dons an apron with oversized pockets, for the same purpose. They rake in $650.

An Italian father, a factory foreman in Duluth, gives each of his four daughters a $10,000 wedding replete with two bands (one Neapolitan, one rock), six varieties of pasta and a $600 gown for each lass.

Then there was the Italian wedding, described in Gay Talese's best-seller *Honor Thy Father,* of Mafia mogul Bill Bonanno to Rosalie Profaci *(her* relatives no slouches in the underworld pedigree department). Three thousand guests jammed the Astor Hotel ballroom in New York, entertainment was by Tony Bennett, a literal truckload of champagne was drunk, thousands of California daisies specially flown in, $100,000 in cash gifts to the young twosome, and a guest list of such "notables" as Albert Anastasia, Frank Costello and Vito Genovese.

The famed Priscilla of Boston claims she has to design

special, super-hardy trains for the bridal gowns of her Greek girls, to deal with the custom of boundless frenetic dancing. She also admits she personally prefers "ethnic weddings" to your usually "boring, uptight society affair."

She has a definite point, the matrimonial mavin. "Ethnic weddings," that is, Italian, Polish, Chinese, Ukrainian, Mexican—the strains of minority culture in America—do seem to possess more color, joy, flamboyance, food, music, tradition and terrific fun than the typical American rite. Why? Classically, where the social cohesiveness of the community is strong, The Marriage is symbolic of that strength—past and present—and the future continuation of the group. And as these minority pockets have remained more tightly knit, less diffused than in WASP America, the wedding to them becomes life's most momentous celebration. Thus it is not unusual to find a Greek or Puerto Rican family who begins socking away pennies for a daughter's wedding on the day she is born. Through the eighteen or so years of her growth they will sacrifice, without question, any number of personal pleasures and acquisitions; they will frequently abandon the alternative of sending her to college for four years in order to provide the infinitely more meaningful value—The Wedding.

If he must, the father will borrow money. (A major New York bank, which lends up to $6000 for this purpose, does a booming wedding business.) In any case, he will not scrimp, no indeed. He will invite *everybody* there is for him conceivably to invite (as, historically, anyone who was passing through the village or within galloping distance was welcome to the festivity). In comparison with his WASP neighbors, his daughter will have more bridesmaids, a more elaborate, lacier, more expensive gown; her wedding will continue on for more frolicsome hours and will be more reminisced about for years to come, remembered as the true high point of the entire family's life.

Too, the ethnic groups have retained a clearer connection

to their roots, so the wedding will be a closer approximation to the original rituals. As opposed to the country club, watercress-sandwich syndrome, it will have many elements of the pure folk celebration, unaltered customs (like the pinning of money to the bride's dress) from wedding history.

We do, however, live in America and not in the sixteenth-century Ukraine. Priscilla is not in the habit of manufacturing authentic Slavic wedding costumes, and the friendly neighborhood caterer evidently has abolished the tradition of family and friends working together to prepare the feast. With growing acculturation and the passage of time, authenticity has been lost. Or almost lost. There is perhaps one group, one sub-society in this country, that has remained startlingly untouched by technology, commercialism, assimilation, competitiveness or most other aspects of twentieth-century life. In every pocket of their activities they have stayed utterly loyal to their historical lore, still living by the ancient, unchanged codes of the past. These are the Orthodox Jews, approximately one million strong in America today.

The Orthodox marriage ritual bears as much resemblance to today's typical American Jewish wedding as it does to a Comanche war dance. Reform and Conservative Judaism— that which characterizes Jewish life in this country—has been culled from both the nomadic course of their history (a bistle German, a little Russian, Italian, Slavic, Spanish, Arabic) and by the dilution of spreading assimilation right here. Jewish middle-class life has become so infected with creeping whitebreadness that there are many among us who assume that ancient Yiddish folk music means the score from *Fiddler on the Roof*. The conventional Jewish wedding carries in it strains of *Gentile Homes and Gardens* welded to some ingeniously flamboyant symbols—like the chopped liver cruise ship—of upward mobility.

Attending an Orthodox wedding, on the other hand, is like stepping into a time capsule and emerging somewhere around the eleventh century in middle Europe. The people one meets appear to have no relation to 1970's America, the "events" of the day no correspondence to familiarity. It is the essence of the true ethnic wedding—abounding with pure passion, primeval symbolism, rollicking joy, solemnity and history. It is also filled with undisguised sexist horror.

I don't know what to expect as the subway train on which I am riding plunges farther into the bowels of Brooklyn, heading toward the first Orthodox wedding I've attended. As a Reform Jew manqué, my only contact with my holier brethren has been on brief jaunts through Manhattan's Lower East Side, where one would invariably pass a gaggle of unhealthy-looking young fellows on their way to or from school or the synagogue ("too much time spent at the Torah," I always thought about those sun-deprived, icky white complexions). You knew they were Hasidim (major Orthodox-niks) by the curlicue sideburns ("payess"), the shapeless, too-big black suits that had a quality of having just been dredged up that very morning from the depths of some musty attic trunk, and by the fact that even as teen-age boys they seemed distinctly like funny little old men. Anachronistic, strange, completely isolated—it would seem—from the surrounding culture. In New York and Brooklyn, the Hasidim live in self-created ghettos much like nineteenth-century Europe; they study Torah and the Talmud, become rabbis or go into particular businesses like diamond merchanting; they attend synagogue all the time, speak Yiddish most of the time.

So, recalling my only associations with Orthodoxy, by the time I arrive at the Aperion Manor hall on King's Highway ("Exclusive Glatt Kosher Catering"—very haute kosher, to you), I feel like a goy. Instantly I make two profound errors, unforgivable breaches of Orthodox law (as we will see, there ain't any *minor* infractions in this crowd): I have stupidly worn a miniskirt—a shocking exposure of thigh—and, even worse yet, I shake hands with Mr. Pruzansky, the owner. Men, you see, are not permitted to touch flesh with *any* woman other than their wives, so I have committed a Glatt

Sin by my aggressive, automatic greeting. Were it not for the fact that I am that magic person, A REPORTER, I would be banished forever to the Brooklyn streets. As it is, the tale of my crime eventually reaches most of the six hundred guests (three hundred of whom comment on it to me); I become, for my transgressions of the skin, the star of the evening, only slightly less fascinating than the bride herself, nineteen-year-old Judith Bucksbaum, the Hebrew teacher.

To the Orthodox Jew, marriage has always been the symbol of existence—both of providing structure to life (the home being second only in importance to the synagogue) and of literal survival. *Every* Orthodox person gets married, without fail. According to Jewish law, it is actually a religious duty—a man who doesn't marry is guilty of diminishing the image of God, and in the past, a single man over twenty could be ordered by the court to take a wife. As one eighteen-year-old girl at this wedding, still unattached but blithely confident, said to me: "Being married, raising a family, running the house, is what we were born for. It's what gives meaning to a woman's life." In the same way that my suggestion of alternative lifestyles is unthinkable, so is anything except a huge razzle-dazzle of a wedding. A young Rockefeller would be more likely to tie her knot in City Hall than a lass of the Orthodox faith; if her parents can't afford it, all the friends and relations will chip in, without shame, to provide The Great Day.

Knowing all this ahead of time, I don't drop dead with shock when, upon entering the reception hall, the first object my eyes fasten on is the bride—perched on a golden throne. Lest you envision the palace at Versailles for this, let me describe the setting. The Aperion Manor is your basic catering hall, found in cities and towns all over America. It is furnished in a style that can only be termed "Bridal Baroque"—that is, a decor peculiar to institutions dealing with weddings: lots of red velvet in unlikely places (walls and ceilings, for instance), wall-to-wall mirrors, chandeliers, crystal doodads, marble statuary. The style might also be called "Bronx Apartment House Lobby Rococo," but its most pervasive ingredient is the Gilt Complex—EVERYTHING is phony gold.

The Aperion Manor can handle three weddings simultaneously on its three floors, but tonight there is only one, the reason being its size. (In the old days the whole village was invited and a wealthy family held two bashes, one for friends and relatives and a pauper's feast for any poor person who could manage to find his way there. The bride and groom were seated with the strangers, ate and danced with them and doled out coins. It was considered good luck to share one's happy fortune. The updated version is the giving of a hefty donation to the temple.) There are degrees of Orthodoxy, depending on how closely one adheres to the thousands of strictures, and on a scale of one to ten, the owner tells me, tonight's gala would measure a solid nine. A true Hasidic wedding would never be held indoors, regardless of weather, the notion being that the couple's children should be as numerous as the stars in the sky, thus one should be close to them. An acceptable approximation for Orthodox Jews has been provided by the Aperion Manor: in the room where ceremonies are held, a small hole has been cut out through the ceiling and the roof above, so that at least eleven stars peer through.

Back to Judith on her gilt throne. There are two receptions taking place simultaneously, prior to the ceremony, in the cavernous room divided in half by a floor-to-ceiling velvet drape. Each half has its own bar and mammoth smorgasbord and the guests do not move from one section to the other. At the "Bride's Reception," the princess is surrounded by girlfriends, people approach the throne to congratulate, pay court, admire her ornate gown (by Priscilla of Boston, I learn). To the earthy music of a six-piece band —no Miami Beach mambo, but true deedle-deedle-dai-dai Yiddish folk stuff—the folks dance in large circles, the hora, the miserloo. Women with women, men with men. At no time do the sexes intermingle. This band, I am told, the most sought-after on the Orthodox circuit, won't work a wedding where there is heterosexual dancing.

For the first moments after my arrival, I recede to the corner, suddenly shamed for my nude legs, to observe with fascination. The pervading aura of European old-worldliness is caused largely by the music and by the way in which the assemblage is dressed. All the men and boys of all ages wear those pawnshop black suits and either yarmulkes (skullcaps) or black George Raft fedoras. Why does everything they have on appear to be four sizes too big? The women's garb runs from "goin'-to-meetin'" dresses to bespangled satin gowns. But decorously covered, you betcha. Not a bare arm, hint of a breast or thigh in the joint. The young maidens truly look maidenly, curiously old-fashioned, unstylish, virginal—the reason being, as we will explore in a moment, that they are all, indeed, virgins. As it registers on my consciousness that the majority of women have exactly the same hairdo—that Pat Nixon plaster-of-Paris bouffant—I remember. These are wigs. Nobody has real hair. Orthodox women are required to shave their heads upon marriage and to wear wigs forevermore in public.

The food is overpowering, leaden, sensational. And, of course, Glatt Kosher. Long tables with cold salads, smoked fishes, fruit, challah; bubbling caldrons of stuffed cabbage, veal stew, kasha varnishkes (don't ask me to explain), noodle pudding, pot roast, chow mein. (Note: When will some hip sociologist do a study of the relationship between Judaism and Chinese food?) As it is, traditionally, the Orthodox feeling that wine should be taken to help rejoice but not to cloud the head from one's studies, people are drinking very little—but attacking the food with unbound fervor. Dinner, after all, won't be served for an hour yet.

I am waiting for Moshe Pruzansky, the thirtyish, overweight (small wonder), highly Orthodox proprietor, to return to me from his overseeing chores, so that I may peek in at the "Groom's Reception," on the other side of the barrier drape. That's where, apparently, all the heavy action is taking place. Where the marriage contract, or Ketubah, is being written, pruned, negotiated and approved. It is probably the most critical segment of the whole wedding ritual.

Historically, a Jewish man and woman were considered married if any one of the following took place: (1) an article of value, such as a ring, was given to the bride, as a gesture of her purchase; (2) a document was drawn up specifying how much the groom was paying and for what (200 silver denarii for a virgin, 100 for a widow); (3) sexual intercourse, with the intention of consecration. The first two were to be executed in front of two adult, Jewish, non-related males. For the third, the witnesses were to wait outside the groom's tent. At an Orthodox wedding today all three conditions must be met, literally or symbolically.

On the male side of the partition no women are permitted. For the heathen reporter, an exception is made. A flock of rabbis, the groom, both fathers (the groom's father is himself a rabbi) and the witnesses are poring over the Ketubah with the intensity of deliberation of WASP corporation attorneys arranging a major merger. In fact, the deed is a business transaction, stating, among other fine points, that Judith is a virgin and specifying what she is entitled to in case of divorce or widowhood. There is nothing mock-serious or automatic about this ritual. It takes two hours this night to agree on terms, to proofread, haggle, bargain, check and recheck for errors. IBM merging with TWA, presided over by fifteen ancient, snowy-bearded Hebrews.

Suddenly there is a great bellowing shriek from the men. The Ketubah has finally been signed. The Hasidic music all at once becomes louder and more frenetic, and then, in an explosion of the most primitive exuberance and passion, the young groom—a thin, pallid twenty-three-year-old rabbinical student—surrounded by his black-suited comrades, dances into the bride's domain. Everybody—six hundred strong—joins in, in exultant, foot-stomping, shouting joy, whirling with him across the room as he goes to claim his bride. When he reaches the throne on which she is demurely poised, he covers her face with a white veil, thereby asserting that she is now his alone, belongs to him, is never again to be gazed on by men other than himself. Until this moment he has not been permitted to see her for seven days. It is now time for the wedding ceremony to begin.

I'm overwhelmed with what I've witnessed in the last minutes. The undiluted, communal joy and eroticism, the utter dominion over woman, the tribal symbolism. (Wasn't that scene, in fact, a re-creation of the Marriage by Capture, with its male machismo and maidenly submission?) It seems to be, in so many ways, the embodiment of the archetypical wedding rite. Right here on King's Highway.

To comprehend anything about Orthodox life, one must understand the concept of the separation of women from men. In synagogue they must sit on opposite sides; at all social events they are split and do not mingle; men and women never dance together, even husbands with their own wives, except in some ultra-liberal sects where each will dance holding the opposite ends of a handkerchief, so as not to touch. They are not permitted any physical contact with a member of the opposite sex, save for their own mates. (This is the ordinance I violated by my klutzlike handshaking.) I am startled to realize, at this incredibly ecstatic wedding, that there is barely any talking, any mingling at all between men and women. And yet the atmosphere is deeply, heavily charged with sexuality. How to understand this?

Some days later it is explained to me by Rabbi Bruce Goldman at Columbia University. "Among the Orthodox

Jews," he says, "there has always been a keen recognition of the power of sex, the force it plays in one's life. If a man is praying in synagogue or studying Torah and a woman were to be sitting next to him, he would be distracted, wouldn't be able to concentrate. Men create a barrier so as to be able to keep their minds on their studies; it's clearly an acknowledgment of woman's sexual powers over men. In the same way, people have nothing to do with any but their own spouses because presumably they'll respond to others, be attracted to them, want to have sex, which will disrupt the home and family. Obviously, this must have been, historically, a problem, for the rabbis to lay down all these injunctions about separation. You don't prohibit something unless there's difficulty."

For the ceremony, men and women take their places on opposite sides of the pseudo-synagogue, a grand room one flight down from the reception hall. There is minimal resemblance to other wedding ceremonies: no bridesmaids or best man, no "Here Comes the Bride." Instead, the groom enters, wearing a white robe over his suit to illustrate his purity, walking between his parents, carrying lit candles. The bride and her parents then march to the floral chuppa placed directly under the hole in the roof and walk seven times around the groom, indicating the seven days a week that she will serve him. The Hasidic band plays—now on flutes and accordions only—very peppy tunes, a surprising incongruity for so solemn a shindig. No English is spoken at all; everything is in Hebrew. A neighbor interprets the goings-on for me: now the rabbi is reading aloud the marriage contract; now a little blessing over the wine and Judith and Yisroel sip together; now each of the honored rabbi guests, thirty in all this night, comes up to add his blessing; now another sip of wine. On and on . . .

The chuppa is one of those nuptial traditions that has interesting multiple symbolic meaning, depending on whom you talk to. Some historians claim it derives from the groom's tent, where the marriage was consummated, then became the mark of the new home to be created by the couple. Westermarck, as we have said, believes it was a symbol for protection of the couple from evil forces from above. It used to be a piece of velvet held up on four sides by four men; more often now, in your normal Jewish jamboree, the chuppa consists of $1290 worth of lavender petunias imported from Honduras.

After seven standard blessings are recited—chanted, really —comes the climax, the most poignant and joyful moment of every Jewish wedding service. The groom stomps on a glass, breaking it, and the couple is wed. (In Reform ceremonies at tacky hotels, a light bulb wrapped in a napkin is frequently used instead, to save money, ostensibly, for the herring. Not so here.) Again, the meaning of this gesture is not entirely clear. The standard explanation is that a Jew, in every instance of happiness, must remember the destruction of the Temple by the Romans and the suffering of all Jews. Another is the symbolic breaking of the bride's hymen. Many cultures have an equivalent—Moroccan Jews throw raw eggs at the bride so that she should bear as plentifully and easily as a hen. At any rate, with this merry sound and the spontaneous shouting of "Mazel Tov!" everybody storms the chuppa, the music becomes frenzied, the same unbridled jubilation as when the Ketubah was signed. The message one gets from this moment, and many moments throughout the evening, is ancient and tribal and profound. Infinitely deeper than the vibrations at today's typical weddings—"Isn't this sweet, isn't she pretty in white, isn't the roast beef tender, isn't Uncle Danny looking well after his operation, wouldn't it be nice if they remain happy, but after all, who can tell these days?" Tonight, deep in the heart of Brooklyn, there is a sense of people fulfilling a primordial destiny. It is not just a splashy, expensive wedding. It is, at least to the hundreds of participants, a Dance of Life.

As the couple walk back down the aisle, almost enveloped

by shouting, embracing, dancing, sweating well-wishers (note: there is still no inter-gender hugging or kissing), they fulfill the last part of the ceremony, a ritual that, to my knowledge, exists only among Orthodox Jews. Led to a tiny room down the hall, in which a bit of food has been laid out, Judith and Yisroel are secluded alone together for twenty minutes. In the old days this custom of "Yihud" was, in fact, meant to consummate the marriage, the final validation. Today it's not sexy but sweet and, to be sure, practical. For this Orthodox couple barely know one another; they have had only a few dates, a very short engagement (recall that in the Middle Ages the Jewish betrothal period was one-half day) and in all likelihood have *never* been alone. They have both fasted for twenty-four hours, in order to cleanse and purify themselves for their future together, so in the Yihud they break fast together, spend their very first moments alone, begin this ordained new life.

A few words about purity: Virginity is still a primary prize in this peculiar universe. The Orthodox wedding invitation reads, "We invite you to the marriage of the virgin Deborah." The insistence upon brief, chaperoned courtships is to minimize sexual temptation. (Boys are not required to be virgins, but since they hardly pass the time of day with ladies anyway, they mostly are.) The whole gestalt of separation between the sexes is related to this focus on purity, as is the accepted Orthodox doctrine of woman as "unclean."

My fur begins to bristle as the zaftig, earthy, bewigged woman sitting on my left at the ceremony explains "uncleanliness." Evidently there are several hundred religious laws—literally several hundred—regarding a woman's status during her menstruation. These are the basis of all Orthodox marital codes of behavior, the premise being that she must be ostracized while "unclean." If any of them are broken, according to a terrifying little manual called the *Code of Jewish Family Purity*, "awesome, frightening punishment, also reserved for such capital sins as incest and violation of the Yom Kippur Fast, cuts off the sinner's soul from the immortality enjoyed by other souls and cuts off from life the generations which have been conceived in sin."

Very abbreviatedly, here's how it goes. During menstruation, a woman must "separate" from her husband. That is, not only is sexual intercourse forbidden, but any physical contact, even the passing of an object from one to the other. She must not sleep in his bed or sit next to him on a couch; anything leading to closer relations must be avoided, hence affectionate conversation is forbidden, as is her singing in his presence.

On the fifth day of menstruation a woman "dons the white"—inserts a piece of clean white cloth into her vagina, to check out whether any blood remains. If not, she begins counting her "clean days," seven days during which the separation rules still apply (she's still considered unclean). At the end of that period she must attend the "mikvah," the public ritual bath, in order to become acceptably pure for her husband.

I ask my neighbor how she feels about (1) being considered virtually leprous for two weeks a month and (2) being able to make love only two weeks a month. To the first question she regards me blankly. And I suddenly know, in a flash of fearful insight, how she cannot in any way perceive the ugliness that I feel so deeply of how women are looked upon in her world. She knows nothing else, is so shockingly estranged—indeed ghettoized—from the forward motions of twentieth-century American life surrounding her on every corner that nothing has seeped in of how others live today. Indeed, there is no sense of today about these people *at all*, and that fact is, at once, what is so enchanting, so fascinating and so horrifying about this wedding. I feel as if I am witnessing the ancient core, the very roots of sexism, peering at an X-ray where outward subtleties and deceits vanish and the gut of inner truth all hangs out. Women are dirty, strange creatures; they possess some devilish sexual power over men which, unleashed, will devour them. Clearly they must be diminished, contained, segregated. Shave her head (such a classic power-divesting symbol) and she will be chained to you. Remind her once a month of her vileness and the better she will serve you.

But there are confusions, ambiguities, still in my mind. My neighbor tells me the period of abstinence is splendid for the sex life: "The anticipation makes it like a honeymoon every month. It's always like the first time all over again." She's been married for twenty-four years, and there is something about her—some quality of contentment and self-caring—that makes me believe her. And yet intuitively I know that if you think a woman is untouchable and dirty you do not love her and on the deepest levels you must not —cannot—enjoy her sexuality.

Meanwhile, back at the wedding, passion is pudding-thick. A ten-foot-tall partition, cloaked in greenery, has been erected, dividing the room into male and female halves. (At Level Ten Glatt Orthodox weddings the rabbis will sit at a table in the corner and put up a barrier around their very own table, so that there is nary a possibility of even catching a glimpse of woman-flesh.) The dinner is heavy and unceasing —the historical product of a people who obviously believed every meal to be their last. Everybody gorges (how? what stomach pocket possibly remains unoccupied?) but indifferently. It's the nonstop dancing, building orgasmically in its fervor, that is turning on the whole joint. In one number, the groom sits on a chair that is then hoisted atop several pairs of shoulders and whirled about dizzyingly. On the bride's turf, the dances are less macho but equally as impassioned, breathless. There is never a time when the music stops, when the fever lulls, when the folks sit down and relax. Old men gambol about with old men, grandmas with tiny girl children. It builds and builds and builds. . . . How odd to suddenly realize that the young couple for whom this tribal revelry is being celebrated will never in their lives, never once, dance together. How odd, and anachronistic and—ultimately—how unfathomable.

If the Orthodox Jewish culture has been bizarrely immune to any trickling influences from the world at large, what can you say about a black wedding in Harlem where the soloist croons "Oh Danny boy, the pipes the pipes are caw-all-ling"? And where a bevy of lady guests are gussied up in blond wigs?

To begin with, you can say the obvious: that the black population has been tragically bereft of its own ethnic identity, its linkage to black history and culture. The emergence of an Afro-American sense is very new, very limited. Then you can make a direct parallel to white society and that peculiar truth about weddings: most "Consciousness III" youngsters, kids who have rejected, at least for the moment, the values of their parents, return to the fold for their weddings. Black kids—whatever their personal goals and politics—do not, statistically, don the dashikis and bone up on African tribal rites for their nuptials; they rent a catering hall, spread out the roast turkey and potato salad and the band plays "Theme from Dr. Zhivago."

Among the poor, where there is little enough romance or celebration or pageantry in their daily existences, The Wedding is easily life's only rainbow. But in the striving middle class, the psychology is like the middle-class Jewish: the wedding is less a manifestation of life's continuum, one of the joyful instants in the pendulum process of joy-sorrow, than it is an undeniable demonstration of the family's success! Status! Position! Respectability!

Barbara Boggs, a professional wedding consultant in Washington, D.C. (Wonderful Weddings is her company), makes the observation that in her city, where there is a large, continually expanding black population, "the big money these days is being spent on black middle-class affairs. The white society is toning down spending—because of the recession and the fact that there are so many parties in this town nobody's much impressed by flashy hors d'oeuvres anymore— but among the blacks, we see more and more tented weddings for five hundred. For them, it's the period of social arrival."

At the New Covenant Baptist Church, on 157th Street and Amsterdam Avenue, on a cool Saturday afternoon in September, Catherine Richmond is marrying Curtis Trueheart. She is a social worker, twenty-nine, and he is a union troubleshooter (whatever that is) of forty-two. Although this is her second marriage (his first), she's having a big splashy blowout. Six ushers, six bridesmaids, ring bearers and flower girls, two hundred guests, Cadillac limousines to shepherd folks to the reception at a catering establishment across town.

A half hour before the ceremony is to begin, the scene is true street theater. A black face and shoulders hangs out of every tenement window on the block. Silent, gleaming black limos rim the curb, making a somehow ominous picture. Excited kids and skinny dogs run back and forth, peering inside the dark, empty vehicles, anticipating the action. Poised on the narrow Harlem street is the ramshackle old church, and from a block's distance one can spot a fierce explosion of color—pinks and purples—on its steps.

There are the six ushers, ushering, and they're gorgeous. Double-breasted maroon velvet Edwardian frock coats, shocking-pink ruffled shirts, black silk bow ties, bell-bottoms. Absolutely spiffy jazzy gorgeous. Seventy dollars to rent for the day, one tells me, boasting.

And the guests, starting to arrive now, bearing gifts in hand, gigantic fancy-wrapped parcels, appliances mostly. What a parade, what costumes, such get-out! Sequined, gilted, jangling, sparkling, beaded, chiffoned, starched. Mink stoles, gold spike-heeled shoes, bare midriff, maxi-mini-midi, fringe, spangles, orange hair, blond curls, an occasional Afro, kiddies with ribbons flowing from everywhere. Eye-boggling cleavage, twenty bracelets on one arm. *Quelle* contrast to the barren, bleak church, with hardly a flower, windows too dirty to see through and a portable fan perched on a table set between the pews. A perfect Manhattan set, I think. The organ is broken today so a lady from the congregation plays a not-too-healthy piano—"Clair de Lune," I think it is —and then another lady sings "Ohdannyboythepipesthe-pipes . . ."

Is there one person here who isn't taking pictures madly? Flashbulbs, the whir of a movie camera, snap, wind, focus. Is this a once-in-a-lifetime spectacle, never before and never since, the Pope's visit to New York, Jackie Kennedy come to the Apollo Theater, an event to be recorded for the millennium?

The bridesmaids make their appearance. Gorgeous too, dressed to kill in shocking pink flowing to the floor, matching cloche caps, dainty white pearl earrings. Dynamite knockouts they are. Now the bride's Cadillac pulls up and she is swarmed over by the street audience. Bob Dylan arriving at a rock concert. Catherine's the celeb today; because of her there's fuchsia and limousines come to Harlem, blocking out the garbage in the gutters and what a mighty show!

"It's just a big dress-up, that's what it's all about," claims the best man. "How often you get decked out like this and have a big blast? The main draw is the reception and then the parties afterward, goin' on all night. You're in the groove anyway, so it's a ball!"

"A weddin' is heartwarming," says the woman sitting next to me in church, wrapped in battle-scarred silver fox. "There aren't too many warm things left in life. No matter how short the marriage lasts, the weddin' is a beautiful thing."

Directly behind the Baptist minister, on the altar, hangs suspended a five-foot color framed photo of himself. His sermon lasts twenty-five minutes ("Sweet and long," I hear whispered at its dramatic high point). His singsong emotion-

ality is punctuated all the way through by the congregation's noisy agreements. "Amen" . . . "Say so" . . . "That's
right, Lawd" . . . "You tell 'em". . . .

"We're here to join in holy matrimony which is mighty
nice. Man gets mighty lonesome." "A-Men" to that one. He
immediately launches into what apparently is his pet topic
of the moment—woman's place. "The Bible says, 'Wives,
submit yourselves to your husbands.' That's where you wives
get off base, not wanting to obey your husbands. The wife
needs to look up to her husband, reverence him, be obedient
to him." ("That's right, right. . . .") "The husband is the
head, the wife is the foot. The head tells the feet what to
do, where to go, and I wanna tell you somethin' right now.
Anythin' with two heads isn't normal." ("A-men, Lawd.
. . ." "Say so. . . .")

"No woman wants this liberation stuff who's got a real
husband. If the woman lets the husband be head of the
house, you won't go downtown to see the lawyer. That's the
truth." Not a soul disagrees with that one.

He bellows a lot about divorce, instructions to avoid it.
"This is what breaks up a home, in-laws who cling too close.
The mother and father's hands have to leave go of their
children." Loudly paying tribute to life's tragedies and trib-
ulations, he gets better, more howling, wailing, every minute,
and the wedding guests really begin to jive: "In this tiiim-
mme, when men and women don't seem to be satisfiiiieeeed
with each other . . ." "A-men, Lawd, Lawd. . . ."

Is this a wedding sermon, I wonder to myself. But, to be
sure, the ability of the black culture to verbalize suffering
is much keener than other groups'. It is clear from this ceremony that blacks hold few fantasies about marriage and the
perfect glories therein. ("I now pronounce you man and wife
and you go on about your business," is his closing.) Have I
ever before heard the existence of divorce acknowledged in
a wedding service? Certainly not. But here it is spelled out
up front, in spades, with helpful hints for prevention.

To the blacks the wedding ritual has less to do with the acting out of notions about flawless, till-death-us-do-part ecstatic future than some other momentous human need. In these gray surroundings, with the aluminum fan whirring an accompaniment to the proceedings, I sense that it's all much closer to a hunger in one's life for color, splendor, spectacle, drama. "No matter how short the marriage lasts," says the realist, who's seen no more carnage than the rest of us, but hasn't learned to confuse The Wedding with Wedded Bliss, "the weddin' is a beautiful thing." To the struggling black middle class, seeking all the U.S. of A. good-life symbols and cut off from its own historical roots, the wedding represents the classic tale of Doing Everything Just Right. Ushers in their $70 rented doodads, the shiny limos, the sit-down dinner at the Savoy Manor Ballroom, the air of rather stuffy propriety, the waltzing. Nice people. Respectable, Making-It Americans.

5. Members of the Wedding

Within the supermarket of wedding styles, the jumbo array
of choices—shall we have it at home, in a hotel, on a hilltop, in church, at the country club, on Uncle Herman's
putting green, on the Staten Island ferry?—certain elements
are fixed, essential, ubiquitous. Nobody, but nobody, has a
wedding wingding without music, or a photographer, or a
cake or flowers. It may be Lester Lanin and the Bachrach
studio, or Cousin Shirley's precocious little daughter on the
accordion and Aunt Beverly with the Brownie Reflex and
the mail-order course in Artistic Photography. The vittles
may be in quantity to stuff the population of Vermont for a
snowbound week, or able to be seen only through a high-
powered microscope. No matter. The American wedding
does not take place without them.

A combination of tradition, spiritual need and external
pressure demands it. Weddings have always been accom-
panied by flowers, a major fertility symbol; to boot, floral
decorations are beautiful, festive, in general connected to
celebration; then, since everybody else's halls are decked with
boughs of flowering quince and baby's breath, what kind of
chintzy fellow are you for denying them to your daughter
and guests?

The battalion of servicemen—the caterer, the cake maker,
the rentals man—thrive on the wedding fiesta. Many grow
exceedingly plump and some, like tapeworms, fatten while

their host starves. Who they are, how they operate, their relationship with client form a key chapter of the American wedding story.

Two seemingly incompatible qualities epitomize the wedding specialists: extreme romantic sentimentality about weddings, and the compulsive, cynical thrust to make you spend more than you want to or can afford. I have seen both in operation: a bandleader in Los Angeles who, after twenty years of wedding-working, actually displayed tear-filled eyes as an unspectacular bride trooped down the aisle at the Brentwood Country Club; I also saw a caterer, possessed with the subtlety of a door-to-door vacuum cleaner hawk, convince a customer that her frolic would be utter schlocksville if the caviar were to be, as she wished, something humbler than beluga.

The vulnerability, you see, is monstrous, the situation laden with intensity and the relationship, hence, critical. One is not buying a pair of rubbers or a new freezer where minor emotional baggage is attached to the purchase, where the salesman is peripheral and the product crystal clear and if it doesn't work you simply return it. The involvement between wedding fixer and wedding giver is more like patient and doctor—you don't know what he's doing until he's done it and by then it's too late. So you must trust. And what you are really buying is a dream.

In this case you are placing your "life" in the hands of a florist or a baker. A mother told me how the floral arrangements on the dais at her daughter's wedding were terribly skimpy, how it ruined the whole day as far as she was concerned. Her lips were pinched in the telling, her eyes visibly moistened just remembering it. And this catastrophe took place twelve years ago, but she hasn't forgotten. Or forgiven. Too much pepper in the vichyssoise and it's declared a National Disaster. A band that plays too loud rock or too slow cha-chas and Mama's life is over.

From terror, or insecurity or childlike faith, the wedding-

thrower tends to leave everything in the mavins' hands—
which is precisely where they wish the power to reside. The
fingers, then, tend to stretch out and grasp more than just
their allotted share. The iffy-piffiest caterer in Los Angeles,
Milton Williams, will go shopping with the bride for her
gown; a florist in Denver also handles the invitations and
hires the parking valets; *everybody* considers himself a consultant, coordinator and four-star general. A photographer
in Houston sends a lackey to help the bride and bridesmaids
get dressed. Ultimately, one forgets whose wedding it really
is.

Then, of course, there is the whole subject of the Kickback. A common enough American sport, it is otherwise
known as One Hand Feeding the Other. It works at all
levels in the wedding industry: you, the caterer, recommend
your buddy the photographer and your other pal the rentals-
supply man and they in turn express their gratitude to you.
The bridal consultant in the department store has her palm
greased by the florist, who in turn gets a little something
from the bandleader, who also has to spread a few dimes to
the hotel banquet manager. The professional wedding consultant, lucky her, gets it from all directions, since she hires
EVERYBODY, but no one's immune to the bug. Should
the seamstress who's sewing tiny beads on the bridal gown
in the back room recommend the fellow she knows who
carves swans out of ice, she gets a kickback from him. According to an executive at Bradford Bachrach, the well-
known portrait photography studio, "Every girl in America
could get married for twenty percent less if this practice
stopped." The funny fact is that every pro admits the existence of the system, deplores it and assures you that he's the
only virgin in America.

The caterers, I must tell you, are the most fun to talk
to. Appropriate words like "juicy" and "spicy" apply. All
obsessively devoted to food, they are, for the most part, fat.

Obviously they adore what they do, even the bad ones and the mediocre pigs-in-blankets-and-deviled-eggs fellows (most caterers, inexplicably, are men). And they will be able to recall instantaneously every menu of their lives, as many a fashion freak can tell you precisely what she has worn to every memorable occasion of the last ten years.

The near-favorite story of Milton Williams, a warm and handsome black man of about forty, is of a society wedding he catered some years back on chic Harbor Island, with guests arriving from all over southern California. Let him tell it: "The hostess's idea of a wedding was a cucumber sandwich and a glass of champagne. I said, 'How can you have the audacity to ask people to drive four hours for a piece of watercress? Is that all you think of your guests?' Well, she gave in and we wound up with three round buffet tables of schnitzel paprikash, barley soufflé, watercress and endive sandwiches and oysters in saki cups, plus cheese and fruit. It was superb."

Now, this saga has several classic elements. The menu, indeed superb and inventive (Milton would rather burn his béarnaise than ever serve a deviled egg), and the exercise of power, sheer intimidating power. How else can a hostess respond to the huffy accusation of is-that-all-you-think-of-your-guests but to lay on the full groaning board?

Milton (*"everybody* calls me Milton") is an elegant connoisseur of good food and good living (he is also a decorator and lives in a spectacular home in the Hollywood hills). He swears, and one absolutely believes it, that he has never created the same menu twice; his phone number has been unlisted for seventeen years, and I have heard him referred to, by worshipful clients, as both "the Tiffany of caterers" and "the Messiah." Which may seem a little exalted for a chef, but then in southern California folks are very dependent on their helpers. Milton does the usual catalog of weddings, grandiose clambakes and wee at-home dinners for 120 or forty or eight plus out-of-town conventions for eight hundred. He is acknowledged to be the most expensive cook in L.A., but won't discuss crass money, never with me and hardly ever with his customers. "I never ask the price of anything that I buy for a party. I only ask quality. If I think enough of you to invite you to my home, then my best isn't good enough." Which is interesting logic since it is *not* his home and he *isn't* paying, but don't tell Milton that. He orders exotic vegetables flown in from wherever and evidently drives baker Gary Hansen berserk with his cavalier philosophy about dough—hiring him to create lavish cake productions but never giving him money guidelines. But then, Milton's clients—90 percent of his business is repeat—probably don't care much either. He has no set fee, bases it on what he has to buy for the party, but says, "Once I give an estimate, that's it. If I say twenty dollars a head and it ends up twenty-five, I feel it's my fault and I take the loss."

In that moral vein he recounts to me the tale of an old eccentric rich lady who, thinking that she was dying (she wasn't), decided to throw a "swan song" party, renting live swans to grace the swimming pool. Milton says: "She insisted I cook all the food early in the morning for that night, and I was foolish enough to give in to her anxiety. Everything was, to my taste, rotten. I went into the living room in the middle of the dinner and personally invited everybody to come back the very next night for another party, at my expense. This little fiasco cost me personally seven thousand dollars."

Milton is a prime illustration of thickness between wedding specialist and host. He has the keys to several swell homes and to several skeleton-filled closets in those homes. "I hear all the 'tsouris' from the parents," he says in a speech that is frequently laced with Yiddishisms. "If the girl is marrying a hippie or a boy who isn't Jewish, I get it all, even Papa's heart attack." But Milton does have such a haimish, empathetic quality that you surely want to embroil him in every "tsouris" of your life.

Because of his power in the catering sphere, he gets away with murder. For Danny Thomas' daughter's wedding at the Century Plaza Hotel—a caterer's services are really superfluous in this case—he went in and cooked with the chef. "It's not allowed," he admits. "Most of these guys are European and, you know, they think they wrote the book." When he does a hotel gala, he brings in his own staff—twenty-two people who work for him as bartenders, waiters and cooks— "to keep our standards up." Also forbidden. And he frequently argues with banquet managers when he feels the liquor bill has been unduly escalated.

His anecdotes all reflect the quality of his needing you infinitely less than you need him: "A very rich, social-climbing woman called me to do her daughter's wedding. She said she wanted pastrami, corned beef, salami, lox and cream cheese. I simply said, 'I don't do this sort of thing. Why don't you call a delicatessen?' She said, 'No, no, Milton, I must have *you*.' So I suggested a smorgasbord with a man slicing Nova Scotia salmon to serve on hot rolls and brioche, a noodle soufflé with mushrooms. Plus some beautiful cold meats if she wanted. But cole slaw, *never*. She said she was convinced, then I told her the price and she was appalled. Do you know this nebbish called back at six A.M. to beg me to do the wedding? I refused, naturally."

In the old days, people "catered" their weddings themselves, or with the help of family and friends (not unlike the principle of the New Wedding). Or they had servants who did it. Now, with the disappearance of both traditions, a new career category has arisen—the Party Professional. People who are paid to help other people entertain. Yet another in the grab bag of technological achievements that cuts us off from our activities. We have our cars washed by machines, our gardens gardened by gardeners. We take our dogs to "boutiques" so that others may bathe them; if we're especially busy or precious, we even hire somebody else to walk them. We surrender control to such a degree that a bride-to-be told me, about the menu for her reception: "I *loathe* Beef Wellington, but the caterer told me he loves to prepare it and it always impresses the guests, so I agreed to have it as the main course. I can always eat before the ceremony."

There are, obviously, caterers and caterers. The Milton Williamses who cook in their own kitchens, shop personally for every item, rearrange the client's furniture, invent everzingier party gimmicks—for a French picnic fete he handdelivered, as invitations, two hundred miniature straw baskets filled with fresh vegetables—and are practically members of the family (a Beverly Hills hostess says it's not uncommon in her circle for a guest to enter, shake her hand and kiss the caterer). And who never, but never solicit business but, on the contrary, make you feel positively *blessed* if they agree to take your case.

Ruth Factor, also in Los Angeles, is the more usual breed of caterer. Operating from an office-cum-professional kitchen, one section of which is for take-out hors d'oeuvres, she tells you immediately that she is the "resident caterer" of Temple Beth-El, an apparent coup. I go to see her one morning, posing as a bride in search of a chef; subsequent to my visit, for the following month, I receive several letters from Mrs. Factor soliciting my supposed soiree.

Ruth Factor is very Jewish, very motherly and very enthusiastic. Depending on how you feel about your own mother, you either trust that she will personally spend five days perspiring over a steaming stoveful of your favorite goodies, preparing them with infinite love and compulsiveness, or you believe that she will unmercifully screw you. In either case, she is a zesty woman whose slogan is "You can eat the decorations." By that she means that items on her platters that look like flowers are really radishes, and things that look like leaves are actually green peppers. All sculpted by Ruth herself. "It's like an artist when you paint a picture," she explains.

When I ask about serving pieces and dishes, she replies: "We're getting away from silver. It's overdone. We use gorgeous plastic platters that cost forty dollars apiece. The most gorgeous things you ever saw in your life"—a phrase also used, I notice, to describe the chicken chow mein.

Thomas Thomasser is THE caterer in San Francisco, but in fact much more. "We're social directors, hosts, a total entertainment corporation. Other caterers just provide food and service; we do everything—give music, produce entire shows. I can even put together a whole party, including twenty guests, in two hours." (Evidently lonely businessmen from out of town frequently request just that service, and Thomasser has a revolving list of what might be called professional guests, or freeloaders.)

He is a very portly young man whose even portlier enterprise (thirty or forty parties every weekend) operates from a wonderful sort of townhouse on a San Francisco hill, and, despite the eighty employees, fifty bartenders and waiters, fourteen chefs and the claim that they can produce enough meat to feed two thousand people every twenty-five minutes, the atmosphere is only slightly less homey than Aunt Jemima's kitchen. When he talks about crepes and soufflés and quiches and mousses—which he does, a lot—it is with such a profound lust that you veer between becoming embarrassed at hearing such intimacies from a stranger and aching to run out instantaneously for a hot fudge sundae.

His father was butler to Templeton Crocker, the great host of San Francisco, the Perle Mesta, as it were, of the Bay Area. In 1958 father and son started their own catering establishment, which in these fifteen years has soared from grossing $150,000 a year to over $1 million. Currently Thomas packages his own line of frozen gourmet goodies, has four franchised restaurants, a retail wineshop in the basement, runs executive dining rooms in banks and has his very own plum pudding oven. He works the catering route from Reno to Santa Barbara.

Caterers generally charge by the person, $25 a head being nifty-high, $15 closer to the average. The admitted profit is around 20 percent. Thomasser, whose vast factory requires more elaborate computations, says he charges five times the food cost or four times the cost of his labor. And he claims he can tell ahead of time, almost to the nickel, what a wedding will run the host by figuring that partyers consume eight to ten hors d'oeuvres at a reception and one-half bottle of champagne if no liquor is served, or four drinks apiece.

A gigantic problem for caterers is the varying of the menu. It is very likely, in this business so highly dependent upon personal recommendation, that many of your patrons will move in the same social cliques, be invited to the very same weddings and dinner do's. The low-end caterers don't care too much and you're liable to overhear guests muttering, "Well, the potato casserole was much better last week at the Johnson wedding, but the chicken fricassee is less salty tonight than at the Wiley party." Classier merchants avoid this depth of tackiness in a variety of ways. Thomasser, for one, keeps vast card files detailing entire menus, one for every person who's ever thrown a party with him. And since he personally knows all the crusty folks in San Francisco, he can quickly calculate who's going to be at Mrs. X's regatta who was duplicated at Mrs. Y's last month and so he'd better not do the caviar omelet number again. And, although he insists "I only serve what I like to eat," over six thousand recipes repose in his repertoire. "We've served everything," he states, "from veal in chocolate sauce to a whole cow. But never steak or spaghetti, and I don't go for gimmicks like colored cream cheese."

The kind of food that's most popular depends, among other aspects, on the area of the country. Los Angeles is more meat-and-potatoesy than San Francisco or New York; in Houston—according to caterer David Moncrief—it's real "Amurrican," with a flash of Mexican. "Egg rolls and sweet-and-sour chicken is about as exotic as we ever get. I do stuffed grape leaves occasionally, but a lot of people think they're old green cigars." Moncrief, I should point out, is the only saintless wedding professional I have spoken to, the only man in the industry who will fess up to taking kickbacks from everybody he deals with.

Getting a florist to describe to you how he puts together a wedding is rather like asking a Mafia magnate to tell you about his day at the office. It's not only the reluctance—which is considerable. It is also the fact that, for most of us, it is as impossible to comprehend forty thousand pink American Beauty roses as it is $100 million. I know what three dozen roses are, but forty thousand? And those are the numbers in which they deal. Five thousand orchids? A hundred dozen blue delphiniums? And who knows what a "blue delphinium" is anyway? Or a smilax, or a stephanotis or a phaleonopsis or any of those other blossoming wonders that are bread-and-butter to the industry?

Throughout history, the presence of flowers at weddings has been paramount—one of the primary earmarks of ongoing life. Orange blossoms, for example, embody the highest of all virtues—innocence, purity, lasting love and fertility—and thus the greatest good fortune. (At least according to the Chinese, Greeks, Romans and the Crusaders who introduced them to northern Europe.) Says *The Folklore of Weddings and Marriage:* "Because the tree is an evergreen, it symbolizes the lasting nature of love. Because it bears both blossoms and fruit at one and the same time, it symbolizes, in the delicate blossoms, the innocence and purity of young love, and, in the fruit, the proved promise of fertility and motherhood."

The bridal bouquet was not originally composed of flowers at all, but of a potent combination of garlic, chives, rosemary, bay leaves and other strong herbs, the purpose being to drive away evil demons threatening the couple's happy state.

Today, flower power is a $1½ billion a year industry, $250 million of that sum gleaned from weddings. If any doubt exists of whether the transformation of a catering chamber into the entire forest primeval works to dispel the demons or ensure fertility, there is certainly no question that flowerage is one of the essential status symbols in the American wedding. Sparsity of floral adornments is, in some crowds, like no food or, in other orbits, like pouring New York State champagne. Chintzy. An insult to your guests, a face-slap to your daughter.

How much the flowers cost depends, obviously, on who you are and where the wedding is being held. Many churches around the nation have outlawed botanical excess under the odd and un-American theory that it has nothing to do with religion. (A florist in Denver told me about a Catholic wedding where the family wanted extravagance and the priest forbade it. They planned the ceremony, thus, for when he would be away on vacation, and installed $3000 worth of flowers. Except that he came back unexpectedly the night before and had them remove every last daisy.)

Hotels, on the other hand, revel in gluttony. The banquet manager at the Pierre in Manhattan tells me "you can't do it properly for under three thousand dollars," implying that one will desecrate his sanctuary by spending a cent less. I viewed the finished decorations for a wedding at the Plaza—a simple but quite lovely forest setting, mostly greens and very few flowers—and watched the banquet manager's frozen assessment of the room, as if he were peering at one of his buffet tables piled high with bologna sandwiches.

Home weddings can be the least exorbitant, unless you are the Beverly Hills tobacco czar who transmogrifies your humble estate into a southern plantation for your daughter's wedding, by gluing billions of magnolia blossoms to the elm trees. Then, too, a half million white roses and five thousand orchids decorate the library for the twelve-minute ceremony; the flower bill is $150,000 and the happy couple is divorced four years later.

Stanley Kersten, a Los Angeles florist, says that the very cheapest he can manage is $1000 at a hotel and $500 in a garden but admits that $10,000 worth of wedding posies "would be rather overdone." Harry Finley, in Beverly Hills, won't touch a job for under $3000 and confesses: "I come to your house and the first thing I do is look in your clothes closet to see the kind of taste you have, froufrou or tailored. Then I decide."

In any case, the flowers are the most variable and flexible of all wedding costs, depending on the season of the year, the part of the country, the quantity, the containers and the dexterity of the florist. Many floral bills should rightly win the Pulitzer Prize for fiction. Some fellows use artificial greenery on the walls and ceilings of a room but charge for real; some, reports the banquet manager of a Detroit hotel, use seconds (day-old flowers) from the wholesale market, which are already in their terminal stages before you reach the peach melba; still others charge for yellow roses but furnish the room with yellow daisies, assuming rightly that the hyper-excited family won't notice. The prime chutzpa is confirmed by reports that Saturday night's white tulips had been seen at Sunday morning's wedding brunch. Each bride had paid as though the flowers existed only for her.

Even the very reputable boys can't estimate what the price will be. Stanley Kersten goes to the flower market in the wee morning hours but can never be sure what posies are available that day or if it's a good crop. In Houston, Bob Galloway has to import everything, as Texas grows no flowers whatsoever, so he's dependent on the airmails, the ice and the reliability of ferns from Seattle, roses from San Francisco and anemones from New York. Kersten, who charges the customer $4 for every $1 he pays, admits that often he has to make out a fake bill for the father, sending the real tab to the mother, who will then pay him the difference over a period of months, from her own pocket. "All the father is interested in," he's noticed, "is where the bar is and how's the booze."

Like everybody else in this emotionally charged, intensely personal industry, most florists are prima donnas. They often insist on working with the caterer *they* prefer, and feel it their moral obligation to command. Harry Finley bills himself "Party Coordinator," which means he has his tentacles implanted in the invitations, the menu and the music. Stanley Kersten tries to talk the family out of banquet tables and into round bridal tables (it's not clear exactly why) and admits: "I walk out on weddings if I can't stand the taste. I just won't tolerate it when it's a formal wedding but they want the bridesmaids to carry baskets. It goes against my grain." Bob Galloway won't work on Sunday, therefore excluding himself from the big Jewish market in Houston, and won't do December weddings because of busy work with Christmas decorations. In addition, he disdains the common practice of moving the floral pieces from church to home. "It's horribly cheap to carry dripping vases, tripping over the guests with a bowl held over your head, shrieking, 'Excuse me, coming through,' leaking water, rushing in front of everybody to plunk a vase on a table. I refuse."

Florists, more than the other arms of the wedding tree, are experiencing changes in taste. Kids are more attracted to field flowers and informal greenery and plants in their natural states than staid arrangements. Enormous flowing bridal bouquets are on the decline and, if you believe Mel Atlas, the movie *Goodbye, Columbus* has killed—or at least permanently maimed—the blossom trade. "That movie murdered us," he says with a fair amount of murderous hysteria. "It's been a disaster for the industry. Now all the time I hear, 'Don't give me a *Goodbye, Columbus* wedding,' from the mothers as well as the daughters. That damn movie is responsible for simplicity becoming In. It's hurt us, since the more flowers we sell the better it is. My average big wedding used to run six thousand dollars in flowers. Now it's a helluva lot less." Atlas' reaction is perhaps so violent not only because his wallet is a bit less bulgy, but because *he* is the villain responsible for the wildly elaborate floral decorations in *Goodbye, Columbus.*

The high point of her life occurred when the mayor of Inglewood, California, proclaimed March 13, 1967, as "Edie Steinmetz Day," to commemorate her appearance on "What's My Line?" What *is* her line that commands such trumpets? Well, Edie Steinmetz owns a company called Doves of Happiness. That is to say, she rents out doves for weddings, flower shows, debutante cotillions and whichever of life's occasions call for the presence of her tiny feathered friends. In any other part of the world but southern California, Edie Steinmetz would be considered a bona fide "crazylady"; here, in Lotus Land, she is just another of your basic bananas. I adored her instantly.

She operates from a store that is closer to being an eccentric's attic in its chaotic clutter. Wrought-iron cages of every possible dimension, fake trees, filigree archways, seven-foot columns, something she's labeled a "floralabra," which is a candle holder made from plastic flowers. All props for her beloved doves—120 of them, each with its own name and each easily recognizable to Edie. "Liberace," for instance, was named in tribute to none-other-than-himself when, during an engagement at the Los Angeles Home Show, the star kept a cage of Edie's birds sitting next to the piano and at each performance bestowed a special honor upon them by playing "La Paloma"—"The Dove."

It all began for Edie in 1959, when she was just a fortyish housewife. A neighbor, she recounts, gave her a tiny wounded baby squirrel (she is the kind of schmaltzy lady who is undoubtedly *always* being given tiny wounded somethings to de-wound). Anyway, Edie nursed "Sally Squirrel" on a doll's milk bottle, getting up every morning at 5 A.M. to refill the hot-water bottle on which ailing Sally slept. Now, what this has to do with doves becomes immediately clear: after Sally Squirrel recovered, Edie went to buy a cage for her and the pet store man asked her to take care of his white dove, Petey, while he went away. Edie, so that the bird shouldn't be lonesome, found him a mate named Polly. "Polly and Petey fell madly in love," says she with a marvelous perky smile, "but they were both males. It was heartbreaking." (Apparently—I learn from Edie's capsulized lesson in ornithology—it is impossible visibly to discern male from female doves. It only becomes evident when one lays an egg. Or doesn't.) "So I searched and searched for two females, and you can't imagine how hard it was to find doves around here." Naturally Edie found them, after driving all over California. Pat and Pam. And a year later she had five additions to the brood.

"The family was growing and what to do with it became my obsession. Nobody was renting doves back in 1959, and when I had the idea, my husband Joe thought I was nuts. 'Mommy,' he said [yes, he calls her "Mommy"; she calls him "Honey"], I think you're crazy, but I'll stand behind you in whatever you do." Edie accumulated, in the first year, thirty birdies. As of now, her nest supports 120 and she takes the eggs away. "You can only handle so many, you know, so you have to use birth control." The platoon is kept partially in her home, in an aviary, and with a young couple who work for her as dove messengers. And a pair sit in the store window at all times. When I ask Edie if she knows specifically which two are here today, she peers at them for just an instant and says, confidently, "Oh yes. That's Princess Margaret and that one's Charity."

Edie, I suspect, is a little bit of a celebrity hound. But who in this town isn't? She did the wedding of Jack Lemmon and Felicia Farr ("our doves were there for that"), David Hemmings' wedding, in which five cages of birds floated in the pool, and Cesar Romero's niece's wedding. She says, "Mr. Romero saw my doves at a luncheon at the Century Plaza and fell madly in love with them." But, she insists, 99 percent of her business is from working girls, girls wanting dove decor instead of altar baskets. And she refuses to do the dove-in-the-cake number. "I'm afraid they won't be able to breathe properly or they'll drop, if you know what I mean," she whispers. I know what she means.

(Doves, in truth, have very dangerous jobs. Every hotel banquet manager has a horror story: having to chase the little darlings when they fly out of the cake and hover menacingly over the guests; the occasional eggs that hatch in the dove centerpieces at dinner; the "flying chuppa" at the Beverly Hilton where doves were contained over the canopy, released with a flourish at the "I do" and all floated to the floor—dead.)

A woman from Long Island called her once, asking Edie to fly in with doves for her daughter's wedding. She refused, on the grounds that the doves couldn't stand the trip. "My doves are cherished and spotlessly clean, bathed every morning. You couldn't be in this business if you didn't really adore birds," she says. Which may qualify as the understatement of the year.

Once in a while a dove lays an egg at a wedding and everybody loves it, since doves are yet another sign of fruitfulness. "But you can't ever tell when it's going to happen," Edie reports. "They just don't look preggy, you know." She always carries a few extra birds to these carnivals, in case one should get dirty. As Edie says, "A dirty dove is like a dirty angel."

Edie's "menus" range from $35 a day for two plain cages, two doves in each, to the deluxe extravaganza of eighteen for $150. Her cages have the breadth of St. Laurent's new spring line: one sits in the arms of a "marble" cherub which in turn sits atop a pedestal; another calls itself a "French Garden Cart"; yet another is an elaborate, flower-bedecked float for the pool. Edie's personal favorite is the "Penthouse Teardrop," a cage-cum-pedestal creation that must be seen to be believed. All are wrought iron, adorned with "permanent flowers"—California euphemism for "fake." In Edie's most lavish clambake to date, she placed twelve cages lining the aisles of a hotel ballroom, with a spotlight effect centered on her doves, whom she refers to, mostly, as her dovies. Birds are always rented in couples, in part as romantic symbolism, and partly so they don't get lonely, a state that—to listen to Edie—happens to doves at least as often as it does to mankind.

If there is a higher power that matchmakes people to their careers, Edie was guided to the pluperfect job. She is so sentimental, so syrupy as to make Rod McKuen come off like Kafka. Throughout our meeting she regales me with dove tales that repeatedly bring both of us to the brink of tears. "I was doing the World Beauty Show at a sports arena," is the beginning of one pearl. "I had brought two rare South American tiny diamond doves, and one escaped. I was miserable to think that poor little dovie would starve to death. Everybody in the place searched for four days, sent messages and pleas over the PA system. On the fourth day, just as we were giving him up for lost, there he was—a little dove perched outside the cage, peering in longingly at his mate on the inside." She sniffles, and I sniffle, utterly relieved for the happy ending, absurdly thankful the little dovie didn't die, after all, of starvation. Or loneliness.

This remarkable quirky lady whose entire wardrobe is, in some way, embellished with her trademark—silk smocks embroidered in doves, silver dove earrings and matching pendant, artificial dove hair ornament—is not only a gooey pussycat. Like a true Horatio Alger American, Edie has stretched what might seem like a rather limited enterprise, a bird-on-the-brain fetish, into big box-office. "My dovies make a lot of personal appearances, have been seen a lot on TV," she brags, referring not only to her "What's My Line?" caper but "To Tell the Truth" also, and a parcel of local Los Angeles shows. She lectures all over southern California, billed as "The Doves of Happiness Lady," talking about the biblical history and significance of doves (Noah, it seems, was brought the news of the flood's finish by a dove with red mud on its feet). She tells the story of Sally Squirrel and stresses the soapy themes of It's-Never-Too-

Late and Life-Begins-at-Forty. "For lectures I use my pet doves, Melanie and Fancy," Edie says. "They're trained to sit on my shoulders quietly. I also do magic tricks, like producing a dove out of fire or out of a balloon. I'm lousy, but most of my audience doesn't know any better."

She is also the inventor of the dove-o-gram—an invitation or announcement delivered, in some manner that I find utterly inexplicable, by live doves.

Upstairs, above the shop, four blocks from the Marriage License Bureau, is Edie's wedding chapel, where she provides for instant ceremonies ($25 for ten guests, $35 for twenty; chapel holds up to fifty). For an extra $5, she'll tape the ceremony, performed by one of twelve on-call ministers; battery-driven candles cost $12 more; the immense white wrought-iron heart posed at the altar comes free, as do the two dovies transported up from the front window.

As we sit in the chapel, Edie recalls another incident from her daily melodrama, this one involving a fifty-year-old Italian woman who came into the store, saying her twenty-fifth anniversary was approaching and she and her husband had promised to renew their vows on that day. They wanted to have a big celebration for all their friends as her husband had cancer and would be dead in six months. The next day she brought him in to look at the chapel and, in Edie's oft-repeated words, "they fell madly in love with it." But they just couldn't afford the $35 and left, dejected. She continues: "That night I couldn't sleep a wink and decided to track them down and give them the wedding for nothing, but all I knew was his first name and that he was the night watchman at a toy factory somewhere in L.A. I went through all the phone books and called ten toy companies until I finally found him. They had a beautiful ceremony with fifty guests, and a party afterward." Tears, at this point, are overflowing Edie's puppy eyes and running down her round and rosy cheeks. Yes, and mine too.

6. The Dream Brokers

The way the story goes, Lester Lanin was conducting his orchestra at a tip-top society wedding. One of the guests approached him during the break, wanting to confirm a rumor he had recently heard. "Lester, are you Jewish?" was the question. "Not necessarily," smiled Lanin and sauntered away.

Lester Lanin is like that, whether or not the tale is apocryphal. Society bandleaders are like that, having been exposed to a lethal dose of the elitism epidemic among their clients. Some, like Bill Harrington (of Tricia Nixon wedding fame), possess a milky indoors pallor that is often a symptom of blue blood; others, like Peter Duchin, are practically movie stars, and having them play at your party is rather like having Norman Mailer drop in. Meyer Davis, known as the "Millionaire Maestro," has played at every presidential Inaugural Ball since Warren G. Harding's, not to mention the absolute cream of debutante do's (the Philadelphia Assembly Ball, oldest in the United States, has been graced by his presence for fifty years) and charity galas. And don't forget John and Jackie Kennedy's wedding and *every* Du Pont frolic since Hector was a pup (he's already booked for a Du Pont debut on June 6, 1986). Lanin, himself no lump in the upper crust, worked the Rockefeller/Percy nuptials, a Mellon wedding and Tricia's rehearsal ("I didn't do the wedding," he claims, "because I had a date that day in

Dayton, Ohio"). His promotional brochure in addition to stating his credo in Latin—*"Optimum in Musica et Festiva"* —lists a soufflé of what he calls his "august clients"—the Tiffany Ball in Newport, the April in Paris Ball in New York, the Fleur de Lis Ball in St. Louis and the Radnor Hunt Ball in Radnor. Never having heard of any of these august events, I am only reassured of the vast chasm between social planets in this country.

But that's the noteworthy thing about society bands. Although the leaders—Lanin, Davis, Duchin, Harrington—are more snobbish than Mrs. Astor's fabled pet horse, and when cataloguing the soirees at which they've worked will *never* talk about Mrs. Goldberg's son's bar mitzvah, nevertheless they have undoubtedly mined much gold from Mrs. Goldberg, not to mention Mrs. Jones and Mrs. Pasquale. You see, Lanin and Davis are among the hugest orchestra corporations in America, and here is one of the few social areas where the top and lower drawers overlap. You cannot get married at the Maidstone Country Club on Long Island if you're a plebeian—even a loaded one. You can, however, hire one of the forty orchestras playing under the Lester Lanin flag and get all the status that comes along with the name. Lanin, in the flesh, of course, you won't get unless you're willing to spend anywhere from $500 to $2500 extra for the privilege.

They're big business, to be sure. And they (that is, their orchestras) work every kind of gig where music is essential, from a dental convention in Atlantic City—Lanin says a four-day convention can gross him $150,000—to the Stop-and-Shop Trading Stamp dinner dance at the Waldorf, to Mrs. Upnose's tea dance at the Cos Club. Lanin says one-half of his business is weddings; Davis tabulates it at 15 percent. Although their activities tend to be busiest in the East, they'll fly anywhere in the world when the client pays transportation costs for leader and band.

Both Lanin and Davis claim to have initiated the whole

society orchestra thing. Lanin's grandfather and father were traveling musicians, trudging by horse and wagon from place to place, often riding three days to play for a wedding. Lester, who is fluent on piano and drums but these days only conducts, had his own band in Palm Beach at the age of sixteen. Where, one assumes, he began to infiltrate the Beautiful People. Now he boasts: "You name the socialites in this country and I've played for them. The Fords, Du Ponts, Astors, Vanderbilts, Whitneys, plus thousands of millionaires you've never heard of. That's top billing, don't you feel that way too? I've played for all of them. I built my business like a doctor does. I never solicited. I prayed to God for it and He answered."

Davis' son, Emory, now runs the store and conducts. ("I'm cheaper than my father," he says.) With offices in New York, Washington, Philadelphia and Palm Beach, he can and does put together fifty bands for any one evening—having diminished from the heyday of ocean-liner travel, when they had eighty—and "employs" over 1100 musicians. Employs, in this sense, meaning free-lance men who are on call to him, allowed to work for other orchestras so long as they are noncompetitive. In New York, for instance, he has 400 musicians, including twelve piano players and fifteen trumpet players.

Most bandleaders throughout America do not maneuver on such a grand corporate scale. Most have one cluster of musicians of which they are the leader and that's it. Most, also, do not leave their bookings to God. They hustle.

At eleven o'clock one night I receive a phone call from one Jack Gerard, of the Jack Gerard Orchestra, headquarters in the Bronx. He has gotten my name from what he refers to as "the central listing of caterers"—as a bride-to-be and, thus, potential customer. (I have, in the course of this work, sent away for all manner of wedding information and hence my name has become a hot property on the marketplace.) He admits that he has had to look up my number in the Manhattan telephone book and has called time after time before reaching me. Have I hired an orchestra yet? No, say I. Good, could he send me a brochure? And might he, while he has me on the phone finally, tell me a little about the versatile Jack Gerard Enterprises? Good.

"We're a contemporary group, not a hard-rock band," he assures me. "We do Top 40, Bachrach, and when I say we don't do Fillmore East and Creedence Clearwater, I mean it sincerely. And we have a 'tummeler,' a rabble-rouser who does terrific jokes which everybody enjoys." When I ask him for references, for people who have used him at their weddings, he balks with: "Listen, we only play music. We're not lawyers or doctors who do this at night for fun. We're all Juilliard graduates."

Two days later a brochure arrives in the mail ("Hop on the Jack Gerard bandwagon for your next party"), again describing their style as combining "youthful excitement" and "old-fashioned elegance" and listing as credits: "Students of the finest artists in the world" and "More than 10,000 weddings, bar mitzvahs, on-the-spot shows, and parties under their belts to boot." Two days after that another phone call, inviting me to a "musical showcase" at Sandy's Lantern Inn in Westchester County. Jack Gerard and his versatile enterprises will perform for an evening, the purpose of which "is to enlighten you in the realm of good music for your wedding or party." I can bring, he says, my spouse-to-be and anybody else I want and the refreshments are free.

Sandy's Lantern Inn is in Harrison, a small suburban town about an hour's drive from Manhattan. Although the village is charming, Sandy's is a tawdry bar/dive/joint, across from the railroad station. Even before I enter, I am practically overcome by an ear-shattering, head-splitting quantity of sound emanating from within. I presume it's the "youthful excitement" part of the evening.

It's all coming from the four "Juilliard graduates": a drummer, an expressionless electric guitarist, a middle-aged orange-headed lady vocalist wearing wraparound shades and a slave bracelet just below the armpit. The maestro, Jack Gerard himself, is a young replica of an old-time music biz Broadway sharpie, with blindingly shiny clothing and a beard that is just *too* manicured. He plays the slide trombone, wiggling his thighs spastically as if he were being compelled to by an electric exercise machine.

In the audience are about forty very young couples, looking to be of Polish or Italian background. Most of the girls are exceedingly dressed up, some are with their mothers and everybody is ordering free highballs with a vengeance. Two women who work for Gerard slither between the tables, trying to sign up business, handing out promo folders, being professionally amiable, hustling.

His act: never have I heard more noise coming from fewer instruments and less exuberance. One would think, to view the musicians' faces, that they were asleep, were it possible to sleep during such racket. Bossa novas, the "Miami Beach Rhumba," a medley from *Oklahoma!* ("We've found this to be a number we've recorded and a number that goes over extremely big at weddings," introduces Jack).

—"A big favorite of the bride and groom is 'More,' " he says. After "More," they play "Till."

—"And now, the very beautiful 'Theme from the Godfather,' featuring Bobbie!"

At one point Gerard asks everyone to write out his requests and one of the helpers goes through the bar collecting them. As far as I can see, he plays none.

To be expected, the Jack Gerard Enterprises, are a bit cheaper than most wedding bands, running $75 a man for four hours on a Saturday night, the prime time. Prices also depend on the hour of the day and the number of hours involved, but Lanin, for instance, charges $125 a man and up ("My prices depend on the business, but I don't soak the rich. I love these people," he croons). And Michael Paige, an L.A. maestro, gets $95 a person, more if he himself presides.

At hotel blowouts the host is also responsible for feeding the band, at the same per-head cost as for his guests.

Many people are interested in hiring a band only if the leader will agree to be present. A hotel banquet manager in Chicago gossips about a popular local band whose chief would never show up, always telling the same story about being summoned at the last minute to the White House to play for the President.

It had always seemed to me, whenever I thought of all the weddings I had attended, that the music was virtually interchangeable for each one. That conjugal combos—bands that regularly work the wedding circuit and not much else—toot through their repertoire of seventy-five ever-popular ditties, plus Aunt Agnes' request for "Don't Sit Under the Apple Tree with Anyone Else but Me," and that's that. Evidently I'm wrong. Evidently there's an art of programming and timing the music for a wedding that, at least to the tune-smiths, either makes or breaks the party. "You have to watch the faces in the room and the feet, all the time," says Michael Paige. "You have to notice if they're happy and swinging or if too many people are sitting down and not dancing. Or if it's only the kids who are dancing and not the adults, then you have to tone down the rock, change the tempos, play the old songs. It's a very subtle thing. My objective is to keep the dance floor filled all the time."

The emergence of rock, naturally, is what's caused the difficulty, the generational gulf. The wedding musicians were brought up on Freddy Martin, Russ Morgan and Benny Goodman; the kids on the Beatles. Bernie Richards, an L.A. bandleader, says: "In the same way that older people just cannot move their bodies like the kids, the adult orchestra simply can't imitate a rock sound. Sometimes, if it's a really huge bash, I use two groups—a string band and a rock group."

Lester Lanin, who insists he was the first to play rock in society ("I remember. It was at the June Ball in Philadelphia"), employs two groups, The Rocking Chairs and The Footwarmers, and Bill Harrington transported two rock players to the White House for Tricia's wingding. But bear in mind that it's tame stuff. At best it's Richards' "polite rock" or what New York bandman Dutch Wolff calls "bubble-gum rock." "You know, it's incredibly confusing," he muses. "Middle-aged people are so afraid the kids will think they're old that they ask you to play acid rock. They want to be *With It,* but they really hate every note, can't dance to it and it gives them a migraine. But if you play a Glenn Miller tune, they get insulted. Anyway, you just don't get in there with speakers and flatten them against the wall at an elegant country club."

Too, a wide gap exists between music for the Jews and music for the Christians. To begin with, Jews like more South American rhythms: Harrington says 25 percent of the evening is devoted to them, whereas at a Gentile jamboree, it's "one cha-cha per night, if that." Then, society kids go to dancing school when young and learn an up-tempo two-step instead of the classic box-step fox-trot. It harkens back to the Scott Fitzgerald era, and Jews—and others who haven't attended Miss Twinkletoe's classes—can't keep up with the beat.

Lanin, by the way, denies all of these variances, saying, "The top society Jews and Greeks and Italians don't want native music. They're the top."

Bernie Richards confesses that he frequently plays the same numbers over and over, says people don't even notice until after the fifth time. His heaviest moral concern these days is in trying to change the protocol of the first dance in which, by etiquette laws, the newlyweds begin, then the bride is claimed by her father, the groom dances with his mother-in-law, best man with the bride, groom with the maid of honor, etc. Very traditional, very rigid. Bernie says: "There's too many divorces these days, and it gets ridiculous. 'Now the bride dances with her real father, no, her stepfather who's the father at the moment, no, the father who's paying.' I've seen weddings where there are so many fathers-of-the-bride and stepfathers-of-the-groom that the first dance goes on for an hour!"

In California, as in other regions of America where the weather is consistently sunny and the living quarters spacious, weddings frequently take place at home and outdoors, and thus the business of equipment rentals flourishes like grapefruit. In Los Angeles, for instance, folks erect tents across the tennis courts, build dance floors across the swimming pools and blanket the world with artificial grass so authentic that even the family bloodhound thinks he's found a brand-new meadow. Many innocents plan home weddings under the assumption that they will save money, won't have to squirm under hotel liquor exorbitances or the call to transform a sterile catering hall into the botanical gardens. The aftershock of, say, a bill from Krupnicks Party Rentals for $4000 reverberates for years: how did it happen? one pleads. A simple garden fete, a few hundred intimates? Four thousand dollars? That's applesauce, says Bob Berman, the Krupnicks man who sent a tab for around $20,000 to Bob Hope for the rentals on his daughter's wedding. Why, according to the $4329.19 bill sitting in front of me, the price of a big white tent alone is $700 and the plot of fake grass comes to $450 and 400 white chairs are $200 and 425 linen napkins are $76.50 and six salad bowls are $51 and six sets of salad servers are $6. And there's eighty-two separate items on the bill and the next morning—like the rotting flowers lying in wait for the garbage man—they're all gone. Right back to Bob Berman's warehouse.

Sitting in said warehouse is enough stuff to completely furnish every house in Massapequa Park. Over 15,000 chairs, 400 tables of every conceivable size, shape and vintage. Four different styles of chinaware, ranging from the very ritzy to the ultra humble with thousands of pieces in each set—my informal estimate says Berman owns approximately 50,000 plates. Four varieties of glassware, two silver patterns. More.

It used to be that rental equipment was ugly; you considered yourself lucky just to be able to *find* 200 matching glasses and spoons, and the fact that the chairs looked like Kiwanis Club Moderne and the tents as if they were stolen from the visiting carnival was irrelevant. Nowadays tents are termed "marquees" and as often as not are lined with silk to match the maid of honor's frock. Rentals people employ experts to do De Mille lighting, construction engineers to build quaint Venetian bridges over the swimming pool, and the array of glories never ceases.

In Los Angeles, Carl Levin (Medico Rents) works with Milton Williams, the caterer, and Stanley Kersten, the florist, and it's *their* show. Tinkers to Evers to Chance. Carl tries to insist that his clients do away with receiving lines and children (in the wedding party, that is) and boasts that his major innovation has been to change the direction in which the bride and groom face so that the "audience" sees *them,* not the clergyman. He also believes that pressuring parents to spend more than they originally envisioned is right. Moral, even, under the flag of the-more-you-do-the-better-the-wedding.

Rentals men benefit even more than most of the servicemen from such conjugal excess. Their warehouses have bloomed in recent years because the family desires special goodies—like the silk tent lining, or handmade skirting for the cake table to match the organdy tablecloths to match the five hundred chairs specially painted white with yellow seats. Levin or Berman arranges for this stuff to be made up—no rental mogul possesses such fancies—the family pays and *he* keeps.

The most outlandish of overdoses is the scaffolding of the swimming pool, in order to provide a dance floor. The pool must first be completely drained. Next the foundation is built up, from the bottom, in steel. It is then covered with a layer of plywood, cut to the exact shape of the pool. The cost of this one-night stand? $500.

For actor Jack Webb's wedding reception at the Ambassador Hotel in Chicago, the cake was decorated entirely with police badges made out of sugar icing and was so immense that it had to be sawed in half to fit through the door. At a summer stock theater in Massachusetts, where Mickey Rooney was starring in a play called *Alimony,* replicas of his six wedding cakes were displayed in the lobby. Fountains gushing champagne from the peak of the cake are beginning to blossom into popularity. (Nobody can seem to explain to me why the cake doesn't become soaked, but that's neither here nor there.) And Sammy Davis, Jr.'s, most recent wedding sported a three-tiered psychedelic cake ("like one of those far-out posters," says the baker), topped by bride and groom figures in icing overalls.

There is no wedding without a cake. Liquor is optional, food not inevitable, but cake—always. It was one of the most ancient parts of the nuptial rite and one of the primary fertility objects. The early Romans prepared a cake—actually a loaf of bread made of barley—as an offering to the god Jupiter. After sharing a wedge, the groom broke the remainder over his bride's head, signifying both the breaking of the hymen and the dominance of the male over the female. The guests scrambled for the leftover crumbs to take home for luck, as insurance of their own fruitfulness.

In early Anglo-Saxon weddings bread was replaced by small hard biscuits, in turn replaced in the Middle Ages by sweet small buns, brought by the guests themselves and stacked in a high mass in front of the newlyweds. The custom was for the couple to try to kiss over the mound; if successful, they were thus assured of lifelong prosperity and endless children. It was in the Restoration period that the transition was made from sweet bun to solid confection: Charles II, returning to England from exile in France, brought with him French pastry chefs who completed the cake evolution by icing the solid squares with a crust of hardened sugar, then topping the mound with toys and figures. What we think of today as the wedding cake is actually the "bride's cake"—frilly, decorative, not meant to be eaten. The "groom's cake" was dark, a fruitcake, practical, substantial. The sexist implications rise like the yeast.

I cannot tell you why, but all the professional makers of wedding cakes whom I have met are the most colorful casserole of characters in the bridal business. Perhaps it's the repeated exposure to all that confection and goo that makes one a bit more whimsical and vaporous than one's fellows. Paradoxically, the creators are infinitely more flamboyant and bouncy than their creations. Wedding cakes are not only visually indistinguishable from one another, but all taste— no matter what the proclaimed ingredients—like wet wallpaper.

In Houston, Texas, one lady bakes every middle- and upper-class cake in town and she is—like Neiman-Marcus—a household word. Mrs. Steude (rhymes with "booty") was the first woman ever to graduate from Rice University with a degree in chemistry: how and why she made the leap from test tube to cake pan is apparently a private saga, but she's been at it now for forty-four years, whipping out an average of 150 cakes a year. She has sent all of her children through college on the proceeds.

She possesses a dedication and high integrity about her craft that I found myself wishing, throughout a long chat with her (she talks A LOT), one could glimpse in politicians or business giants—folks with the real power. Cakes are to her, in some way that is as obvious as it is incomprehensible, real and living things. "I never send out a cake unchaperoned," she says. "Either my daughter delivers it or my friend from college whom I've known for forty years and I can really trust. And I *always* go to the wedding myself. You know, people at a reception drink or get a little carried away and

they can assassinate or mutilate a cake. I'm a troubleshooter."
And she's serious besides.

I first meet Mrs. Steude at a very posh reception at the
very patrician River Oaks Country Club. I spy this white-
haired, grandmotherly but determined lady entrenched amid
begowned and bejeweled revelers, poised immobile, arms
crossed over chest. Guardian of the cake table. Wearing black
flat ballet slippers, a beige lace dress and a hearing aid, she
seems to me to be the embodiment of all those characters on
the radio serials of my childhood: Aunt Jenny, Ma Perkins
and Stella Dallas. Except that she is, at this moment, an
army general, a secret service man and a German shepherd
all melded together. Formidable. Eyes darting about the
room to ascertain, I suppose, which frolicker is liable to be
drunk enough to "multilate" or "assassinate" or otherwise
endanger the cake. Protective, wary, in charge, on the alert.
She will let no other person cut or serve the cake, executing
the surgery with a silver knife festooned with flowers ("We
never touch anything with our fingers," she prides) and with
the solemnity of a Houston heart transplanter. This particular sweetmeat costs $190 and will ostensibly feed six
hundred Texans.

When she finally relaxes—that is, when most of the cake
has been served and her guard duties thus over—we sit and
chat. (If only she were not watching every mouthful, every
chew, every swallow I am making of the gigantic slab she
has cut me with a Portnoy's-mother's absorption, conversation would be easier.)

She outlines her *modus operandi*. "First," she begins, "I
interview the customer for two hours before taking the job.
To make sure I like the people. I do everything myself, you
know, and it's very important. Some weeks I bake for a
thousand people, which means I could use ninety dozen
eggs. You know how many eggs that is to break yourself?"

Mrs. Steude has two kitchens, $1000 worth of cake pans
which she designed herself, and diagrams every cake on paper.

"Just the setting up of the cake is an engineering project," she says, "but it's all a matter of organization." She begins working on Monday for cakes due the following weekend, by ordering the eggs and chopping the pecans. She makes only two kinds, white and chocolate, her own recipes, decor.ting them with handmade sugar orchids or stephanotis. "I always turn off my hearing aid when I start to bake," she says, "and sometimes I forget to turn it on again." She prefers, above all, Jewish weddings, where "there is served a complete repast."

I would like to be able to tell you that Mrs. Steude's cake that night was as delicious as she. It was not.

Gary Hansen is the U.S. Steel of southern California bridal baking, what with four chefs, a basic "line" of a hundred different models and a Beverly Hills showroom in which a pretty young girl hands you a brochure describing flavor choices—"Pure Bridal White, Daring German Chocolate, Classic Italian Marble and Secret Danish Gold"—and leads you to the cellar where a hundred plastic replicas of the styles reside on tables, each looking, to my eye, exactly like its neighbor. Nonetheless, Hansen, who descends from six generations of pastry chefs, including one who baked for the King of Denmark, believes that a great revolution is taking place in wedding cakedom—a quiet, bloodless, but truly potent rebellion. He speaks about his subject with the exhilaration of an architect who has just invented the skyscraper. "We're making really big breakthroughs," he says, barely able to bottle his enthusiasm. "We're going to be using fresh flowers on our cakes, for what we call our 'flower children cake.' It started as a joke, you know, but now we're really excited. Kids are rebelling against their parents' traditions and want something truly revolutionary. And we're giving it to them. Like a cake that's going to be covered entirely in chocolate chips. Another in solid fresh strawberries. Now we're working on root beer and scotch flavors, but we're having problems with the dissipation of the scotch taste.

"You know, we innovated chocolate wedding cakes in L.A., to keep up with the new freedom of expression. But it really upset some people. It's wild what we're doing, but who says it has to be the same old four-tiered white cake year after year? The times are changing, you know? We just hope people will accept such far-out ideas."

Hansen, whose family started this business thirty years ago, makes cakes priced from $3 to $1000 (the average is $150) and claims he has done and can do *anything*. Frogs cut out of cake, Boeing 707s. For $160 you can get a confection adorned with hearts, cherubs, bells, roses and doves—all edible. His kitchen shelves are stacked with boxes of decorations, labeled with such oddnesses as "boy tennis players," "bowling pins," "motorcycle" and "teen-age dancer," and he brags that he can prepare a complete wedding pastry for three hundred people in one hour.

He created Governor Reagan's birthday cake, which duplicated a portrait of the ex-movie star in icing; the cake for Marlo Thomas' twenty-first birthday was seven feet tall, with crowns, fountains and an icing pillow. His fondest remembrance is a concoction for a party at a movie studio. They wanted a life-sized naked lady, made out of cake, lying on a six-foot marble slab. It took one man two full days—the longest time spent on the breasts, reports Hansen. When it was finished, a white sheet was placed over the sweet body on the slab, and it was delivered to the studio in a rented hearse.

It is not uncommon for him to ship bar mitzvah cakes to Israel, purchasing a separate seat for the goody; cakes floating in swimming pools are already yawny trite in this part of the country, and doves are standard. "We use white finches, however," says Hansen, "because doves are too docile." He proceeds to explain something many of us have been dying to know—how you get the doves in and out. Evidently there are three ways to encapsulate them, the most effective (and least lethal) where you push a lever which then opens the lid, the doves being on a spring inside which then shoves them out. A good-sized cake can hold up to fifteen birdies.

"Every year we come up with styling changes," says the cake pioneer. "This year we're stressing water fountains very heavy and next year our big push is the chocolate. We always try to break with tradition; you know, we consider ourselves culinary artists." To accompany this grand vision, he is in the process of installing, behind the kitchen, an art department with drafting boards, and hiring artists to create new designs.

Hansen bubbles about the NOW wedding cake: "We've gone to artificial plastic roses, the petals all hand-shaped, to look like the sugar roses of fifty years ago. We're using advance styling methods to get back to the grand days of culinary art, to get that wonderful elegant look. With labor costs today, you can't do the real thing anymore. We're putting the pilot model in the showroom now, and we'll just wait for the public's reaction. I just hope it doesn't take them two years to accept it."

I am agog, cannot wait to glimpse the outcome of this cultural revolution, feel like a fashion editor getting the first advance peek at the miniskirt. He shows me the color transparencies of his new models, his NOW line, the cake contribution to future shock, and again, all twenty-four numbers look to me just like every wedding cake I've ever seen in my life. "Like cars, we go into a model change every year," he says with uncontained excitement, but it's all the same old Edsel to me.

Pity the poor photographer. He is, not uncommonly, the most detested presence at the wedding. The pain-in-the-neck intruder, the leech, the homeless stray mongrel, hanging around, whining for the table scraps. He arrives as the bride is dressing, hovers over the events of the day like a relentless bill collector or—to quote one disgruntled groom—"an anxious buzzard." In some extreme cases he has been known to poise himself mid-aisle, like some wedding guest gone berserk,

commanding *"Hold it right there"* to the advancing attendants, snapping, clicking, popping flashbulbs. Sometimes he
slinks up behind the altar, in back of the clergyman, and
shoots blindingly into the couples' faces amid the "I do's."
He has, on occasion, the omnipresent neck-breather, been
known to usher the newlyweds into a deserted room to
click-click while the welcoming throngs await outside; to
interrupt climaxing rumbas, lurk around Aunt Lillian's
ample décolletage, haunt kissing twosomes who should not
be kissing. But what the hell. Solemnity is not his business.
Making pictures is.

There are more photographers in the wedding business
than in any other sphere of photographic work in America.
The prospects are built in—and the required talent is minimal. All that's demanded is a Rolliflex, a bathtub and a dark
suit. Competition, therefore, is bloody ferocious, as is the
hustle. When a girl's engagement announcement appears in
The New York Times, before the ink is dry on the page
she will receive a phone call from a representative of Bradford Bachrach, the biggest operation in the East. Heaven
alone knows where the salesperson (they prefer "bridal consultant") gets the telephone number—there are those who
suspect a conspiratory friend at the *Times*—but brides report
the pitch to be fierce. One says the lady guaranteed her
Bachrach wedding photo would appear in the *Times* (Bachrach denies this, insisting, "All we say is that we have better
glossies than other photographers, and if that's an influence,
well . . ."). Another bride, saying she had already hired
so-and-so, was told, "Oh, him. He probably has his studio
in the men's room," then continued the recital of so-and-so's
cheating, taking kickbacks and general ineptitude.

Fred Winchell, a remarkably tall vice-president of Gittings,
the largest portrait photography outfit in the West and Southwest, claims: "We have to go after our business more aggres-
sively than other people because brides don't think about
photography as a necessity. People spend thousands on flowers

and music and booze—the things that will show and impress
—and then have Uncle Marty come to the wedding with his
Instamatic. We have to convince them that in future years
they'll want a marvelous permanent keepsake of the wedding.

"We try to tell our story to engaged girls and their mothers.
We have women on staff who maintain contact with the
bridal coordinators in the stores, the jewelers and so on.
They go to all the weddings with the photographer and find
out who there is engaged, as we stay in the flow of people
who are of marriageable age. If you're an upcoming bride, we
would like to come to your house and see you the morning
after you've gotten your ring. We want to take your engagement portrait for the paper, your bridal sitting shots and
your candids at the wedding."

Gittings ("Candid coverage from garter to getaway"), with
traveling door-to-door salesladies in sixty-five cities, is primarily in the portrait business, only 20 percent of their
volume coming from weddings. "But that's where it all starts,
that's the cornerstone," explains Winchell. "We photograph
the bride, then she has children and we photograph them.
Then the graduations, debuts, family portraits, et cetera."
Apparently the industry is on the wane: more amateurs are
becoming camera hobbyists, preferring their own candid account of Junior's evolution to the formal studio approach.
Then, according to Winchell, the decline is symptomatic of
bigger societal trends. "Our country is heading more and
more into the disposable—new cars every year, people moving
to new homes every few years. We're less and less concerned
with the permanent, the lasting. Our service is for people
who want to treasure and preserve happy times, the family
unit." What haunts one is the fact of the booming divorce
rate, which makes even the family unit disposable.

This is perhaps the moment to mention that how Winchell
(as well as every other wedding photographer) "preserves
happy times" is by exorcising every wrinkle and every blemish from the family unit, adding pink cheeks where there

are none, eliminating paunches where they predominate, creating Barbie dolls from faulty human beings. Wedding pictures are to honest photography what number painting is to art. Shallow and lifeless, unreal and predictable. Each album bears the same standard tritenesses: bride and groom sipping champagne from the same glass, him fooling around with her garter, the cutting of the cake, feeding it to one another, rice-throwing, riding away in the car, Daddy holding his pants pockets out. Then there's Aunt Harriet dancing with Uncle Ben, Grandpa waltzing with the bride, the two seven-year-old flower girls jitterbugging with each other. Winchell says it's because the same things go on at every wedding. "We're not making cliché pictures, but pictures of clichés, all the customs that have been done at every wedding for hundreds of years."

Financially, most photographers operate in fairly standard manner. You must guarantee a minimum order, and they guarantee a minimum number of shots. Bachrach will take at least eighty; you must purchase thirty prints. "Our philosophy," they say, "is that a photo must be salable or we don't shoot it. We don't do receiving lines, for instance, because nobody ever buys that one. We only shoot every guest at the tables if the family promises to buy them. Otherwise they ask us to do it just to impress the groom's family with what sports they are. And then we're stuck with ten pictures of Aunt Pauline." For Jack Huff, in Los Angeles, the minimum is $175; for Bachrach it's twenty-five 5 x 7 color shots in a leather album for $200; William Figge in Glendale, California, charges $185 for twenty 8 x 10s.

None of that, however, matters in the slightest. *Everybody* orders more than he has to. "What we're selling," says Jack Huff, "is sentimentality. The bride's mother looks at the proofs, all the glorious memories come flooding back, and she wants pictures of it all. We have to depend on her being sentimental, or we don't make money." Huff's average order thus falls between $300 and $400, but for the extravagantly romantic customer each photographer has his deluxenesses. The acme is from Gittings: "A life-size Imperial Sovereign Colour Portrait embedded in artist's canvas . . . The portraits resemble early paintings by the Old Masters, particularly of the Dutch school"—sells for $1800. A life-size portrait of the princess, combining all the romantic fiction of a Vermeer with all of the airbrushing known to modern science. . . .

Most brides want a classic portrait, and one for her parents, and his parents, and all the grandparents and perhaps the society pages. The whole clan has to have a wedding album each and the maid of honor wants that color candid of her where she never looked better in her life—and the cash register just keeps ticking it all off.

A mother of the bride in Milwaukee talked to me the morning after her daughter's wedding. Recalling, ecstatically, every detail and every nuance of the event, she said: "I just can't wait for the pictures to come so I can live it all over again." And I realized *that* was all that remained. Her memories would, as they do, dim. The flowers were already buried, the champagne digested. The only indelible record of all that toil and money—all those dreams and plans—the only permanent keepsake of the wedding would be the photographs. That's all.

7. Deep in the Heart of Excess

Why does everything—the quality of life itself—seem bigger, noisier, tougher, richer, in Texas than anywhere else in the country? Texas is a silly exaggeration, a distortion of reality, L.B.J. hoisting up his shirt to boast his belly scar for the entire world. The King Ranch and H. L. Hunt, De Bakey and Cooley, the Houston Astrodome and the Texas Book Depository.

One hears of fabulous weddings, oil-gusher extravaganzas that could happen only in a paperback novel. Or in Texas. They're still chattering about the Blaffer shindig—Blaffer, as in Humble Oil—a mock Italian Renaissance court pageant, music by the Houston Symphony, costumes by Mr. John, who flew down from New York for last-minute nips and tucks. Or the John Mecom (also oil) wedding, where one thousand nearest and dearest were served a sit-down filet mignon dinner and a thirty-foot wedding cake, and the flower bill alone came to $28,000. Or the Cone affair in Lubbock, for which a Manhattan hairdresser and two assistants were imported for one week prior to W-day (at $1500 a day) to do daily coiffure repairs for the four hundred lady guests from all over America who were being treated to seven days of breakfasts, teas and golf.

Or the double wedding in Houston, a prominent doctor's two daughters, for 1400 guests. One of the grooms was from Madrid, so a jet was chartered to cart over their Spanish

guests, along with a fifteenth-century carved-wood pulpit—
a priceless church relic purchased just for the ceremony.

A Houston caterer, who has of late been doing divorce-
announcement dinner dances for six hundred (and whose
mark of local renown is a dolphin carved out of ice, its
gullet overflowing with imported caviar), tells of the most
lavish wedding in his history, held in a home "already as
big as a country club." In order to accommodate the eight
hundred invitees indoors, the host had added a ballroom on
to the house, which cost $20,000 to build. To boot, the win-
dows were removed from the living and dining rooms, for
easy access to the garden.

The classic Dallas hoop-de-doo of the last fifteen years,
wedding of Texas multimillionaire Sid Richardson, sported
an unbelievable array of flower decorations: 2300 camellias,
1700 Easter lilies, 500 gardenias, 1000 bride's roses, 1000
snapdragons, 1500 peachblossom stems, 500 bunches of vi-
olets, 200 azaleas, 170 white lilacs, a dozen pink magnolia
trees, five flowering peach trees and a dozen flowering-crab-
apple trees. The posies were flown in from Los Angeles,
Chicago, Mobile, San Francisco, Birmingham, North and
South Carolina and Belgium.

Even White House weddings—normally the models of solid
burgher respectability and politic propriety—took on a Texas
flair under L.B.J. If Tricia's was like a Grosse Pointe country club dance, Luci and Lynda Johnson's had about them
at least a smidgen of San Antone rodeo. Luci and her
twenty-six attendants marched down an aisle the literal
length of a football field plus a basketball court, in the
largest Roman Catholic church in the United States.
Its 56-bell carillon pealed for one full hour before the
ceremony. Lynda Bird's fete, truly humble by comparison,
cost $62,000 and was preceded by twenty-one prenuptial
parties.

In much the same way that the ethnic wedding—the classic
celebration of the culture—speaks volumes about the be-

havior, history, tastes and values of that culture, so do the
ways in which people marry in various parts of America
reflect the character and idiosyncracies of our geography. As
regional cooking has a distinct entity, so do regional weddings.

Bridal fashions, for instance, show clear variances from section to section. In the South fabrics are sheer, silk organza.
The climate surely accounts for part of this; the southern
image of Blanche DuBois floating femininity, provocative
yet ethereal, the rest. In the Farm Belt girls tend to buy the
most elaborate lace-tiered gowns—inexpensive, but heavily
beaded, with sweeping cathedral trains. True costumery,
galaxies removed from one's daily earthbound garb. In engagement and wedding rings, styles in New England are
strictly conservative, the South likes lots of men's pinkie
diamonds, and in the West, where ring fashions originate
(along with most new fads that envelop the nation), prefer-
ences are for rougher textures, newer substances, more inno-
vative styling.

Then, wedding styles themselves differ from place to place.
Washington, D.C., a town devoted to hearty socializing, is
not knocked out by yet another big party with yet more
leaden cheese puffs. A city of no industry, no movie or oil
magnates, no bankers, few millionaires, but abounding with
good-taste diplomacy, the social modus is restrained, understated. Ellen Proxmire, copartner in Wonderful Weddings,
describes Washington nuptials as "simple as they can be.
Washingtonians don't use a wedding as an excuse to produce
a spectacle. The kinds of splashy weddings that are *de
rigueur* elsewhere would be considered grotesque here." A
"typical" wedding in D.C. would be held in a church with
a hotel reception afterward (hotel catering is considerably
cheaper here than in other cities), a light buffet and quiet
music for quiet dancing. Good Taste.

By contrast, take Los Angeles, cuckoo capital of America.
Where else, except in this nest of paradoxes, extremes and
eccentricities, could you attend a wedding where, following

the eight be-pinked bridesmaids down the aisle, marches the family white toy poodle in a pink organdy "dress" and at the dinner the mashed potatoes are also dyed pink; where, for a Pasadena society bash, the bride's mother decides that the green interior of the church doesn't groove with her yellow plans, thus paints the entire church yellow the day before the ceremony, repaints it green the day after? Where, for writer Budd Schulberg's marriage to Geraldine Brooks, the swimming pool is emptied and completely refilled with one solid ton of oranges?

The lifestyle in southern California is, even within its most rigid social castes, freer, more eclectic, crazier than in the East. The fact that, at a Hancock Park/Gentile/oil/conservative wedding, the couple and their friends interrupt the sedate ceremony to sit down in a circle and toss the I Ching coins does not make Grandma faint or necessarily find its way into the local society column. In Philadelphia folks would be dining out on that shocker for the entire winter, but in L.A.—even haute Hancock Park—it's a mild yawn.

Architecturally, L.A. boasts incredibly flamboyant houses and decors alongside the faceless boxes which spring up overnight and envelop the landscape like giant ant armies. Both styles, however different, carry the same message: "We came to the land of the golden dream to Make It. Fast. Flaunt it, spend it, build a house quick, let every buck all hang out." There's no sense of tomorrow here, certainly no yesterday. Tradition is what we left behind.

San Francisco, on the other hand, is light-years farther away from L.A. than its 425 miles. A tradition-bound, staid, essentially tiny town, it is characterized, by a knowledgeable local caterer, as "still a village. There are only ten thousand people who run the city, spend the money, dominate the cultural and social life. And they are very concerned about their image. Their emotional ties are with New York and Boston and they'd rather die than be linked with Los Angeles in the same breath."

The San Francisco psyche is of stern stuff—rooted in the utter horror of that not-quite-definable demon of "bad taste." There is a huge quantity of money in San Francisco (which is *never,* heaven forfend, to be called "Frisco"), but it's old, or if it's new it arrives at a snail's pace and results, appropriately, from the Protestant ethic of Working Damn Hard. Or the nearly Protestant ethic of inheriting it from Daddy who Worked Damn Hard. In any case, it clearly isn't acquired in the Los Angeles fashion of an overnight real estate boom or from owning a casino in Vegas or from being a show-biz agent who had a client who made it big in one B picture, never to be heard from again, but in the meantime you've bought a FAB-U-LOUS manse with a sauna and radiant-heated floors and a bed suspended from the ceiling on chains. My, no indeed.

In San Francisco people spend their loot at one-third the rate of citizens anywhere else. A wedding in this area is graceful and elegant, bereft of poodles and tricky lighting. While the kids of the rich are sometimes going the peasant route in dress—how quaint, really—and getting married under the trees, their weddings often resemble the one at a Walnut Creek ranch, a very rural setting to be sure. The entire barn was decorated with field flowers (not *actually* hand-picked in the field, mind you, but purchased from a chic florist), French champagne was poured from eight-magnum bottles, a barbecue pit with electric spit was constructed and whole lambs skewered therein, all to the tune of a string quartet from the Oakland Symphony. The tab was $60,000—for 160 guests. San Franciscans who attended love to describe that gala as a "hippie wedding."

Now there's Texas. Witness a Texas wedding—your average middle-class home garden wedding. Could be happening, at that same instant and without much variation, in Larchmont or Dubuque. Only here, in Houston, on a steamy Friday evening in August, there's a difference: the guests, blanketing the green lawn, number 1200. Twelve hundred bodies and that's not even ranked, in Texas, as a circus maximus. It is not possible, I have decided, scouring my brains for the names of anybody I'd ever met even once in my life, to know 1200 people.

"My biggest problem in planning this affair," says Mrs. Quisenberry, mother of the bride, "was in cutting down the guest list." She's not kidding, one sees, as she continues: "Ah have hundreds and hundreds of deah, deah girlfriends—from college, from various clubs and organizations and from working on political campaigns. Many of them Ah haven't seen in ten years, but they're still mah very good friends." And what better place to gather them together—all of these "deah, deah" buddies from twenty-five years ago's Theta Chi house —than at your Ferberesque jamboree/barbecue of a daughter's wedding.

The fact that a "friend" is defined as somebody you knew three decades ago, haven't kept in touch with, but wouldn't dream of throwing your daughter's wedding without, is distinctly Texas mentality. The famous Texas hospitality tends to be indiscriminate, the cordiality instantaneous, the warmth expansive but skin-deep. There is about this state a profound flat emptiness that begins with the land and ends with its citizens.

"HAIIIIIII. HOW ARE YOOOOOO? GLAD TO SEE YOOOOOO!" is drawled, by the aging prom-queen hostess, to every approaching guest. Watching, fascinated, as she repeats the saccharine refrain 847 times with unflagging vim, I am convinced that she has no idea who one-third of the assemblage is. And they continue to arrive and arrive and arrive. . . . A mini-battalion. Twenty-four classy black maids shuffle to and fro along the drive of this simple, comfortably inelegant home, dispensing champagne. The spacious lawn has been completely tented for the bash (green and white— the tackiest tenting, points out my sociologically observant escort). But ostentation, flash, gaudiness is evidently not the ticket in bourgeois Texas. The flowers are skimpy and middle-aged, the food—barbecued beef, mushy cheese on soggy crackers, fruit hunks impaled on toothpicks—is strictly hospital tray, the costumes and sets unspectacular. What's unique about a Texas wedding—any Texas wedding—is the hugeness.

It bespeaks the social life of the community. In cities smaller than New York, Los Angeles or Chicago, people do tend to know more numbers of people. There's a clearer sense of cohesiveness, less anonymity, a hundred congregating spots from country club to Knights of Columbus. People *belong* to things, participate, erect an active extracurricular structure to their lives. Then, too, folks rarely seem to abandon Texas. They're deserting New York by the caravan, *everybody* in California is a recent transplant from somewhere else, but Texans stay put. The Texas chauvinism is— God only knows why—ferocious.

Another reason for the massive population at weddings is the high divorce rate, which produces multi families instead of the normal two. I witnessed one fete in Dallas where there were, in attendance, seven sets of "parents." You see, Texans are so relentlessly genial that naturally not only would the bride's father's current (third) wife be invited, but also his second wife, who, after all, practically brought up the girl and has a new husband (her fourth) who obviously must be present. Now, when you add the groom's familial complexities, and throw in a caldron of grandparents and step-grandparents, you can see why the first ten pews in church were filled before one non-related guest even entered.

Mrs. Quisenberry tells me she is invited to at least one wedding a week, two or three in the height of the season. She expresses amazement at my amazement: "But that's our whole social life. That's what we do on Friday and Saturday nights. Where else would we go?" And it perpetuates itself, naturally. If you have 1200 folks at your clambake, you can expect at least one wedding invitation back from each of them over

the next few years. Yep, that's sho' a lot of busy—if interchangeable—Saturday nights.

One would expect the Quisenberry celebration to be a rollicking, hog-stomping, yip-yip-yipping, shoot-'em-up Texas
jubilee. Wrong. The ceremony is held at 8:30, the bride and
groom disappear at 10 (after *not* being greeted by a majority
of the stranger-guests) and by 10:45 the tacky tents are de-
escalated. Hardly anybody dances, gets drunk, becomes obnoxious, or appears to have a particularly peachy time. A
traditional, bland, pretty, lifeless American wedding. A big
TWO on the Terrific Party Scale of ONE to TEN. Twelve
thousand dollars, an Astrodome full of ostensibly festive folk,
and the most exciting event of the evening is when a barrel-
chested man in a ten-gallon hat takes out his pearl-handled
pistol from his jacket pocket and his wife simultaneously re-
moves her matching one from her powder-blue beaded purse
and, pointing them at my brains, cordially assure me that
they *always* carry weapons, everywhere they go, since their
last trip to New York City.

Let me tell you some facts about Houston, Texas. To begin with, it is the sixth largest city in America, the largest
in the Southwest. As the fastest-growing city in the country
(Lloyd's of London predicts its population will surpass that
of New York by 1980), Houston is now first in the manufacture and distribution of oil equipment, as a refinery center
and in pipeline transmission. In the Southwest it leads in the
number of scientists, retail sales and private planes.

The population of Houston has increased 40 percent since
1960, this huge leap coming about mainly as a result of giant
corporations moving their headquarters here: Shell Oil, three
major divisions of Standard Oil of New Jersey, M. W.
Kellogg Co., the food division of Coca-Cola, to name just
a scattering. Then, too, there was the construction of the
Manned Space Center, which created an entire new city
twenty miles south of Houston, complete with avenues named
after astronauts.

Houston produces 80 percent of America's synthetic rubber, houses 25 percent of all natural gas pipeline companies, is third in the nation's manufacture of chemicals and is responsible for the refining of 1,396,750 barrels of oil a day.

All of this is to say that there is a quality of brand-newness and buzzing, swirling movement about Houston as in no other metropolis. Building takes place everywhere—shopping centers, condominiums, housing developments and office complexes materialize overnight where yesterday lay only the bare, apathetic Texas land. Even more than Los Angeles, Houston has the sense of not having existed five years ago. And, unlike California, those who arrive daily with their lifetime cargoes in tow come not with some airy dream of riches and the unspoken promise of ceaseless Pacific sun. Here, the oil is pumping away with tick-tock regularity, and you smell it and the chemicals, the sulphur and the rubber from Neiman-Marcus' parking lot. The prosperity is real.

How it plays against the essentially sleepy, humid atmosphere is really the only quality that keeps Houston interesting. In New York, one hears the death-rattle echoes of this great defeated giant on every corner. Houston is in the throes of labor, and struggling to emerge is an entity that doesn't yet know who it is.

Have you ever wondered what happens to forty-two-year-old college football heroes, or Miss America contestants from 1954? They're all here, in Houston. It's a boomtown carved out of the gray Texas flatness and populated by slightly-over-the-hill Sandra Dees. The faces in Texas are startlingly beautiful—startlingly because *everybody* is beautiful. Middle-class Texas women are lean, tan, flawless; every piece of apparatus—from pants suit to shoulder bag to matching eye shadow—is endlessly thought out and, as a result, nothing looks as if it moves, the clothing appears to be glued to their bodies. It's the kind of perfect beauty that comes from never ever being smacked, or even really touched, by real life.

And the beautiful men. Not handsome and cowboyish and rugged, like your memories of Texas movies might dictate, not even handsome and square and straight like astronauts. More like male models—weak and cold and vain. Even dangerous, a bit. Guys you don't want to be anywhere near when they're shitface drunk.

You smell the flow of money in Houston, as in any boomtown. Even when it's not visible, its existence charges the air. Like the implied presence of gold in them thar hills that would set the valley towns atingle with anticipation, with the lusty possibilities. Houston's like that. Incredibly greedy, in its own friendly drawling way.

Take the afternoon I went to interview the Camerons, whose daughter Emily was about to get married the following night, Saturday. The Camerons live in River Oaks, one of the rich sections of town. It's where you find the best country clubs (Emily's reception will be at the River Oaks C.C., which is not so hotsy-totsy as the Bayou Club but a lot more really top-drawer than the Houston C.C.). *Everybody* in the ascending middle-to-upper-middle class belongs to a country club. For one thing, until the laws were changed just recently, it was the only place you could get a drink, and God-bless-'em-Texans sure like a nip of the sauce now and then. But, also, Texans are exceedingly clubby and many folks belong to several.

River Oaks is where the fancy churches are (Emily's ceremony will be held in St. John the Divine, biggest church in Texas), the swell stores like Neiman's and sprawling redstone ranch homes (was the expression "ranch home" invented in Texas?) that all tend to look exactly the same.

Emily Cameron, twenty, is your quintessential high school cheerleader; giggly, peppy, cute, bouncy—all those adjectives. She is less beautiful than most Texas lasses, indeed much less so than any of her six knockout bridesmaids. Never mind. At this moment in her life she is a true princess, and they are but ladies of the court.

I am totally unprepared for what follows my knock at the Cameron front door. It is opened by a massive policeman, heavily armed (that is, the gun slung over his Texas hip looks like it ain't kiddin'), and I am led into the living room which, at the moment, is indistinguishable from the housewares department at Macy's: a room perhaps forty feet long whose furniture has been removed and replaced by white-clothed tables that are utterly blanketed with gifts. There are seven or eight of these long tables, every inch taken up by silver, crystal, china, indefinable doodads. A sterling silver caviar dish here, a set of pot-de-crèmes there. A porcelain ostrich, an ornate silver samovar. Just what we've always wanted. Sterling napkin rings, a Sony stereo ensemble. Mrs. Cameron escorts me through room after room, all the same scene, muttering, "Isn't it purty?" about every $500 antique silver knickknack. A set of twelve Baccarat crystal goblets, $40 a glass, she says. From the groom's grandma. A bad oil painting from Lyndon and Lady Bird (Mr. C. is a lawyer and an active Democrat in town), a silver something from the Connallys. *Quelle* bonanza! What loot!

One room houses only kitchen appliance gifts, many doubles and triples. Three ten-speed electric blenders, an electric ice-crusher, electric can opener, electric knife, electric juicer, grinder, whipper, mixer, masher, shredder. If there's a power failure, we starve to death.

More rooms, more silver, a set of artichoke plates, a satin bedspread. A sterling punch bowl with twelve cups to match. Exactly what a cheerleader and her twenty-two-year-old student hubby need to get started in life, in their pad at the U. of Texas.

Finally, reaching a room mercifully bereft of goods, Mama explains the mechanics of a middle-class wedding. She has invited a thousand of her dearest friends, expects only 750 to attend and has already received that many gifts. Emily has registered, it seems, at five local stores (oh, Texas! Elsewhere two is considered the very maximum before unpardonable gaucherie), and every single day for three months the trucks have been pulling up with bounty. The armed guard was hired three weeks ago, will stay one week beyond the wedding, until all this cargo is stored away. ("We'll never use *any* of it!" giggles Emily, surveying her $30,000 worth of love offerings.)

Mrs. C. has organized the gifts with computer efficiency: she's erected a card catalog file, alphabetized by name of the donor and specifying the gift and date of arrival. The store's tag is clipped to the back of the card, to expedite returns. Then, in a lined notebook, she has a cross-reference system which in no way can I understand, except that each gift has a number and the number is then pasted somewhere on the object itself for identification. Brilliant. Terrifying.

At this moment a uniformed messenger arrives with an envelope/gift, which Greg, the groom, opens. It's $100 in new one-dollar bills, and Greg has to ask Emily who's Mr. and Mrs. So-and-So. Emily hasn't the slightest idea either, but Mr. Cameron, who's just come home from the office, does. A client.

Then Emily bounces back in, bearing yet more boxes of just arrived stuff and a scrapbook to show me. Pasted inside are thirty or so invitations to parties given in her honor, which have run in an unending river for the last four months. You see, deep in the heart of Texas, the actual wedding is only a tiny part of the whole shebang. The pre-conjugal frolicking begins with engagement parties (plural). "Lots of friends offered," coos Mrs. Cameron, "but we only accepted the very minimum. Three." Then, as the wedding draws near, the social momentum crescendoes furiously.

Emily shows me their schedule. Ready? A barbecue given by the Connallys at their ranch; a kitchen shower; a linen shower; a "Honey Do" shower for the groom ("Honey do this, honey do that." Gifts for him, for around-the-house chores. Cute?); a brunch for out-of-town guests; a stag party; a bridesmaids' luncheon; a rehearsal dinner; a recipe shower (Emily chirps: "That doesn't count, does it? There weren't any gifts"). Note that those presents brought to the above events have zero to do with the required wedding gift. Mrs. Cameron misses the irony of her following admission: "We were thinking of having a tea for everyone to look at the gifts, but that seemed like overdoing it." I ponder the philosophical dilemma of whether invitees to that gift-tea would have been expected to bring a gift. . . .

How did Emily in her splendiferous whirlwind miss another uniquely Texas custom, the Trousseau Tea, the plot of which revolves around inviting lady friends to review your new slips and underpants, hanging there from a rented clothes rack which has been decorously covered with white satin?

All during the afternoon neighbors troop in and out to view the gift display. It's apparently the hottest tourist attraction in River Oaks. Oooohs and ahhhhs for everything, but the big hit of the day is a rococo, gold-plated teapot, an item which in no way relates to the life of this giggly couple currently buzzing around the house in their madras Bermuda shorts (matching) and sneakers. Today, one observes, the couple doesn't even matter. The stream of neighbors totally ignore them, the supposed superstars; many don't even know who the bride is (somebody even mistook *me* for Emily). Grooms are traditionally invisible, but the bride's supposed to be the celeb. Not here in Fat City. The star of this Hollywood spectacular is the Merchandise.

What does it all mean to Emily and Greg? I wonder during a quiet moment in this regatta. How do they hold on to any sense of solemnity or joy in the blinding face of all that sterling silver? Well, apparently they don't, because Emily says she sees the whole pageant as "just a big shindig." Perhaps a perky, simply *fabulous* extension of Homecoming Weekend. Texas U. has won the big game and she's the queen of the dance. How the Camerons feel about their daughter's wedding I can only surmise, since their effusive Texas cordiality works to belie honest expression. The Wedding, I think, symbolizes to them pretty much what it does to every parent: we have lots of deah friends (750 to be precise), we're respected members of our society (look at the picture Lady Bird sent us. Isn't it purty?) in which we've participated for twenty-five years, we're loved (that china and crystal is *really* for us, you know) and we've Made It (look at that truck from Neiman's pulling into the driveway, and take a gander at my card catalog file).

The wedding itself, the next evening, is certainly an anticlimax, merely the inevitable playing out of the game, although it *really* ended with the fifteenth party and the nine hundredth gift.

It is again, inevitably, a painfully hot night. Summer heat must have as much to do with molding the Houston psyche as anything else about the place. For the heat has its own persona in this city. Wet, heavy, relentless, it governs every possible act of free will. It sits on your head and arms, putting you agonizingly in touch with the dripping, sticking extrusions of your body. Then, as supposed relief, but not really, there's the air conditioning. Everything in Houston is air-conditioned; natives, in fact, think nothing odd or creepy about telling you that they never step outdoors for one minute for days at a time during the summer. Impossible? It is possible, with the construction of this city, to go from air-conditioned house to air-conditioned garage, to air-conditioned car, to air-conditioned underground parking lot in air-conditioned office building, to office, to restaurant lunch in building, to car, to home. No wonder Houstonians are a touch sluggish, vague and unreal—like prisoners whose existences are confined to an artificial universe. All that super-refined, phony cold air day in, day out. Freezes the soul.

The Church of St. John the Divine, then, air-conditioned, with icy stone white walls and floors, resembles a church not at all, but a *House Beautiful* ranch. "HAIIIIIII. HOW ARE YOOOOOOO? GLAD TO SEE YOOOOOOO!" the 750 guests greet one another. Have they not all seen one another at last week's wedding, or last night's? No matter. Backstage, in a room reserved for the "cast," Mary Ann Maxwell, the bridal consultant from Foley's Department Store, where the gowns were purchased, runs about, coordinating all the details to make opening night a triumph. Stage fright is a big problem, as are any teeny but crucial imperfections. A brand-new pimple on the nose here, a dirt speck on the glove there. The nervous bride is a costumed kewpie doll. Wind her up and she gets married.

Mary Ann isn't in such hot shape herself, what with dressing the frantic ladies-in-waiting and coordinating the intricate split-second timing of the limousines which will dash the wedding party from church to country club so as to arrive before the guests, so as to be in receiving-line position early. But Mary Ann goes to lots of weddings—her store alone is doing 115 this month—and she's cynical. She quietly points out to me that all the girls' corsages are ever so slightly wilted, a characteristic of the cut-rate florist the Camerons have hired; she also snipes that Emily's gown is last season's and bought on a half-price sale.

The ceremony itself is standard, much less interesting than the gift carnival of the previous afternoon. A dreadful harp-organ combo hails "Here Comes the Bride," the Episcopal minister, cursed with a Walter Brennan twang, mutters perfunctory vows, and that's that.

The reception, at smart River Oaks Country Club, is also standard, oddly short-lived and lackluster. Egg salad and Ritz crackers, champagne and bourbon. Where is the joy in Mudville tonight? Where is the passion and the holiness of this, life's paramount celebration? Back, perhaps, in the air-conditioned ranch house, reclining on white tables, watched over by the begunned Texas fuzz?

Need I tell you that there is no evidence in Texas of the New Wedding, of kids opting for the personal over the cliché? Earlier I've asked Emily if she ever for a moment considered *not* doing it the way she's doing it, or if any of her friends have had nontraditional weddings. "I know of one girl who got married in a cave," she giggled. "But she's weird to begin with. Her husband tripped on his hair." Not one of her pals is writing her own ceremony (although one wanted a more personal service, Emily relates, so she hired a sorority sister who was a creative writing major to jazz up the old vows); no one is doing it outdoors (are you kidding? in Houston heat?), and nobody she knows has small weddings, ever. ("Oh, yeah, one. About three hundred people.") Emily herself has never considered, until I mention it, the possibility of having music other than Mendelssohn.

The western minister tells me he's had only one request from kids to add something to his basic ceremony. He refused to marry them. "I think there's a great danger in letting young people have their own contemporary standards, instead of Biblical standards," he drawls. "It's not that we don't trust young people, but the vows ought to be more meaningful than they are yet capable of understanding. Our Episcopal service has an eternal quality, and young people don't know yet what love and marriage are."

In its oversized, overstuffed, oversociable grandiosity, it is the Thing-orientation of the Texas wedding that overwhelms one ultimately. The final understanding that the most extravagant and cherished and indeed *happy* aspect of the wedding is the gifts. The getting, not the giving, the accumulation, the piling of more silver upon more silver, the heady, greedy fever of acquisition. The orgiastic worship of the object. The incentive is not to honor a relationship but to complete the silver service.

How come these children, in the seriousness of pledging to commit their lives to one another, have dedicated so much zestful energy to the parties and the presents and not one instant's thought to the vows? You enter the prenuptial home and there you are dead-center on the sixth floor of Bloomingdale's. And there they are—the happy couple— yellow roses of Texas, 21.1 years old, gleefully tossing crisp green bills (one hundred of them) in the air, then returning to the numbering of the brandy snifters for the card file. And you get the feeling that *this* is the marriage. This is what it's all about for them, what's binding them together. The tie is the Baccarat crystal; if it doesn't work out, the awful crisis will be who gets the silver samovar.

8. All Decked in White

When I was between the ages of six and eight, my best friend, Lois Brenner, would come to my house every Saturday morning. We followed, for virtually all of that period, the same ritual. We would go to my room, shut the door, turn on the radio to Archie Andrews and "Let's Pretend," and we would draw. Hour after hour, sprawling amid papers and crayons, we drew one thing and one thing only—girls in wedding gowns. Finishing one, we would compare, criticize, correct, reject and then go on to the next. The ladies on the paper had marvelously curvaceous bodies—like the bodies we knew we would have someday—with breasts and cleavage and minuscule waists and rivers of Veronica Lake hair. We experimented with styles, V neck and short sleeves on this one, bouffant skirt and scoop neck on the next, with the professional intensity of Givenchy turning out his new spring collection. For us, like the little girls who now play The Bride Game, it was a very serious enterprise. The fantasy of what our own wedding dresses would be had to carry us through those slow, often terrible childhood years until the magic time when we would finally be grown up—and to that perfect moment when we would at last be brides.

Then, for many years, I also had my bride and bridesmaid dolls, with little dresses that my mother would periodically take off and wash and iron so that they always looked fresh. For my birthday one year she bought me a completely new bridal wardrobe for my synthetic friends.

That's how it all begins. Way back in those early days when we get the messages about what's important and when the playthings that engage us are working to shape our future lives. When I started to plunk the piano at age three, I recall, one of the first melodies I picked out with my index finger was "Da Da Da-Da"—"Here Comes the Bride."

A few months ago, in the bridal salon of a Cleveland department store, I saw a young girl come in—she was perhaps eighteen—wearing her jeans-and-sneakers uniform, but there to shop for her wedding gown. I stood by as the bridal directress brought several long white rustling garments into the dressing room, politely advising the girl to comb her hair and apply makeup before proceeding. She did, slipped into the first dress—a lacy, beaded affair—peered at herself in the mirror for a long moment—and burst into tears. "I can't believe it," she sobbed joyfully. "I've always dreamed of being a bride and looking just like this, and it's really come true. Is this really *me*?"

At a bridal specialty shop in Chicago, when the young customer tries on a wedding tog, she then models it for the entire staff—emerging through a curtain to float down a long ramp, while an organ recording plays "The Wedding March" and the salesladies gasp and sigh, as per instruction. One such saleswoman reports that eight out of ten girls buy the very first gown they don—so overcome are they with the initial vision of themselves.

We never, in our childhood play, concerned ourselves with the flowers and decorations, planned the menu or gave a thought to the gifts. Even the man—aside from possessing several of the combined perfections of our various movie gods—was unclear. How we would look walking down the aisle with all eyes upon us was the essential fantasy. And for almost every young woman getting married in America today, it still is. She is transformed, this day, from whatever she was to utter radiant beauty. What divine magic. She doesn't need a nose job, silicone or Weight Watchers; she doesn't even have to be rich. She only needs a flowing white wedding gown—that exquisite embodiment of all the romantic dreams of her life.

Item: The largest of the bridal manufacturers, Alfred Angelo, receives hundreds of letters each year with the same theme: "I've been carrying around this picture from *Modern Bride* of one of your dresses for five years. Now I've finally met a guy and I'm getting married. Do you still have it?"

Item: The Brides and Bridesmaids Apparel Association (a trade organization of manufacturers) held an essay contest a few years back for recent brides, on the topic of "Why I Chose My Gown." *Nobody* answered "because it was stylish" or "because it made me look thin." Over 90 percent replied, "It made me look like a fairy princess," or similar sentiments.

Item: Somebody recently invented an electro-optical device for stores, a gadget that is installed behind mirrors and electrically combines the reflection of the girl's face with a projected image of a bridal gown in her correct size and full color—all with fancy, romantic lighting. Thus she can determine how hundreds of gowns will look, at their most flattering, without having to try them on. This "Fashion Mirror," as it is called, is leased to retailers for $7200 a year.

Item: Thousands of brides each year, following the wedding, send their gowns to Heritage Traditions Laboratories in Los Angeles for "restoration." A dress is, in effect, embalmed for posterity—cleaned by a special ultrasonic process that guarantees preservation for a hundred years. It is then put to sleep in a container whose resemblance to a coffin is impossible to overlook.

To the extent that marriage and weddings are involved with idealized departures from reality, the wedding dress is the key metaphor. "Happiness is getting married in just the look you want," claims *Bride's Magazine,* in describing a bridal frock on their pages; a recent Alfred Angelo collection was called "Garden of Dreams"; some copy in *Mod-*

ern Bride declares their pictured finery "harbingers of glorious days to come." Experts say the key word is "memorable": every bride wants, above all else, to look memorable, that is, to remember this supreme experience for the rest of her life. What she will recall most vividly, and most wistfully, in the years to come is not the peach melba or the pink petunias or how Cousin Charlie got plastered and did the Charleston, but how utterly beautiful she looked—indeed what a vision she was—on her day of days.

Eighty percent of all first marriages in the United States last year were formal weddings. That is to say, 1,411,200 girls got married in bridal gowns, as opposed to pants suits, street dresses or jodhpurs. Eighty-seven percent of these garments were floor-length, the average price spent was $164 (including the headpiece) and 94 percent were white or ivory.

The color white, so deeply glued to our current notions of bridedom, has not always been used and, in fact, is not today in other cultures. During the American Revolution brides wore red, the symbolic color of rebellion; Chinese girls today don red as an expression of happiness and permanence. Spanish peasants wear, of all things, black, and in Norway green is the most popular shade. White, however, has historically been connected to joy—not purity, mind you, until the Victorian era, but rather to celebrate great joyous events. The early Romans decked themselves in white at births and for feast days; the Patagonians painted white decorations on their bodies for every happy occasion and on the eve of wedding ceremonies they simply covered their entire bodies with white paint. In early Saxon days and through the eighteenth century it was only the peasant girl who came to her wedding in a plain white robe—a public statement that she brought nothing with her to her marriage and that therefore her husband was not responsible for her debts. Today the Japanese bride wears white, but the message is dual: also a mourning color, it indicates that she is "dead" to her parents and that she will never leave her husband until she goes to the grave.

Now, of course, we have come to associate white with chastity, and the symbolism hangs on with a deathlike grip. The fact that wedding etiquette will staunchly not permit a second-time bride to wear white implies, naturally, that first-timers are virgins. Flying in the face of what we know to be the truth, Tradition, nevertheless will Out.

And it is here, in discussing the wedding gown, that we clearly see how little is really changing in the American Way of Wedding. How tales of paper wedding dresses and plastic dresses and gaucho pants and hot pants and scuba-diving suits make for lively reading in *Life* magazine but have nothing to do with what's really what in our country. When a lass dreams about the magic moment, she is not visualizing herself in see-through-micro-mini with vinyl boots. She is the fairy princess, period.

Hear George Morrissey of *Modern Bride*: "The vast number of first-time brides get married in an unaltered traditional fashion. A very significant statistic is the one which shows that each year there is even a higher rate of white wedding gowns sold than is accounted for just by the increase in the number of marriages. More and more people are having formal weddings every year. It astonishes even me." The publishers say that girls buy bridal magazines primarily to look for wedding garb, and one cannot help but notice that the doodads portrayed throughout those pages, month after month, year after year, are white, long and conventional. The concept, the gestalt of the wedding dress remains as it has been for 150 years.

Bridal consultant Mary Ann Maxwell says: "I was out of the bridal business for three years recently and when I came back I could have sworn I'd just been out to lunch."

Granted, the media deceives us. It would clearly be dreary for the woman's pages to repeat incessantly the same fashion story, to wit: "Miss Beauteous Bridal Frocks held their spring fashion showing today. 142 brand-new, hot-off-the-presses gowns were revealed. Each one was pure white. Each one hung to the floor. Each one had some lace, some beads, some organdy, some seed pearls, some peau de soie. Just like last season. . . ." Ho-hum. Much flashier copy is a piece on the bridal apparition in hooded mini monk's robe, or leather jump suit or mammoth crepe tent. And a candid manufacturer will tell you he only designs these bizarrenesses tongue-in-chic. Showpieces, conversation stoppers, intended to call attention—like the naked waitress in Schrafft's—to the solid bread and butter. Brought out for fashion shows and on television, meant to carry the message that the company is "with it," "now," but then sent off in cartons to the used-clothing drive.

"The most important thing to remember about the bridal field," says an executive of Alfred Angelo, "is that the worst-selling dresses are the up-to-the-minute fashions." A peculiar atavistic reversion seems to take over in almost all young women. Regardless of their lifestyle at the moment, when it's time to get married they harken back to some ancient tribal voice. Store after store reports the same behavior: lass enters as a tie-dyed hippie, leaves as a vanilla ice cream cone. And one has to assume that eight minutes after the last wedding guests depart it's riches-to-rags again. "How kids get married has to do with the values they grew up with, not what happened this year in college," explains the Angelo man. "We recently ran an ad campaign where the copy read, 'Be the kind of girl you want to be, but be an Alfred Angelo bride.' It showed a girl on skis, then with a guitar, then in our formal wedding gown. It was enormously successful."

There's also the All-Brides-Are-Beautiful myth to account for the quirky transformation. It is, sadly, an untruth that every bride is ravishing, regardless of the basic equipment. There are some things that even Priscilla of Boston, with all her White House drag, cannot control. But this is certainly our one big chance for that treasured golden apple; if we're ever going to be able to get out of our own drab skin, this is the day it'll happen—or never. The bridal magazines stress this fiction ad nauseam with articles on how to decide on your special wedding hair style, how to drop fifteen fast pounds, how to correct any posture defects for that major walk. Excessive narcissism, purple vanity, fixation on the few square feet that comprise one's physical self, is expected, encouraged, exalted. When else?

In an article that *must* be the quintessential psalm to self-centeredness, *Harper's Bazaar* advises the bride to start working on her wedding face three weeks prior to the day "with a full measure of salon attentions." She must begin a series of facials "to bring her complexion to the highest possible burnish—and also to give her three rehearsals, under professional guidance, of her wedding makeup." The story goes on to insist: "This is one of the most exacting cosmetic problems she will ever face."

On the wedding day, the experts advise, her masseuse and hairdresser should be there to lighten her inevitable tensions.

Small wonder that an upcoming bride who spends her waking life in dungarees will have no interest in white satin pants for her wedding. Or shorts, or miniskirts, or anything else that feels familiar. In fact, whatever her money situation, it does not matter in the least that the gown will never be worn again. Practicality is not for princesses; several brides have told me, in fact, that they deliberately chose apparel that could never be restyled or shortened or altered in any way to become "real" dresses.

Fashion is always a cultural barometer for what's going on in the society at that moment. Are we into flights of color or sobriety, sexually flaunting or repressed? Are the skirts long or short—and does that mean the stock market is up or down? The metaphor is less true in the bridal industry with its particular idiosyncracies and demands; but like the nurse's uniform whose hemline occasionally trickles up or down, only in the most minor ways is the wedding gown subject to the fads and fancies of fashion.

Two-thirds of all wedding dresses are purchased—the rest are borrowed, hand-sewn, handed down or rented—and sales of bridal finery totaled $150 million last year. In a most fundamental sense the bridal apparel biz is as far removed from the operations of the ladies' garment industry—whose gabardine ghetto on New York's Seventh Avenue it shares —as it is from the workings of Campbell's soups. First of all, it is a tiny subcategory, less than a hundred manufacturers in all. Then, it is dealing with a one-time customer who is buying only one dress in her life. The bridal guys can figure out, from population statistics, the finite number of potential customers each year. And, for them, it's now or never.

As one dramatic result, there is a desperate competitiveness and fierce bitchiness among bridal clothiers not unlike a battle to the death for the last seat in the lifeboat. In my travels I never—but never—heard a tender word from one for another. (One manufacturer says about Priscilla, "Glop is her forte; her attempts at fashion have been feeble"; somebody else says Pandora's dresses are cheesy; Priscilla claims responsibility for practically every bridal innovation but the cotton gin.) Another contributant to ferocity is the difficulty in making head or tail of the market. If you manufacture, say, little basic $100 cotton shirtwaist dresses, you know whom you're selling, whom you're excluding; you know what towns and what stores in those towns in which to place the garments. But, in bridal wear, it is often the poorest girls who spend the most money. And they have totally disparate taste from wealthier girls and do not shop at the same emporiums. So what kind of $500 dress do you design to suit both mentalities, and which stores will buy it? And how do you promote and merchandise it?

The biggest contrast, however, between the bridal kingdom and the rest of fashion is that it is *not* a ready-to-wear business. Except for the low-end dresses—those under $100—every gown is more or less custom-made. Mori Lee is the exception. The second largest house ($6 million a year), their togs retail from $50 to $125, their major customers are J. C. Penney and Sears. Functioning exactly like their ready-to-wear cousins, they cut and ship 3000 carbons of one style at a clip, no custom craft whatsoever. They sell 80,000 gowns a year—a very hefty portion of the bride population—and claim that 90 percent of the girls in Omaha get married in their dresses.

The Alfred Angelo line is more to the point. With gowns ranging from $100 to $295, the only garment produced in advance is the sample, sold one to a store. The customer's actual getup, the one she will wear for her wedding, is cut after she places the order. Not only to be altered to her size, but to accommodate her styling changes as well—a longer train, a little lower in the neckline. In addition, most of the dress is actually hand-made. Beading, lacing, the lining are all separate processes, executed *for every individual gown* by ladies sitting in huge factory rooms sewing on tiny beads, one at a time. It is, in an era of no-human-hands-have-touched-this-product, a startling concept. At the Angelo factory in Philadelphia there are three hundred of these ladies. As it has been explained to me, the usual street robe will be cut in quantities of several thousand, with a total of perhaps twenty pairs of hands involved with the entire procedure. In bridal, every dress is handled by over a hundred pairs of hands. That's why the markup is 100 percent or more, as opposed to the ordinary ready-to-wear escalation of 42 percent.

Buying bridal finery is the sole experience with the luxury, the elitism, of custom-made clothing that most American girls will ever have. Hence it is no accident that the bridal salon is often the fanciest nook in the store. Nothing hangs limply on racks, nobody shoves, salesgirls do not sniff or grump.

The sale of one gown involves anywhere from three to ten fittings; if the bridesmaids' rigs are also purchased there —which, naturally, is the store's prayer—the involvement is even deeper.

The bridal apparel industry is native to the United States, and only of the last thirty years. Before that gowns were not manufactured at all but were either hand-made by dress-makers or handed-me-down by grandmas. Then the small bridal specialty shop was developed, where several seam-stresses were employed to concoct each costume from scratch; one-half of all purchased bridal dresses today come from these marts. In Europe there is still no wedding gown in-dustry to speak of.

With the nuptial boom, the overall growth of the garment business and the bridal magazines, which provided a show-case for manufacturers, came the industry. Until the end of World War II, however, only twelve or fifteen manufacturers existed and those few were in serious danger of extinction when the government rationed fabrics of "nonessential" in-dustries. Luckily, the bridal powers convinced Uncle Sam that there is hardly anything MORE essential during war-time than the stability of marriage, so the quota was removed. As the war ended, the marriage rate soared (1946 is still the biggest year in history), and with it came the frock factories.

Sometimes termed the General Motors of the field, Alfred Angelo, Inc., is the oldest, as well as largest, corporation. They have seven subdivisions and cover every inch of the bridal globe—economically and culturally. Their total vol-ume is over $10 million a year. To study the workings of Alfred Angelo is to uncover a fascinating story of American sociology, of who gets married and how in our country.

It's a mama-and-papa candy store that "just growed"; Al-fred Angelo is Alfred Piccione, who began a bridal shop thirty-five years ago. Today, between him and his wife, Edith, and their four children (who have worked on and off since age seven), their operation comprises three factories, 750 employees, four wedding dress lines, two for bridesmaids, one for headpieces.

"Each of our companies has its own special market and its own particular philosophy," explains Edith Piccione, as we trudge through the massive confines of her main factory in North Philadelphia. "To understand bridal design you *must* understand the background, the religious connections, the individual psychology, as well as the economic status, of your girl." With that, we sit down in her airy office, strewn with pencil sketches of females in long gowns (she does it too, eh?), and watch a fashion show—a one-hour parade of models in white. At the beginning every doodad appears virtually the same to my virgin eye, but by the time sixty or so costumes have passed by and Mrs. Piccione has—to her credit—conveyed her extraordinary knowledge of the game, I am a wiser person.

We start with the gowns from Bridallure, their budget and volume company, prices ranging from $50 to $110. Bouffant, sequined, lacy, these are, without exception, highly gingerbreaded dresses. Yards and yards of train, layered skirts that stretch three feet away from the body, and veils completely covering the face—an old-fashioned and anti-quated concept. My first reaction is surprise that the cheapest, those that are *not* custom-made, but factory-produced en masse, should be so elaborate. Edith clears my head: "The customer of Bridallure is the girl who cannot afford a five-hundred-dollar wedding dress but it has to look that way. This girl is undoubtedly from a background of foreign-born parents or a group of people who hang on to all of the old traditions. On the West Coast she is probably Spanish; in the Midwest she is from a really small town and is likely to be Polish or Italian. She wants ruffles, glitter, the top-of-the-wedding-cake look. That's her image of a bride."

She is a girl, according to Edith Piccione, who is not in-fluenced by or even exposed to fashion trends. She is a movie magazine reader, is very affected by television—Edith does a lot of local TV fashion shows to reach her—and doesn't get to department stores to shop. She is strongly knit to family convention and will have a gigantic wedding, for which her parents will have been saving for years. If she's Italian, the groom's family will pay for part, so it's got to be even more extravagant. The Bridallure bride has hardly, if ever, worn a formal gown before; she is the most vulnerable to purchasing the very first she dons due to the socko impact of witnessing herself in so much lace (lace is the key feature of this line), all that mantilla and veil and a train longer than the Super Chief.

Again, vogues in fashion don't at all affect this line. "When we try something new, it frequently bombs," says Edith with regret. "We're always looking for something different, a new fabric and a little oomphier design, but it doesn't work, these girls don't want it. We have one dress that we've kept in the line for ten years, and it's still one of the heaviest sellers."

Bridallure dresses are always pure, snowy, virgin white.

The Alfred Angelo line—$100 to $295—is, by contrast, 50 percent white, 50 percent ivory. The fabrics are of finer quality: imported chantilly laces (it's domestic in Bridallure), imported organza instead of nylon, silk-faced peau de soie (verboten in the cheaper). The big difference between the lines is the fashion styling. Straight or A-lines replace the Scarlett O'Hara look, trains are short or nonexistent, a headpiece is often dispensed with entirely.

The Angelo bride reads the bridal publications, *Vogue* and *Seventeen;* she's more likely to be in college than the Bridallure girl; she's best found in New York, New England or larger Midwestern cities where there are vast department stores (the Bridallure kitten buys from a specialty mart). Although her dress will be more expensive, her wedding will be smaller and simpler.

The two couturier lines are Piccione Bridal and a series

of gowns, inaugurated in 1970, by Oscar de la Renta. (Wedding rigs designed by French biggies are a new wave—and thus far not a very successful one. They do not seem to understand, with Mrs. Piccione's clarity, the American girl.) Whereas Edith alone creates all the Bridallure and Angelo robes, a young designer named Ron LoVice chisels the Piccione line, selling from $250 to $600. "We started Piccione three years ago," says Edith, "in response to what we sensed was a great need for the highest up-to-date fashion in quality gowns. We use, here, the finest silk fabrics, hand beading, and laces that I design myself." The Piccione gowns are 80 percent ivory; the styling is untraditional—low backs or décolleté do well in this batch—and exceedingly less fussy than the Bridallure. Every gown herein is constructed to the measurements of the bride.

The costumes are sold in a variety of ways. At the couture level, only one store in a city is allowed to carry the line; Angelo will not sell *the same style* to two stores in the same city, and Bridallure is most likely to be as commonly found as the proverbial cold. Exclusivity, you see, is a noteworthy fringe benefit of affluence.

It is in the elite dresses, from *all* manufacturers, that one tends to observe whatever leaps from convention are being taken. The girl in this bracket is very modish and devoted to looking original. *Not* micro-mini-plastic-peekaboos, mind you. Not nutsy inelegant, but distinctly memorable and even —God help us—sexy! Eleanor Robbins, a young dynamo who has revolutionized the dreary bridal department of New York's Bonwit Teller since taking command two years ago, says: "My girls want uniqueness. They want to feel they're onstage, and naughtily provocative. My kids are kicky!" Her kicky kiddies are among the few in America who will buy pantaloon outfits, hot pants and mid-length gauchos. "If you give them the best, marvelous fabrics and design, I can educate them to love it—even if it's far out."

The man from Mori Lee—second only to Alfred Angelo

in yearly volume—capsulizes this apparel business neatly for me: "I could take a Piccione four-hundred-dollar dress and copy it down to sixty dollars—and I couldn't give it away. The sixty-dollar girl has a completely different vision of how she wants to look and it doesn't matter that she's getting a bargain. She wants something that *looks* expensive, and in her book that means with a whole lot of goop all over it. I always have to remind myself that you can never underestimate the American taste."

There is a little company in the wedding world called Pandora Bridals, run—in the haimish tradition of Seventh Avenue—by a father and son, Nathan and Gerald Mantell. It has been described to me as the outfit which is most forward-thinking in terms of design and merchandising and, interestingly enough, it is budget-priced, so I decide to pay them a visit.

Pandora costumes sell from $89 to $398, their strength being in the middling $140 area, their experiment being to create a fashion look more in the lower than in the upper prices. "We gear ourselves," says the junior Mantell, "to sell Altman's, not Neiman-Marcus. The better stores, like Bergdorf's or I. Magnin, play it safe, jump to orthodox gowns. Gimbels, Alexander's, the budget stores, all are getting young, fashion-minded buyers."

Pandora's young designer, Frank Rizzo, only a three-year veteran of the bridal realm ("It's really a challenge to have to do everything in white!"), plays with unheard-of fabrics: piqué, matte jersey, clingy sexy materials, the no-bra look, helmets, parasols. "We believe—no matter what everybody in this business insists—that kids want something different, trendy. The clue, as far as I'm concerned, is that the wedding dress has to be a little sexy, with a bit of breast showing. Girls are obsessed with bosom; they start taking birth control pills six months ahead of the wedding just to increase their bust two inches."

While I am there, wandering among the white, impressed with the real flair of his designs, the Pandora people stage a fashion show for themselves, of next summer's dresses. The purpose is to select an appropriate garment for the cover of *Bride's Magazine* and to pick out gowns for their own ad campaigns. Nine execs are present, and two models, one of whom is in real life the switchboard operator. A financial barracuda-type sitting next to me, frenziedly doodling figures on yellow bits of paper, clues me in to the momentousness of selecting the pluperfect gown: a cover of *Bride's* can mean $500,000 in additional business, or 25 percent of their total year's volume. I become appropriately solemn. The modeling run-through commences.

A Seventh Avenue dialogue is now taking place, a "shmatte" shorthand that is as incomprehensible to an outsider as overhearing a gaggle of brain surgeons wrist-deep in brain surgery. "Saki is meaningless at forty-nine dollars," is somebody's opening line as the befuddled switchboardist shleps in wearing an ill-fitting dress. Somebody explains that saki is a fabric but that "at forty-nine dollars she wants worsted." He also explains that $49 is a wholesale price; manufacturers always talk in terms of wholesale, not retail, figures.

Another costume appears. "That's a pretty dress, Gerry, but I think you're hurting it with the gold braid. Remember number two fifty-nine, that twisted belt? *That* was a good number." Nodding agreement.

And another. "That's a knockout, Vinnie, at twenty-nine dollars. That's that ruffle they're screaming for. We'll sell it as a bridal, we'll sell it as a formal. You know what makes that dress, Charlie? The print. The print." (It is, surely, an enchanting, low-necked chiffon print.)

"Once you talk thirty-nine dollars, you know who you're knockin' out. You're not talkin' twenty-nine." I'm beginning to catch on. "The gown is oversimple," Vinnie responds to an oversimple dress that joins the parade. "The headpiece has to have something zippo." The designer makes a note. Something zippo for the headpiece.

"Now, THAT dress is gonna sell. It has visual value, a total look. Oh, yeah, that's a knockout. At forty-nine seventy-three, the girl's gonna bust her wig over it."

The climax—the dress that's favored for the coveted cover —arrives. A very sweet cotton lace ditty with matching mantilla. Agitation fills the room, as in those racetrack movies where the unknown horse has just finished a phenomenal trial run around the track and the owners realize they have a winner. "It's an item!" shrieks Charlie. "It's definitely an item!"

One cannot, I suppose, explore the bridal apparel game without mentioning the superstar, Priscilla Kidder—Priscilla of Boston. Because she has achieved a public prominence through her association with White House affairs (she befrocked Luci Johnson and Julie and Tricia Nixon), there are those who believe Priscilla to be the *only* bridal designer in the country. She herself may be one of the staunchest believers.

Priscilla is a chicly gotten-up, clever, giddy, tough, good-looking dynamo in her mid-fifties. Although she may or may not be responsible, as she claims, for (1) introducing the wedding band neckline ("I did it in Luci's dress—now it's a staple"), (2) burying the hoop petticoat, (3) inventing the princess line, (4) reincarnating mantillas and, in general, elevating bridal dumbness into lofty fashion, she is, without doubt, the savviest go-getting promoter in an industry not known for its zip. Her company creates not only the usual array of variously priced attire, but also a line of mother-of-the-bride dresses, flower girl dresses, duds for the under 5'3" and Priscilla Veils. She owns two retail stores in Boston in which she herself spends a goodly amount of time, she acts as wedding consultant for her more socially notable clientele and she jets around the country running three-hour fashion showings and preaching that no store should employ a bridal buyer over the age of twenty-five. Other manufacturers, as to be expected, think Priscilla's designs old-hat, matronly and "gloppy"; other manufacturers, on the other hand, have not been asked to create historical splendor in the White House.

The bridal gown biz is infinitely more personal—not to mention romantic, sentimental and mushy—than any other huge industry in the American technocracy. If you purchase your finery in a department store, the salon ladies will, statistically, spend four and a half times longer with you than any other salesgirl with any other customer. In Houston, you will very likely purchase your gown, and those of your attendants, at Foley's, not because it's the best emporium—it isn't—but because everybody knows Mary Ann Maxwell is the hippest bridal dame in town and for no extra charge she'll coach your whole extravaganza right through to the wilting end. In New York, Monica Hickey at Bergdorf's is so "in" that Piccione will invent special laces *just* for her clients. And across the street, at Bonwit Teller, I witnessed the arrival of a Santa Fe oil tycoon and his daughter, who flew there because the news has spread about the new terrific bridal buyer.

But half of the brides in America will acquire their robes from wee-sized bridal shops, like Rose de Paola's Bridal Aisle, on Fourteenth Street in Manhattan. Rose, who earns around $70,000 a year, and caters primarily to Italian, black and Puerto Rican working girls, is a rare leftover from the days when Grand Street—in the Italian ghetto of the Lower East Side—was the wedding garb nucleus of New York, when there were no manufacturers, no department store bridal nests, and everything was hand-sewn by the little women in the back room. She has been in this profession for forty years and in all that time has never accepted any payment but pure cash. A fat chunk of her business is still custom-made—and those dresses start at $350. "I won't buy a Priscilla dress," she says. "I'd rather copy it myself and make a bigger profit." Rose has noticed, in four decades, only microscopic changes but one solid consistency: "Once a bride-to-be sets her heart on a dress she usually buys it, no matter what the cost."

A newly sprouted tentacle is the franchise bridal shop. A sort of Kentucky Fried Chicken in white organza, it is the same precise concept. Modern Bridal and Formal Shops, one of the speediest-spreading franchises, had fifteen stores a year ago, sixty now, mostly in towns of 100,000 population—like Muskegon, Michigan, where previously girls had to travel forty miles to Grand Rapids to find a single white getup. These shops have been grossing an average $90,000 a year, and since—they figure—the wedding rate rises 10 percent each year, the dough will rise accordingly. In hamlets of 30,000, where even a tiny bridal shop would be unfeasible, this outfit is moving its wares into ladies' homes and selling from there.

One gets the overall feeling that the bridal trade today is rather like the garment center of forty years ago. A bunch of folks—a little out of touch with the times and the possibility of exciting lifestyle changes—sitting around in dusty cutting rooms turning out the same rags every season. Edith Piccione sums it up: "The industry has not gone forward because the wedding is *so* bound up with tradition, they refuse to acknowledge any shifts at all. At meetings of the apparel trade association, instead of talking about the future of weddings and marriage, they argue about how to buy cheaper boxes."

Despite the blinders, and the imprisonment in the past, let's acknowledge some key shifts. Barbara Donovan sees faint glimmerings of the wedding costume beginning to move in on the formal gown. "A dress that reflects one's self-image rather than strict tradition. There's more gaiety, not quite so much solemnity in dress." Among urban, sophisticated girls, the subtle trend is away from the vestal virginal —even Tricia Nixon's conventional getup displayed a hint of chest.

The color changes are indeed subtle—white has a magical grasp on the American soul—but here and there we find a quiet blue sash, a muted yellow underskirt, a suggestion of pink thread. (In a *Bride's* survey of 1967, *nobody* reported wearing anything but white or ivory for a formal wedding; in 1971, the same survey disclosed that a small but probably significant 4 percent had some amount of color in their gowns.)

In bridesmaid's garb, however, there is a mini-revolution occurring. When I was bridesmaiding frequently, in the early-to-mid-1960's, one bought *THE* bridesmaid's uniform —easily recognizable because there was no other situation in which you would conceivably wear such baroque ugliness. It often cost as much as $75, and then you had to buy white satin high-heeled shoes which you dyed to the color of the dress. Eleven minutes after the wedding was finished you cut up the dress for dishrags.

That's all changed. Bridesmaid's togs are high fashion today, inexpensive (the average girl spends approximately $35) and absolutely wearable again. Some of my fashion-hippest friends, in truth, shop for their long party frocks and at-home gowns in the bridal salons.

What are the wedding apparel guys' provisions for the second-time bride? The third- and fourth-timers? None. Zero. The rallying call of the entire industry—from the diamond ring merchant to the caterer to the honeymoon heaven to the sterling silversmiths—is, "You're Only Married Once." But nowhere is the fiction more keenly exhibited than in this business of the bridal gown. Dresses, without exception, are designed with the seventeen- to twenty-year-old girl (clearly her first marriage) in mind; it is nigh impossible to find one whose lines are suitable to, say, a woman of thirty-five. Then, too, wedding etiquette either ignores or scorns the second wedding. The *Bride's Book of Etiquette* dismisses it in five short paragraphs, saying: "A second-time bride—no matter what the circumstances of her previous marriage— should not try to imitate a bride marrying for the first time. A second marriage is an occasion for dignity, sentiment and tradition, but not for pomp and circumstance. Neither a formal ceremony nor a large guest list is proper when the bride has been married before." *The Wonderful Wedding Workbook,* written by a group of professional consultants in Washington, D.C., does not deem it fit to mention at all.

Miss Jones, the primmish bridal buyer at L.A.'s I. Magnin, is adamant to the point of hysteria that second marriages not be in white, and *sans* veil, a train, processional and attendants. "It *must* be an underplayed occasion," says she with a disdain implying that such a wedding is the union of two lepers. Neither Magnin's nor practically any other store in the country will provide for the poor pariah. "We just *can't* stock appropriate dresses for the divorcée or widow," says one frank buyer. "It would take a lot of the glory out of it for the young bride to see, for example, a short beige cocktail suit hanging next to a heavenly white lace gown. It's sort of depressing for her."

But how else to perpetuate our deeply romantic mythology? If one acknowledges the icy statistical facts, that 40 percent of the enchanting young Cinderellas and Prince Charmings who make their dreamy-eyed ways up the aisle of enduring love and forever marriage—two out of five of those couples—will, at some future point, sever their foreverness by divorce, well, then, what on earth happens to the white wedding gown? To its symbolic hookup with the Continuance of Tradition, the Perfection of Marriage, the Happily-Ever-After?

The message is clear: YOU'LL NEVER REPEAT THIS EXPERIENCE. Do it up big NOW. And how can we sell the story that This-is-your-most-monumental-once-in-a-lifetime-day if we add the phrase: until next time, or maybe the time after that? Does indeed tend to take the oomph, the juice, out of wanting to spend hundreds or even thousands that one can't really afford on a dress that will be worn for six hours and nevermore. Certainly does take the juice out of it. . . .

9. In This Holy Estate: The Catered Affair

The scene is a chapel. A wedding ceremony is in progress; the attendants have made their entrances and are in position, waiting. The three hundred guests are silent, the organ throbs softly and the lights are dim. Suddenly a misty red spotlight appears, focusing on the side wall where there seems to be a round pedestal, raised seven feet off the ground. It is enveloped by a filmy net curtain behind which there is a person poised, an ethereal silhouette, with its back toward us. As the organ begins a long crescendo, the pedestal starts revolving, very, very slowly, until the figure is facing us, bathed in a warm rosy glow. The curtain opens then to reveal none other than—The Bride. Gasp. Ooooooh. Aaaahhhhhhh. As she steps down, her father is there to escort her up the aisle. En route, her feet activate a treadle mechanism hidden under the carpeting which causes flickering colored lights to play on her face and gown all the way to the altar.

No, we are not on a movie set watching the shooting of *Gidget Gets Married*. We are at the Huntington Town House, on Long Island, and we have just witnessed a real-life production that will be repeated approximately twenty times this same weekend. There are those who, noticing the decor and theatrical embellishments, label the Town House a Wedding Palace. Others, remarking on the assembly-line turnover, a Wedding Factory. It all depends on how you look at these things.

In any case, the Town House and its cousins—Leonard's of Great Neck, the Narragansett Inn, the Fountainhead, about fifteen in all—are a mushrooming phenomenon of the eastern seaboard. They are an outgrowth of the boom in suburban living, the increased spending capability of the suburban middle class and the rise to power of a new breed of American, The Caterer.

If you live on Long Island, or in New Jersey or lower Westchester, and you want your daughter to have a bang-up blowout for three hundred of your nearest and dearest, where do you go? Well, you can go to a Manhattan hotel, the Plaza or the Waldorf, say. That is, if you have $20,000 to spend and are Jewish. (Christians always hold their ceremonies in church, and it's a far trek from West Orange to Fifty-ninth Street.) You can do it at your country club, that is, if you belong to a country club. Or on your back lawn, if you happen to live on a football field. But why not choose a place like The Manor, a grand catering establishment decked out like the Vatican—"where the Hospitality of the Old South meets Continental Cuisine for gracious dining in suburban New Jersey"—where weddings are sold as budget package deals ($19.95 per person includes not only unlimited drinks, hors d'oeuvres, and a châteaubriand dinner but a candelabra for the head table and a dressing room for the bride) and everything, but everything, is arranged for you. This is where you get your super-duper gilt-edged flambé extravaganza of a circus at discount prices; the Sears, Roebuck of the wedding biz.

And they are immense, these palazzi. Leonard's—the Taj Mahal of catering temples—cost $5 million to build, has twelve banquet rooms, can handle 1000 folks for each party and plays host to 30,000 revelers a month. The Town House holds 850 cars in its parking lot and does 1500 weddings a year. The Manor, resting on twenty acres, pays a light bill of $6000 a month and figures annual glassware breakage at $16,000. Any way you slice it, that's a lot of chopped liver.

Let me describe the ambiance. Several of the palaces were designed by the same New York architect, Richard Bellamy, inventor of the Materializing Bride—a geniusness inspired by the Metropolitan Opera production of *Lohengrin,* in which the swan boat glides out of the mist and onto the stage. He calls his style "eclectic"—"English Regency, French Provincial, Louis XIV, and sometimes all three together." It is that mode previously described in these pages as Bridal Baroque and elsewhere tagged "Bourgeois Royale." The philosophical premise of this school of decor is that nothing should be left simple when it could be froufrou'd up, nothing subdued when it is at all possible to be gaudy, everything that *can* be painted gold *must* be painted gold. Leonard's is populated, both inside and out, by naked marble cupids with water spouting from any one of the various orifices; The Manor is a "Southern Plantation" with a fake greenhouse, fake wine cellar, fake birdcages, fake stained-glass windows in the chapel, a fake Torah and a Greek love temple on the lawn for outdoor ceremonies. Well, the man *did* say "eclectic."

Crystal chandeliers are a big number. One could perform open-heart surgery by the light of the chandeliers in Leonard's lobby, and the Town House boasts a custom-made one that cost $56,000, copy of an original in the Schönbrunn Castle in Austria, with crystals arranged in tiers thirty feet deep. Balconies are good, grinning marble cherubs are classic, fountains very crucial, as are ornately spiraling stairways. (At Leonard's, one stairway leads to a glass tower, a choice spot for bridal photos as it offers a panoramic view of downtown Great Neck.) Fake filigree gold meanders all over the place from the borders of the omnipresent mirrors to the faucets in the powder rooms. A neat selling point is the cascading indoor waterfalls, switched on for weddings only. Your very own plastic Niagara Falls. . . .

There are people who fall in love with catering castles merely on the basis of the powder rooms, the management tells me. Some have their own sculpture museums (more nude marble cupidness) and toilets so exotic that one truly forgets why one came in there in the first place. At the Town House the powder room is called the Lavoratorium.

The aim of the decor, explains architect Bellamy, is "to create a Cinderella-like setting for the bride and her handsome prince. We want to give her all the trappings of a fairy tale."

Not that weddings are the only activities, bear in mind. At the Huntington Town House, although nuptials comprise 75 percent of their business, they do lots of organizational fetes on weekdays ("We have the Heart Fund, the Mentally Retarded. We've had Nixon and Agnew. They all come here," brags the manager) and bar mitzvahs, sweet sixteens and anniversary parties on weekends.

Leonard's has three floors, four rooms per floor, and on a Saturday night or Sunday afternoon every room is occupied in a state of nonstop Mardi Gras. In and out, in and out. Three P.M. wedding reception in the Tiffany Room, bar mitzvah next door in the Champagne Room, engagement party at four across the hall in the Parisian Room. Assembly-line frivolity, three thousand frolickers carrying on at any one time. Like New Year's Eve in Times Square, only this hysteria doesn't end a few minutes after midnight. Stories abound of guests looking for the Miller bash who wandered into the wrong room and spent the next five hours celebrating the wrong wedding. And if you stand in the lobby on any one of the levels, you hear all the bands playing simultaneously "Theme From Love Story Sunrise Sunset Hava Nagila What Kind of Fool Am I."

Each palace has its own package deal, but they're just variations on the same theme. At Leonard's they stress the "yarmulkes-are-included" feature, at The Manor you get seconds in your main course ("We're the only ones who offer that bonus"). The Fountainhead, in New Rochelle, does an original theatric: "We bring in a gigantic bowl of salad, instead of serving it on individual plates. We lower the lights and then the spotlight hits the chef in his white hat as he tosses the whole salad right in front of you. It's *very* exciting." To his credit, the banquet salesman has made this event (one which I would not have thought previously to be especially riveting) *sound,* in fact, exciting. At several places, if you buy the most expensive package, your waiters will wear white gloves. At budget prices their hands go naked.

Here's the basic at the Fountainhead, explained to me by the pudgy salesman as I posed as a potential customer: "First you get your drinks and smorgasbord. Now, you can have that after the ceremony, in which case people are often too full to do justice to the really fabulous seven-course sit-down dinner. Or you can have it before, in which case you miss it because the bride's not allowed to be seen. Some people are afraid that if they have liquor served before the ceremony, their guests will get rowdy. I never worry about that if it's a Jewish affair. Jews are looking for the food, not the drinking.

"Anyway, the butler serves the hot hors d'oeuvres. All good items. Egg rolls, kreplach, chicken/pineapple/peapods—we call it c.p.p.—your Nova Scotias and herrings, your egg foo yung and your sweetbreads Regency. All nice. Incidentally, there's a bubbling fountain in the middle of the smorg table. Very exciting."

(I must interrupt to tell you that, like all caterers, this fellow is lustily involved with food and is clearly reaching some fever pitch of excitement as he proceeds with his lecture.)

"Then we go in for dinner. For your appetizer we've gotten away from the fruit. It's a cliché by now. We go for a hot appetizer, like your duck flambé is a good item. There's rolling bars during dinner. Wine is a dollar more per person, but it's a superior boojoolay."

Ultimately one reaches the main course—which accounts for

the greatest variance in the price of the package. Chicken is the cheapest, prime ribs the dearest, with turkey, pot roast, squab falling between. Nobody chooses chicken, I am told, because all his friends know what it costs.

Prices also depend on the number of guests (they go down the more you invite), the day of the week (a reception for 250 can be $1100 cheaper on a Thursday than a Saturday night) and the time of the year (summer months are most expensive). Photography and music are not included in the deal, but—surprise, surprise—all the joints have photographers and orchestras on the premises. The Fountainhead recommends Precious Moments and Steven Scott (who has over fifty bands and works all the halls). Leonard's suggests their photographer; they don't push, mind you, but a Bachrach photographer claims that when he has a Leonard's assignment they won't let him park in the lot and guys somehow keep tripping over his camera cases.

So the packages run anywhere from $11 to $22 a person, infinitely cheaper—perhaps one-half the price—than any fancy hotel. The sum includes all the food and booze (unlimited liquor), minimum flowers, the ceremony—although some charge extra for this—wedding cake, personalized matches, waiters' tips and cigarettes. Most customers, however, choose some of the splendid extras: the "intermezzo" (a sherbet between courses) for $1 per person, champagne at the reception, 75¢, fruit cup sitting in a carved Rome apple instead of silver bowl, 50¢, ice lovebirds, $25 to $50 apiece, flambé first course, $1, Viennese coffee table (a giant buffet of pastries, candy and sundae fixings, served immediately after the wedding cake which is served immediately after the Cherries Jubilee) at $1.95 per head.

Volume is the key, of course, and business is colossal. Witness the basement banquet offices at Leonard's of Great Neck on a rainy September Sunday afternoon. I am waiting my turn—again a poseur—in an anteroom jammed with folks planning social do's. Thirty-five minutes pass before I am ushered into an office by one of the five banquet managers, each wearing a different-colored ruffled shirt—fuchsia, gold, robin's-egg blue—a shiny black suit with velvet bow tie. The telephone, ringing incessantly, is overseen by a tough, ash-blond receptionist who knows everything in the world. "I can only tell you, madam, that whatever your budget is we can give you a party for it, but I can't discuss any more on the phone." Bang. Despite her "catering," Leonard's is booked solidly for the next three months and hardly an hour is available for June—nine months away.

The crowd is very talky; many seem to know one another from the neighborhood. Parents accompany their kids, but the adults are clearly in charge. Specifically Mama. They chatter about why they're here and every event is referred to as an "affair"—wedding, shower, fund-raising luncheon. "When's your affair?" "Who's doing your affair?" "What are you wearing to Sylvia's affair?" I ache to ask the gang, What do you call AN AFFAIR? but don't.

Two youngsters for whom a wedding is ostensibly being planned sit in the background while Mama operates. Filling out the application, she forgets how to spell her future son-in-law's last name and screams "HOWWWWWIIIIIIII-EEEEEEE" across the crowded room to where Howie and his lady have retreated, immobile, permitting their "affair" to be totally manipulated and controlled by somebody else. It seems to me, at that very moment, to be a terrible relinquishment.

But that's precisely why so many people choose Leonard's et al. In a home, hotel or church wedding there are a zillion decisions to be made. Blue candles or yellow? Pigs in blankets or miniature quiche? What kind of flowers? It is imperative that one's wedding be perfect, so every choice engenders the deepest of anxieties. A party on such a grand scale is utterly out of sync with the manner in which most people live. Which of us can bear the possibility of making fools of ourselves, being social klutzes? Mrs. Heathersnit from Newport was reared to throw little galas for five hundred; it is in her genes. The suburban housewife fears her inadequacy in this department and yet it is even more urgent to *her* that she create an impeccable, spectacular occasion. Desperate for help, she reads thirty-two issues of *Bride's,* confers with anyone and everyone who's ever organized a wedding, searches for *somebody* to assure her what's right, what's good taste. In this state she can be—and is—sold anything. Comes along, on his white horse, toting his tray of forty hot-'n'-cold hors d'oeuvres, Big Daddy the Caterer from the Wedding Palace who promises to take care of everything.

Some joints do everything but supervise the wedding night. The Parkway Casino—"Custom Caterers for All Your Social Occasions"—not only takes command of your entire frolic ("Full-Course dinner including Manhattan cocktail . . . 4 pitchers of beer per table") but if you have two hundred guests, they throw in a one-week honeymoon in Florida. All for $9.50 a head. At the Governor Morris Inn in New Jersey, a twenty-four-hour-long weekend wedding reception for a hundred guests, at exactly $2990, includes "50 luxurious air-conditioned double rooms," brunch the next day and use of the pool.

The prize package of all, that is, the deal leaving absolutely nothing for Mama to do—not the tiniest loose end to strike terror in her heart—is offered by the Thatched Cottage, also on Long Island. For an additional $474 over the cost of the reception/dinner, you get your invitations, flowers for the wedding party, ten table centerpieces, personalized stirrers, a limousine AND—relief of reliefs—your wedding gown and groom's tuxedo. Of course you don't get to choose what you really dig, but then the price is right, after all, and at least we're sure we're not screwing up.

This package thing threads its way through the whole American scheme of life. Leonard's of Great Neck is only an extension of the average home, in which everything is instant, frozen, packaged, canned, and even our yogurt now comes pre-stirred. The palace wedding is a TV dinner where not only don't you have to cook but you don't even have to decide what frozen vegetable to serve with what—Mr. Swanson has much more experience and know-how; he knows how to combine meat loaf with tomato sauce with potato nuggets with a chocolate nut brownie for a yummyeasy meal. Not a loving hand participates in preparing the bread for the table, but then personal involvement takes too long and requires too much energy.

Back at Leonard's, the salesman whisks me on a rushed, impatient tour beginning with the three chapels—one on each floor, one for each of your major faiths. In the rear of every one is a customer's viewing room, with a one-way mirror, reminding me of the way psychiatrists observe the inmates at play. "There's the chuppa," he explains, "your Jewish awning effect," and hurries me away before I even have a chance to spy the revolving bride. (At the Fountainhead a more cordial atmosphere prevails, and they operated the entire show just for me—chimes to announce the coming of the bride, jazzy lighting gimmicks controlled by more than a hundred different switches and, in lieu of the pedestal, a long curtained runway down which the bride floats as a filmy apparition.)

We scurry past a jewelry shop, positioned for last-minute gifts or forgotten wedding bands, and then, after much prodding on my part, I'm allowed a moment's peek into two adjacent banquet chambers, two distinct bar mitzvahs, 500 separate partygoers. At first I insist that I have been led into the same room twice, by different doors. You see, not only are the sets and the cast and the plot interchangeable, but—and you'll just have to take my word for this—both bands are concurrently belting out the same song, "I Left My Heart in San Francisco," in the same precise key.

Wedding palaces cater to both Jews and Gentiles, with the scales slightly tipped toward the Jewish. Is it odd then that *all* the food is kosher? And that the Town House has on the payroll several rabbis who, by some Talmudic law or other, must be present to supervise the kitchen whenever it's in operation? In order to make certain, one supposes, that not a thimbleful of butter finds its sneaky way into the territory of the brisket. "The Gentiles don't mind," assures Vinnie Ferraro, operational manager. "They never complain about no butter on the table, and we use a coffee mix instead of cream, which they never even notice." The Fountainhead fellow reports: "Our heaviest complaint is from guests who want brandy alexanders and we can't make them." Wedding cake, at its best not the most ambrosian of tasties, suffers unmercifully at the hands of cream substitute and phony butter.

Despite the fact that the Town House clientele is 40 percent Christian and the owners are Italian (*all* owners of *all* catering châteaus in the East are Italian; enough said about that), they close down for Rosh Hashanah and Yom Kippur, "out of respect for our Jewish customers." I cannot really explain to you why the kitchens are strictly kosher, since in this generation of New York suburbanites the percentage of observers of the ancient laws must be minuscule. One suspects, however, the roots to be economic, as The Caterer is nothing if he is not practical.

The Town House is the only one with two menus, a "Basic" and a "Jewish." Sociologically, it is interesting to compare them. For the cocktail hour and smorgasbord, the Jewish has a champagne sherbet punch bowl, the Gentile doesn't. The Gentile cold canapés include tuna puree, olive spread and stuffed celery; the Jews don't get any of that. To be Jewish means getting silver trays of gefilte fish, sable carp, smoked whitefish and Nova Scotia salmon. (Fish has traditionally been a wedding fertility symbol, and an Oriental Jewish couple would jump three times over a platter filled with fresh fish to insure a lot of babies.) What is termed "liver strudel" and "potato knishes" on one menu is "liver pattie" and "potato soufflé" on the other. Only Jewish galas get "Carving Chef Serving Hot Sliced Prime Steak." ("The Jews expect it," Vinnie explains. "Gentiles aren't accustomed.") In the hors d'oeuvres category of "International Specialties," Jews have Hungarian stuffed cabbage and Tongue Polonaise while Gentiles get Beef Hawaiian and Chicken Cacciatore. Jewish folks get the bar, while to begin dinner, Gentiles are served a Manhattan cocktail, followed by a punch bowl *and* rolling bars.

"Let's face it," confides my chubby Fountainhead friend, "the Christians aren't interested in the smorg. They're looking for the whiskey and the beer." All the managers make the same distinction. At The Manor, where they have computed the median liquor consumption to be 2.9 drinks per person, higher for you-know-who, the man claims: "In a Polish wedding they drink like they're going to the electric chair. The Irish drink with both hands. The Jews, on the other hand, eat anything that isn't nailed down."

Let me take you then to the Huntington Town House on a Saturday evening in early September. As we pull into the vast parking lot, it is difficult to remember that we are in a sleepy Long Island town, thirty miles outside Manhattan. The immediately overwhelming garishness of the surroundings and the incredibly bright artificial lighting remind one of Las Vegas or Miami Beach—both unreal burgs whose lives are also dedicated to mass frolicking. How doubly cuckoo to find Caesar's Palace or the Eden Roc poised amid tiny homey delis, ramshackle neighborhood gas stations and tract homes.

It is 7 P.M. and hundreds upon hundreds of people are streaming into the main lobby. Comparing the crush to Wrigley Field ten minutes before a World Series game is to begin, or an airport arrivals terminal during a snowstorm or Penn Station on the Friday night of July fourth weekend, would not be inappropriate. Only everybody here is rhinestoned to kill and there is an odor of perfume, 177 brands all melding into one icky sweetness, that permeates the entire vastness. Some of it, granted, is residue from the afternoon fireworks, in which four weddings, three bar mitzvahs and an anniversary party took place. Tonight, beginning shortly and continuing until 2 A.M., are scheduled one bar mitzvah, seven Gentile wedding receptions and three complete Jewish weddings. The respective ceremonies will occur in the chapel at eight, eight-thirty and nine, exactly.

The airport aura is certainly not diminished by the fact that the loudspeaker is never silent. "Will all the guests of the Schwartzberger affair please return to the Windsor Room? Your dinner is being served," it commands. "The O'Riley cocktail hour is now beginning in the Hampshire Room," it proclaims. Like the authoritative unseen pilot, the voice blares instructions, directions, it organizes, forestalls calamity. You see, it's even more complex than you can imagine just by knowing that eleven carnivals are going on concurrently. Old stuff must be cleaned away and the new stuff set up, so at various intervals the merrymakers are shipped out of their ballrooms and into the lobby for fifteen minutes where they must fend for themselves.

Thus the lobby tableau one witnesses is a torrid brouhaha of arriving guests scurrying about to find their proper floor (Promenade, Colonnade or Cascade) and correct room, already-tipsy revelers shuffling out for fresh air, lost sheep milling around waiting for dinner, waiters dashing across the floor with trays of food, brides and grooms posing for formal pictures in front of the waterfalls. As I am not gowned and eyelashed I'm evidently assumed to be an employee and am approached every few minutes for directions to "the Bertolini affair" or "the Levineberg bar mitzvah." It is an atmosphere of barely contained chaos that I can only compare to my fantasy of something gone amuck at the Sara Lee plant where suddenly walnuts are being sent into the cheesecake and the croissants now have a banana icing.

And the noise, oh my friends, the relentless stereophonic cacophony of feet thundering, bands trumpeting, party voices squealing and shrilling, dishes clattering. One of the ancient weapons to drive away the evil spirits believed to be threatening newlyweds was that of loud noise. I think to myself that with the volume here, there couldn't possibly be an evil spirit still breathing anywhere east of the Rockies. At one point a squadron of women traveling from their fete to the powder room encounters a flock of pals—guests at another fiesta—en route to the chapel. The shrieks of jolly greeting that arise between the two could be equated perhaps to the mass mating call of five thousand sea gulls.

"Everything goes off like clockwork," claims Vinnie. "We have to keep that feeling of smallness, intimacy, the sense that there is only one affair going on at a time in the building. After all, brides certainly want their privacy on this day." Management is very sensitive to the "Wedding Factory" label, the assembly-line stigma that would be hard to overcome and obviously bad for business. That's why they lie. Why they insist that the activities are so brilliantly staggered that no two parties are waiting in the lobby at the same time. Why they insist you can't hear the music from one room to another and the closest thing to the Town House is getting married in Grandma's cottage in the woods.

It is time for the first of the three ceremonies of the evening. I am blessed with permission to attend all of them. The chapel-in-the-round is enveloped in artificial flowers and rimmed with fake stained-glass windows that also turn out to be fake windows. The chuppa—which the management also titles "the gazebo," depending on your persuasion --graces an altar that is lit by dozens of phony candles. Off to the side, you remember, is the whirling pedestal. The crowd is chattering noisily—unaware for some reason of the holiness of this setting—and has a small glow-on from the cocktail hour which has just preceded. One grande dame has transported a plate of hot hors d'oeuvres with her—Lord knows she does not need one more cheese puff to pass through her body in this lifetime—and nibbles greedily, while neighbors look on with jealousy for her acquisition but awe for her foresight. The organ, meanwhile, belches piety into the air. The lights go dead. It is time. Pandemonium barely diminishes a decibel as the double doors creak open and enters the rabbi wearing—you'll just have to believe this incredibleness, too—a SEQUINED prayer shawl.

The processional is uniquely grotesque for a number of reasons, not the least of which is a perspiring photographer who has stationed himself right in the middle of the aisle and snaps, clicks, flashes and gallops to new positions without cease. Another horror is the opening and shutting of the big twin doors for each member of the wedding party. Apparently the din in the lobby will not allow for doors to remain open more than an instant, but these creak and crunch and crash without mercy. Enter the groom and his parents. CREEEEEAAKKK. CREEEEEEAAKKKK open for the maid of honor. CRRRRRRUUUUUNNNNCH shut. The ultimate offense is the organist who clearly received his training at a roller skating rink and thus deems it fitting suddenly to change the music without warning, to prevent boredom, I suppose. As each bridal party member enters through the clanking doors he strikes up a new tune— despite where he was in the previous one. So that at one instant he is booming an up-tempo martial ditty for the bouncy best man, abruptly switching to "A Pretty Girl Is Like a Melody" for the bridesmaids, followed immediately by a tune from *Fiddler* as Grandma and Grandpa toddle down the aisle. All punctuated, naturally, by creeeeee-kiiiiing, crashing, clanking.

Luckily, everything seems to progress very fast; indeed, it is like a mini Keystone Cops movie. But of course we must be out in exactly twenty minutes and thirty-five seconds for the next scheduled ceremony.

At the dance of the revolving bride the audience makes the required gurgles despite the evidence that most have seen this Hitchcockian ritual scores of times. It's like clapping at the end of the show—you do it because you do it. A ghostly bride materializes on a misty pedestal and you gasp like it's the Second Coming of Christ. Incidentally, this part of the service is optional; your bride can also arrive in the normal fashion. But, they tell me, only one out of five hundred passes up the pedestal.

In this case the young bride—she looks to be fifteen but is nineteen—is weeping noticeably throughout, clutching onto Daddy for dear life, continually wiping her eyes. Jerry, whose official title is Marriage Director, confides to me later that three minutes before the ceremony she hysterically insisted on backing out, canceling the whole thing—a not untraditional happening in wedding annals. Thank God for Jerry and Vinnie and Larry and the army of banquet managers who flew to her, convinced her she *had* to proceed as planned, thereby saving her from the fate of having to eat stuffed derma and potato pancakes for the rest of her life.

As the folks file out—the still-shaking bride having fulfilled her moral obligation to the caterer after all—the next shift is already waiting, pacing impatiently, anxious to get it over with and get back to the roast beef. What do we need this for? hangs in the air. We were having a ball, a few mambos, a couple whiskey sours. Why do they have to interrupt the party?

Same procession, seedier crowd. Charlene, the bride, has a bobbed nose; apparently she also has a cousin who once took flute lessons because he is now tooting "Here Comes the Bride" replete with unauthorized trills. In this wedding the maid of honor sobs her eyes out. The sequined rabbi from the previous scene plays cantor in this one, with a voice rather like Frankie Laine chanting "Mule Train." The rabbi speaks exactly like Dr. David Reuben.

In-out-in-out. Twenty minutes and thirty-five seconds later it's over, right on the nose, precision timing (although the rabbi *did* have to scurry through the last part of his blessing in order to make the schedule). An exiting woman passes an arriving woman in the same green chiffon gown and for a moment matters get very tense. Then they both giggle and exchange where, when, how much technicalities. This crowd —250 of them—is mucho gay and some new summit in noise pollution is achieved. Even when the lights go off and the photographer, who is now sweating absurdly, begins his snapping, flashing, clicking and the doors begin their crashing, whining, the gang *still* won't knock it off. It takes an organ blast of "Pomp and Circumstance," outvoluming them into submission, to provoke silence. This rabbi fellow is all in black, has an accent that hovers between British, Old Testament and the west side of Chicago, and calls the bride Margery instead of Marilyn.

Just at a moment of sweet solemn silence—one of the few in this entire ritual where one could recall why we were here —through the walls filter the rumba strains of the band right next door and a baritone crooning: "You can do it on a Monday a Monday . . ."

On to the merrymaking. Vinnie leads me from sanctum to sanctum, cha-cha to cha-cha. "For a really big wedding, you can take the entire lower floor," he explains, "and have your own lobby, chapel and men's room." Makes sense, of course. Then at least the jostling and shoving offenses will come not from total strangers. Vinnie carries a remote-control beeper device which buzzes every time he is needed and he must then run to a house phone, stationed every fifty yards, to handle the crises. It buzzes incessantly through the evening as he solves all the catastrophes of an obnoxious drunk here, a missing portion of capon there. On our long odyssey, an adventure that fast wears me out with its commercial and impersonal frivolity, he imparts to me teeny professional and sociological gems, the accumulated wisdom of umpteen years locked up in a catering castle. "Gentile weddings last much longer than Jewish—they get out once a year so they really take advantage." Or: "Italian weddings are bigger than Jewish. But the Sephardic Jews spend the most of all; they really know how to get the best." Two further tidbits, one being that the Town House has advertised only three times in thirteen years, thus all their business obviously arises from word of mouth; the other their notions for expansion—plans to seat three thousand at a time with dancing, and with motel facilities on the premises. Onward and upward, new peaks in eternal wedding bliss.

Each cave that we enter swells and bursts with eatables and there is never a minute in the five-hour marathon when the celebrants are not eating. The quality of the fare may fall somewhere between economy-class airplane and summer-camp dining hall; the omnipresent Swedish meatballs are fairly easily confused with the beef stroganoff à la Russe, which itself is indistinguishable from the Hungarian stuffed cabbage. But never mind. Look at the array, table after table, silver tray upon silver tray. It just keeps coming, and besides, it's a well-known truth that, among Jews and Italians particularly, the eleventh commandment states that the more you belch the better the shindig, the bigger the heartburn the groovier the party.

What we miss in gourmetdom we more than make up for in conspicuous consumption and sheer show biz. In the Madison Room a picnicking army awaits the arrival of the duck flambé. Lights dim, folks are commanded by the PA to "Please be seated while your course of duck is being served." The band strikes up a spritely "Bridge on the River Kwai," the cue for the entrance of two waiters hoisting flaming spears of carrots, leading a parade of ten waitresses bearing fiery trays of duck and rice. They goose-step around the room to the music, everybody applauds wildly. My God, is this or is this not an "affair" to remember?

When it's cake time, we get the same popular choreography. The wedding cake arrives—an astonishing gooey replica of an altar, with a cake priest, cross and cake bridesmaids. Oddly enough it's called the Cathedral Cake, is one of the Town House super deluxe extra goodies, and there is apparently a Semitic version. Anyway, its entrance is marked by climactic music, the standard waning lights and the top of the cake flaming away.

I ask a new bride, an eighteen-year-old Italian girl marrying her sixth-grade sweetheart before 275 witnesses, how she likes the Wedding Palace. "Oh, I love it! Everything is so beautiful and you get so much for your money. I just loved standing on the pedestal and whirling around. It's just like Hollywood here!" Hallucinations of grandeur is surely what it is. On a beer budget, the middle-class family is being served up delusions of Dom Perignon. Lay on the flambé and they'll forget it's an assembly line. Give 'em cupids and waterfalls and gilt and maybe they'll believe this is elegance and forget the words "package deal."

One can go no further than the Wedding Factory to escape the ancient marriage rituals and customs. The feast of joy in which everybody participated and contributed has given way to the impersonal, frozen hand of the caterer. One senses that more romance, sweetness and human contact is to be found in the bareness of City Hall than in the lavish accoutrements of the Huntington Town House. There is an essential meaninglessness to the occasion here—the caterer's occasion—no difference at all in spirit between a wedding and a rowdy, overstuffed, utterly forgettable New Year's Eve.

10. The American Spectacle: Hollywood and the White House

Hollywood is both a reflection of and the cradle for American values. I grew up thinking—and still utterly believe, in that deepest part of me that defies knowledge and experience— that every life situation has an "ending," a point at which the screen darkens and that particular drama is over, resolved. When we're good and noble, it all ends happily. But even if not, even if a nice girl like Ali MacGraw fades away gorgeously from a terminal case of Movie Star's Disease, it is somehow "all for the best"—"everything works out in the end." Hollywood has, among other perversions, bequeathed us the ridiculous legacy of Ultimate Justice.

I also still believe that someday my Paul Newman will come, that someday I will be perkymerrypeppy like Doris Day and able to stay underwater as long as Esther Williams. I know in my heart that I have failed abysmally in life for never having had a "grand amour" quite on the scale of Bergman and Bogart's in *Casablanca*. I am also certain that sometime in the future I will be a divinely famous actress.

We've even acquired much of our wedding psyche from Hollywood. The wedding day is *the* chance that Miss Average U.S.A. gets to play Star, this one moment possessing all the excitement and anticipation of a Broadway opening night, minus the pain. No chance the audience won't love her, no possibility of bad reviews; the bride is a sure-fire smash hit. She is Miss America and the Academy Award winner and the about-to-be-crowned princess and Judy Garland at the Palace, all at one moment. The closest she will come to fulfilling the impossible golden dream of Hollywood.

If Hollywood so colors our fantasies, what about its citizens? It is perfectly obvious that movie stars live their lives not like real people but like characters from movies; they mold their existences to play either like a Busby Berkeley technicolor musical extravaganza or like a 1942 Joan Crawford tearjerker. Mae West is a person or a character from a film? The lives of real citizens have "plots" like Elizabeth Taylor's? Don't be silly. Movie stars act out *their* fantasies on screen and off, without distinction between the two worlds. And we the people eat it up.

Hollywood is, after all, the only nobility America has ever known. Our kings and princes are mogul producers and superstar actors, and from the reading of those lives we can define the flaws and triumphs in our own. Sinatra may have all the wealth and glamour in the world, but poor fella, he doesn't have a wife (Mia Farrow walked right out on him, a lot of good his money did, you know what I mean?) and he's getting old and bald just like the rest of us, and he'll be alone one day too, despite his houses and jets and power and fancy friends. Cluck, cluck.

There is a profound symbiosis that exists between movie stars and us. We need to care, I mean really *care,* about Barbra Streisand's blood-strewn divorce. We need to ponder over whose fault it was (her ambition or his competitiveness), how the child will be affected, who's more unhappy, who will remarry first, what's what and who's who. We need to feel wistful because the stars have glitter that we can only touch through the pages of *Silver Screen;* but then they screw up and fail in a much more melodramatic way than we do and we're vindicated, our own lives are safely tolerable once more.

And Hollywood royalty desperately needs our love; without us they do not exist. Knowing that we are hungry tigers who must be fed or we turn on them, they will do anything. Anything. You're having a gallbladder operation, you hire a press agent to spread the word. Getting a divorce? Hold a news conference, hope it'll make the wire services. Getting married? Well, that's the best of all. Everybody loves a wedding, Hollywood adores a spectacle, so why not combine the two? Money in the bank is what it is. Better than John Wayne licking The Big C.

Celebrities' weddings, like their lives, are frequently bigger than life. Johnny Cash's *fifteen*-year-old daughter decides to get married, and eight days later Hendersonville, Tennessee, is rocked by a gala for six hundred in which participate a maid of honor, eight bridesmaids, three junior bridesmaids, a best man, a head usher, six ushers, one junior usher, a Bible boy (five-year-old Kevin Carter Jones—in tails), two candle-lighters, two guest registrars, two program attendants and nine hostesses. At the reception later held at the Cash lake-side mansion, no liquor is served, only grape juice flowing from an electric fountain.

When Florence Larue of the Fifth Dimension singing group marries Marc Gordon, the group's manager, they do it in the parking lot of L.A.'s Century Plaza Hotel. With the minister, they leap into the gondola of a hot-air balloon, the service is performed fifty feet overhead, and when the rope is ceremoniously slashed, the celestial couple sails off into the blue to the band's rendition of "Up, Up and Away"— the group's then current hit record. The minister (to tie up any loose ends) is the boy who wrote the song. A supreme public relations shtik? Life imitating Art?

What are we to say about Tiny Tim tiptoeing through ten thousand tulips imported from Holland, as he takes his vows with his seventeen-year-old Miss Vicki before twenty million devotees of the Johnny Carson "Tonight" show? Perhaps, simply, that it is sensational, crucial publicity— what could be a more opportune bonanza, a wedding and a circus—for a man whose success must rely on blessings other than his talents. Perhaps, too, the game of celebritydom demands that there be no division between public and private existences or that there not even exist a concept of "private." Every human event is grist for the Show Biz mill, nothing is sacred. If one out of every ten Americans, strangers all, is to be a guest at our wedding, then when the TV restrictions loosen up, will we have John Chancellor cover our wedding night?

Is it different from the heyday of the fan magazines when *Photoplay* paid for Janet Leigh and Tony Curtis' wedding, in exchange for an exclusive story? Or when one of the Lennon Sisters recently allowed a photographer to come along on her honeymoon, the deal being that he foot the bill in exchange for all the pics he wanted?

It's really in perfect harmony with the manners, the lifestyle, of Hollywood. Bob Hope's daughter gets married, he sends out news releases (she's not in the business, but what the hell. He is). Actress Brenda Vaccaro moves in with a guy and her press agent puts out a release to the papers. Now, the question arises, does *his* press agent (he's the son of Kirk Douglas and an actor himself) do another release emphasizing *him* instead of *her?*

For some, the wedding is not just an extension of the hoo-hah attendant to their careers; it's the only splash they will ever get, so all the stops are pulled. A dancer on the Lawrence Welk Show was marrying the accordionist's daughter on Valentine's Day. On the show the prior Saturday the entire nationwide audience was extended a "personal" invitation to the wedding. According to one of three photographers who came to cover the jubilee, "Every senior citizen in Long Beach showed up at the church." Thousands milled outside where they could hear the actual ceremony, due to the thoughtfulness of the groom who had arranged for a PA system. The photographer recalls that as the rite drew to a close the minister's voice boomed over the PA: "Ladies and gentlemen, Mr. and Mrs. Bobby Burgess. You may applaud."

Marilyn Beck, a syndicated Hollywood gossip columnist, reports that she's constantly receiving invitations to weddings of actors she's never met, sent out by their press agents. The nuptial of Don DeFore's daughter—a non-show business chick—was one. The press coverage was intended for him. Callous, or part of the game?

Sometimes the Hollywood bride merely lives out her screen image. Sex siren Raquel Welch costumed herself, for her nuptials, in a predictable white crochet see-through mini-dress, sans underwear. And when starlet kitten Edy Williams, of *Beyond the Valley of the Dolls* "fame," wed soft-core porny producer Russ Meyer, she wore skintight white lace, cut deep over her thirty-seven inch amplitude and high up over her thighs. Perfect.

In Hollywood's prime time, the glorious golden years from the thirties through the early fifties, weddings reached a pinnacle of extravagance. That kingdom of old is dead; so indeed are the old weddings. Never again will the world witness—no, be a part of—a pageant like the marriage in 1928 of movie idols Vilma Banky and Rod LaRocque. The couple had originally planned a simple elopement, but her boss, producer Samuel Goldwyn, took command and produced a Real Life Spectacular, with who else but Cecil B. De Mille (Rod's boss) as best man, and a regiment of cops to keep under control the fifteen thousand waiting, swooning, crazed fans. A gargantuan reception boasted mammoth hams and turkeys that later revealed themselves to be plaster-of-Paris creations, specially prepared, as was the wedding itself, for the photographers and press. The bride was extremely late, it seems, as Goldwyn had held her up with work at the studio; in the meantime the band played continuous music from De Mille's latest epic, *King of Kings*.

One must understand the climate of Hollywood then, the machinations of the system. In the Golden Era, the star was *literally* the property—privately as well as professionally—of the studio, the supremely powerful, frequently tryrannical studio. The publicity department created her stardom, manufactured her image, considered everything about her existence to be under their control. She was a public object, and the public of course wanted to know—indeed believed it was their *right* to know—every teensy thing that concerned her. What she ate for breakfast, did she sleep in the nude, who with, and on and on and on. Naturally the wedding was a reflection of this outlook. The studio's aim, in staging a wedding, was for more and greater publicity, and the fans —having been hyped to believe in the intimate connection between their idols and themselves—assumed they would be included in on the festivities.

Thus, when Elizabeth Taylor married Nicky Hilton, it became a worldwide circus. Hollywood veteran costume designer Edith Head remembers it as "the charge of the light brigade, thousands and thousands of fans—many in evening gowns or tuxedos—waiting outside the church for even a glance at the gorgeous, rich, magic couple. People fainted, screamed, the press went utterly berserk."

The press always attended star weddings; when, as in the case of Lana Turner and Bob Topping's, they weren't invited, they presumed the right of the fourth estate to ferret out news wherever it happens (and what could be juicier news?) and leaped over the high walls surrounding the mansion. Once inside, they were accorded guest treatment, witnessed the life-sized statues of the bride and groom carved out of ice, and the baked hams with "I Love You" spelled out in pimientos.

When Norma Shearer married Irving Thalberg in 1928, an airplane soared overhead after the ceremony, showering the newlyweds with rose petals.

John Agar and Shirley Temple were practically dismembered by the three thousand fans who had gathered outside the church in blistering heat at 3 o'clock and waited until 9 P.M. for a glimpse—until they finally stormed the church doors.

For Grace Kelly's wedding—a gala that combined all the splashy elements of Show Biz with the *haute* regality of a European coronation—the princess's gown was "produced" by the MGM costume department. Thirty-five seamstresses spent six weeks in its execution, confronting 300 yards of lace and 450 yards of satin.

Edith Head, whose office on the lot of Universal Studios is drowning in Oscars and whose memory bank is overflowing with luscious tales from historic Hollywood, has designed hundreds of wedding dresses—in movies and in real life. "The further back you go, the more colorful and dramatic the weddings were," she says. "As the star system disintegrated, as the studios declined, so did the Hollywood wedding."

She reminisces fondly about one which she costumed—that of Veronica Lake to millionaire André de Toth. "It was in the days—the early fifties—when you still took weddings very seriously in this town. She was at the height of her career and it was the superstar in the superdress in the superwedding. It was held in a Bel Air mansion with pools and sunken gardens. Everybody in town was there and the whole house was lit with candles, like a Gothic castle. Veronica was a great beauty, he was dark and dashing—a truly romantic beautiful Hollywood couple. When she came floating down a long winding flight of stairs in a candlelight-white satin medieval gown, well—it was just absolutely perfect." Enrapt with her emotion-filled recollection, I suddenly realize I am watching this scene, in my mind's eye, as if it were a movie. A divine, sublimely romantic, 1940's Hollywood sudsy saga, in which this magic moment is the final scene. The music swells, the screen blackens, and we all go home, thrilled to death. Needless to add, the couple lives happily ever after.

"It was simply another era," Miss Head continues, "the era of extravagant living, extravagant movies, extravagant clothes. Those kinds of big palatial weddings would be incongruous now, have nothing to do with the current way of life in Hollywood."

Of course, she is partly mistaken. Hollywood people who remember the old days think today's Tinsel Town lifestyle is humble. With classic naïve distortion, they believe today's Beverly Hills is Middle America, U.S.A. (Doesn't *everybody* out there have a sauna, dahling?) On the other hand, the Golden Era, with all its incomprehensible showiness and opulence, is indeed finished.

"I *hate* doing Hollywood weddings. The people are crazy and they don't pay their bills," snipes a Beverly Hills florist. Says the tip-top society wedding consultant, Gertrude Doran, "The weddings I do I like to feel the people are quality. Movie people aren't quality; they don't do things with taste." From Milton Williams: "Show Business types don't spend the most money. They all have business managers who won't let them splurge. I'd much rather do a Brentwood sweet sixteen any day of the week."

The mavins of the wedding industry all concur: Hollywood weddings are not where it's at. The profits, for them, come from the bourgeois businessmen with the oversized Bel Air castles and a compulsion to make their friends drop dead. There's also dough in the hills of hotsy-totsy Pasadena, and often even in the ascending black middle class. But, in general, Hollywood/movie star/showbiz weddings are, money-wise, dead donkeys.

Somebody once asked a Hollywood costume designer named Donfeld if he knew so-and-so, a well-known actress. "She's my favorite star," he replied. "I go to all her weddings." This, too, is a fat reason, according to the industry pros, why Hollywood razzle-dazzles are diminishing. "Most of the girls here go through so many husbands they're embarrassed to have weddings," Donfeld continues. "Who ever heard of a movie star getting married for the first time?" Then, too, it's a hustling political town, whom you know being as critical to your career—more so, one suspects—than what you do. So whom do you invite to a monstrous wedding or, more to the point, whom *don't* you invite? And how many of that legion of bodies will have been married to other bodies who wind up next to them at the hors d'oeuvres table? Serious embarrassment, heavy stuff, bad news for the host, very nervousing. Better yet, forget the whole thing. Elope to Vegas.

In the younger, hipper Hollywood, more kids are living together unwed. And even if they're not issuing press-release proclamations, it's still more open, less of a stigma, than in the old days. Famous unwed lady stars parade mushrooming bellies on network television; one celeb is quoted by a gossip columnist as insisting she won't marry her boyfriend until they want a child and she won't have a child until she's been married for a while. Actor Roger Moore finally marries his girlfriend, eight years and two kids later; the star of a long-running TV series divorces his wife of twenty-two years, marries his pregnant leading lady right on the sound stage, attended by a battalion of reporters. Weather-beaten Hollywoodites insist it's no different, no freer, today than when Nelson Eddy sang "I Love You Truly" at Jeanette Mac-Donald's wedding to Gene Raymond. The same stuff went then as now. But now it all hangs out.

Naturally there are periodic exceptions to the fabulous-weddings-are-dead rule. But they exist primarily among the offspring of celebs. Dinah Shore's daughter's wedding (*only* $12,000 for flowers, grumps Harry Finley, Beverly Hills' chicnik florist), Danny Thomas' daughter (800 for dinner at the Century Plaza Hotel), Lucie Arnaz (the hot awaited moment was when Mama Lucy danced with ex-hubby Desi). All lavish affairs, heavily weighted with the old-time Hollywood tycoonery, all a paradise for autograph hounds and the press, all splendiferous in food and champagne and daisies. But NOT a Sam Goldwyn shtik on the premises.

Two Hollywood weddings of recent vintage stand out; both brides were the offspring of stars. Bob Hope offered his daughter, Linda, $25,000 instead of a wedding. She refused.

So he sent out a three-page press release, detailing the flowers ("white orchids flown from Hawaii"), the attire ("The bridegroom's mother, Mrs. Robert Greenblatt of Augusta, Ga., will be attired in an Alice Berman original gown in pale rose Dupioni, in princess style, with long, sable-trimmed sleeves, and floor-length skirt. She will wear a matching Emme hat, and bronze-colored orchids pinned to her bag") and the guest list (Ronald Reagan, Spiro Agnew and Toots Shor). Bob Berman, the rentals man, recalls: "It was the largest wedding ever done under a tent. Every rentals person in the country competed for this job, and the fee to us came to over twenty-thousand dollars. It was all done on Hope's own golf course."

Insiders talking about Nancy Sinatra's wedding to producer Hugh Lambert like to describe it as "small," "restrained," "simple," "unpretentious." Perhaps for the Sinatra clan it was all those things. Perhaps compared to her opening-night party at Caesar's Palace, where Harry Finley's decorations cost $65,000, it was. After all, it was not even her first wedding and she *was* married in a Palm Springs church that used to be an army hospital. Understated, yes; but then the bride wanted a candlelight ceremony at two in the afternoon so in order to transform a daytime infirmary into a night-time cathedral, the entire building—windows and all—was covered with vines and shrubbery, $25,000 worth (well, okay, that *does* include 10,000 white roses at the altar). The super-rich *do* have special powers, I am reminded once more. Poof: day becomes night. Simple.

Come with me on a brief trip through an understated Hollywood wedding, as told to me by Donfeld, who not only designed the garb for *The Cincinnati Kid* and *They Shoot Horses, Don't They?*, but also for Nancy Sinatra, her mother and her kingpin father, for her wedding. "She didn't want to do the klieg lights number," he says. "She wanted a tasteful, quiet affair, like a nineteenth-century country wedding. I did twenty-five sketches of her gown before she accepted one—a silk georgette over a slip of white crepe-backed satin.

Fifty different kinds of laces. All made by hand." This country maid's frock tallied in at $3000.

The reception for two hundred was held at the Sinatra compound in Palm Springs—five houses in all. Sinatra's three jets were used to fly Donfeld in from L.A., a hairdresser from Las Vegas (each had his own bungalow on the estate) and the guests from who-knows-where.

Barbara Stanwyck said it was the most beautiful wedding she'd ever seen. Another guest observed it was "a sleepy gathering for a Sinatra vaudeville."

Other countries have royalty; we have movie stars for heroes. Other cultures have bigger-than-life political figures, with total power and longevity; we have politicians who are here today, gone next November and are generally lower than extras in the celebrity hierarchy. Many of us don't even know who the Secretary of the Interior is, much less being able to recognize him in a restaurant. Martha Mitchell became famous, chattered about, recognizable, because she carried on like a Hollywood fruitcake. But other than Martha or a *really* succulent divorce, what other personal goings-on of our politicos really turns us on? Their days lack the essential fantasy, the dazzling glamour and dizzying drama of our Hollywood gods and goddesses. The Secretary of Labor puts on a suit-'n'-tie every morning, takes his multiple-vitamin pill and goes off to a gray office like the rest of us. So what.

The Kennedys, of course, were movie stars—beautiful, rich, young, perfect. Captivated by every last, minute detail of their days, we molded them into super culture heroes, invested in them a portion of ourselves never before or since granted to our first families. They had the magic chemical formula: they were infinitely more spectacular than we, but also reachable. Not like the remote Nixons or Eisenhowers. A newspaper photo of Jackie in dungarees and sneakers and, by God, she IS flesh-'n'-blood real folks.

But most Presidents and their families are totally unavailable to us. Their public profiles are all we see, those and the inadvertent slips-of-the-face, and the unfathomable power. We do not read or hear gossip about their marital hassles ("The Night Pat and Dick Nearly Split Up" will never see the light of day in *Modern Screen*), her nervous breakdowns, his financial worries or their personal heartbreak at the death of their pet Doberman. We know only what they want us to know, and that is far too skimpy for our needs to become immersed in lives more exciting than our own. It's also invariably tedious, never delicious like Steve McQueen's divorce followed by his being seen kissing in Beverly Hills nooks with Natalie Wood, who's at the same time dating her ex-hubby Robert Wagner, whom she will eventually marry again. *THAT'S* satisfying stuff. Such flair, such convolutions of the human operetta. How truly, terrifically luscious!

We are never privy to dirt about White House dinner parties, who wore what and who danced with whom. On the other hand, we sense that they're fairly stuffy—nobody falls in the pool, we assume, the place never gets raided for marijuana and the Prez probably toddles off to bed by ten-thirty. Yawn. His vacations, who cares? No Bel Air tennis courts for the Potomac Prince, no yachts off Corfu, villas in Acapulco, fabulous absolutely fabulous Puccis and Guccis and the best top beautiful people and rivers of champagne and wit. Save for the Kennedys, our First Families have recently tended, to understate the point, toward the pedestrian.

No, we need glamour and exotica to nurture our fantasies and we rarely get it from the White House. Except in one situation: the White House Wedding. It is the one event in the President's private orbit to which we can relate with passion. The wedding is a kind of common denominator between us and the most inaccessible man in America; in this most classical ritual, its elements crossing all social and cultural barriers, the President's daughter is brought down to our mundane level or we up to hers. We can have the rare opportunity to empathize, in a human way for a human happening, with this superhuman family. The family understands the force of this deep identification and thus a White House Wedding becomes more than what it is—it becomes a Political Act.

It can do as much good for a President's current popularity as a quick troop withdrawal or a little minimum-wage boost. Indeed, after Tricia Nixon's blowout, her father's image went soaring, say the pollsters. On that day the President was Everyman—the bumbling, blushing, semi-reluctant, wistful daddy losing his firstborn to another man's hearth. Touching, you'd have to call him. More vulnerable and appealing than we ever witnessed him, before or since.

No one will ever be able to explain, for sure, why Julie Nixon's reception was feted in a quiet, no-reporters soiree at the Plaza Hotel in New York (the florist, by the by, accuses the Nixons of cheapness; only $700 was spent on floral decorations) and Tricia in White House splendor. Could it be that at the time of Julie's nuptials the newly elected President, who would be inaugurated one month later, felt a kingly outpouring of personal funds to be politically inopportune? But that three years later, at a troubled time when the Chief was running short in the brownie-points department, a big beautiful Rose Garden wedding catering to our love of pageantry, a family ceremony on a national scale —the closest we come to a coronation—*this* sort of production might be exceedingly helpful, career-wise? No one knows. One can only speculate.

Tricia Nixon's wedding did have a tremendous effect, at least temporarily, on certain aspects of American life. Votes in the bag for Daddy, money in the till for the bridal gown manufacturer who threw together an instant copy of Tricia's dress, available in stores three days later, and sold thousands upon thousands to upcoming young brides. There was a sudden run on the California champagne served at the reception, and a New York psychiatrist reports that every single female patient, the week following, was fixated on discussion of Tricia's wedding—mostly with envy.

There is, naturally, an American tradition of White House

weddings, Tricia Nixon's being the sixteenth. The first, Maria Hester Monroe's in 1820, was attended by forty-five guests and recorded with a concise thirty-five words, two days later, in a Washington newspaper. (Tricia's wedding day made headlines in every leading newspaper in the world; the television coverage reached one out of every four Americans.)

In 1874 Nellie Grant married Algernon Charles Frederick Sartoris, in a gown costing $5000, on a priceless rug donated by the Sultan of Turkey. All opulence faded, however, next to Algernon's own resplendence: he carried a bouquet of orange blossoms and pink roses and a banner emblazoned with the word "LOVE." It is rumored that after the couple departed President Grant retired to Nellie's room and sobbed his eyes out, which may or may not have been due to a clairvoyant peek at the future—after four children and fifteen years, she abandoned Algernon to his bottle.

The most sumptuous White House bash to date—Tricia's has been labeled a "simple spectacular"—was that of Alice Roosevelt to Nicholas Longworth, in 1906. One thousand guests crammed the East Room, and there were no bridesmaids as Miss Roosevelt was highly competitive. She need not have worried: all eyes were fastened on the two, not-one-but-two, diamond necklaces adorning her throat, gifts from the groom. According to a newspaper report, "Miss Roosevelt looked as pretty as she ever did in her life and that's saying a good deal. As for the sturdy and good-humored fellow who won her, he was one broad beam of sunshine from that much-advertised bald head to his feet."

The subject of wedding gifts has always had heavy political significance in the White House. (Nellie Grant accumulated $75,000 worth, including a $500 handkerchief.) But at no time was this as keenly felt or exaggeratedly exhibited as in the Roosevelt picnic. The President of France sent a $25,000 Gobelin tapestry, the Pope sent a mosaic table and the city of Cincinnati delivered a team of horses. The government of Cuba planned on giving San Juan Hill to the couple, then decided instead on a $30,000 pearl necklace. Somebody donated a $1500 Boston terrier, which arrived with an engraved silver schedule of the dog's daily regimen and a complete wardrobe of suits, petticoats, furs and canine sandals. A punch bowl, given by the Ohio delegation, created such a to-do with the Women's Christian Temperance Union, who held a special prayer session to deal with the crisis, that congressmen were forced to take stands on the issue. A loving cup was finally substituted.

A White House wedding often reflects the social personality and tone of the Presidency. Luci Johnson's wedding, as previously described, was a classy Texas barbecue to which, as comedienne Edie Adams quipped, "only the immediate country was invited." (Speaking of gifts, Luci's favorite was a jeweled Pakistani nose ring, symbolizing female submission, given by Orville Freeman.) There were 700 guests, a 100-voice male choir, a 300-pound cake, Peter Duchin, cold beef sirloin, and the gang had a nifty time. The same for Lynda Bird's. "The Johnsons loved yippee parties," says Washington's Ellen Proxmire. "They had more of them than the Kennedys, less glamorous, of course, but most people said theirs were more fun." "The Johnsons weren't wildly chic," says Barbara Howar, wildly chic D.C. socialite, "but very convivial. When the Johnson girls got married, there were wonderful parties for them—the Harrimans gave showers in that glorious house with ten million dollars' worth of paintings and smart people. The Nixons—well, do you really want to go to a party where Martha Mitchell is? I would kill to avoid a Nixon wedding."

Barbara, a onetime girlfriend of Henry Kissinger and a good weather vane for Potomac social climate, insists "the Nixons have driven this town's social life into total lethargy. They're stolid, dull people. *Nobody* goes to the White House anymore." What's implied, of course, by *nobody* is nobody-who-counts, or nobody-who's-zippyfun, or nobody-who's-anybody-you'd-at-all-want-to-spend-one-second-with.

True, Tricia's wedding had about it the unmistakable instinct for middle-of-the-roaddom. I was there, having been assigned to cover it for *Life* magazine, and it was your standard WASP frolic—less fun than a hippie shindig held on the Malibu cliffs, and less funny than anything happening at Leonard's of Great Neck. But fundamentally like all other weddings. Sweet, joyous, utterly predictable. Splendid, regal, elegant and absolutely inoffensive.

The interesting—okay, incredible—aspect of Tricia's wedding—the third interchangeable White House rite in only four years—is that, on June 12, 1971, it was the biggest news event in the world. A planetary super-spectacle. From beginning to completion, from the day in March when the engagement was officially announced to W-day in June, this event took on the celebratory whoop-de-do of Caesar's triumphal march into Rome and the minuscule complexities of the invasion of Normandy. Why? Certainly not due to the personnel. Tricia was not one of the more colorful young women on the American scene and Edward Finch Cox was, as far as we knew, a nice, bright, clean rich boy. She had been, this moppet of blondness, the target of satire for some years: "A twenty-four-year-old woman dressed like an ice cream cone can give even neatness and cleanliness a bad name," poked one reporter, thereby getting herself excommunicated from the wedding. "Politics slightly to the right of Ivan the Terrible," quoted another, remembering Tricia's animated support of Lester Maddox. As "One of the best-dressed children in America," she was recipient of the annual Goody Two-Shoes Award from a children's wear manufacturer.

No matter. Our First Family is aristocracy—in a kind of ho-hum pumpkin pie way—so anything that concerns them personally becomes of public, and ostensibly historic, consequence. We do not require adoration of the participants. We just worship the pageantry.

How this wedding, devoid of any inherent drama, became international news was a victory for the media. Did we reflect the country's interest or create it when there was little? Take the episode of THE CAKE—that notorious sugar alp which achieved lasting fame upon its repeated failure at the hands of *The New York Times* food staff. If not for the press, it would undoubtedly have been just a cake, a foam rubbery wedding cake, an archetypic cake like every wedding cake through history. Instead it became a star, a carrier of plot and melodrama and campy humor. Will it finally turn out? Will it be a tragic failure? What will it taste like? What will be the surprise decoration on top? Minutiae escalated into crisis. The ultimate triumph of trivia.

How to transform a whitebread, suspenseless occurrence into a News Event was our dilemma, as well as the White House's. We reporters looked for *anything*—any microscopic tidbit. I even made an appointment (under a false name) with Mrs. Nixon's hairdresser at Elizabeth Arden, hoping she would drop some fabulous behind-the-bedroom-door plum. After three hours and $20, I emerged (having curtly declined her offer of a large bow to be pinned among my new, un-requested Shirley Temple curls) with a Pat Nixon cement hairdo—a look I did not particularly cherish—and no scoop.

Nothing was too small for news, no event too banal. Three hours before the ceremony, on my weary way off the White House grounds for lunch with four other reporters, we had the glorious fortune to encounter the three White House dogs—Pasha, Vicky and Timahoe—being walked by the White House Dog Person. Began the hysterical race for key info: "Is Tricia taking hers away with her?" Pens are poised, the air vibrates. "Who did his flowers?" (Referring to the Irish setter's little neckpiece of yellow carnations.) "Where will they be during the ceremony?" Anything, we'll take any crumb, anything.

They tried for theater, they really did. Climactic, mon-umental issues were surrounded by an impenetrable shroud of secrecy. We were not, for example, allowed the teen-siest knowledge of the wedding gown (surprise, surprise world! It's whorehouse red lace, boobs exposed!) until minutes before zero hour. Where it was being sewn—at Priscilla's Boston factory—an armed security guard kept solemn watch; every night it was locked in the vault; Priscilla brought the finished production to Washington strapped into a first-class seat beside her; at the airport she was met by Secret Service men who whisked the dress away to the White House via black limousine. When it was finally unveiled, this mystery of the Orient, this classified Top Secret secret, there it was— a long white wedding dress.

What can I tell you about the wedding? The media made the message in several zillion words, and you know it all. A White House wedding has about it the aura of history, and like all affairs of this sort, this one became—despite itself— a magical, irresistible business. There certainly have been, compared to Tricia's, weddings more elaborate, original, kookier, more jolly. But whether it's the family who borrows from Chase Manhattan to provide their daughter with her promised one day in white, or the White House family determined to provide the nation with a day of historical significance, a wedding is—after all—a wedding.

On the other hand, when guest Alice Roosevelt Longworth was asked if Tricia's wedding brought back the past, she sniped: "It didn't bring back one goddamn memory." So there you are.

11. White Bread and Upper Crust

The very rich are, to be sure, different from you and me. The very rich who are also High Society are even more different. To begin with, they have family trees whose roots stretch way back into American history. Then they possess some ephemeral goods called "background," "social prominence" and "breeding." Like puppies, they have pedigrees, but the actual requirements are somehow much clearer for beagles than for people. They are indubitably—need it be stated?—white, of Anglo-Saxon heritage, and Protestant.

Society girls have special names, like Buffy, Muffie, Mimsie, Missy and Ba-Ba. The men often have Roman numerals following their surnames and their surnames are *never* unpronounceable. They have their very own sports activities, like water polo, and their very own social activity, the Debutante Cotillion.

Frequently labeled by the media as the Jet Set or the Beautiful People, they travel in a rigid social sphere that they like to call "exclusive"; they tend to go to the same schools (which are the schools attended by their ancestors), belong to the same clubs, have second and third homes (summer and winter) in the same fashionable playgrounds, dine in the same French restaurants, shop at the same boutiques, use the same interior decorator, barber and gymnastic instructor, and see the very same 78 or 122 or 247 folks every single night of the week at either a cotillion or a

charity ball held to raise money for some esoteric disease
that nobody can even spell and that NOBODY that anybody
knows has surely ever had.

Their approach to their money—the way in which they
spend it—is different not only from you and me but from
other rich citizens who do not have pedigrees. As contrasted
with the If-You-Have-It-Flaunt-It ethos of the lower echelons
and the *nouveau riche* (who are often substantially more
loaded than they), blue bloods prefer to bury their gold
rather than splash in it. From an abhorrence of ostentation,
a dread of being thought "showy" or newly rich, they have
cultivated a lifestyle that is "understated," "simple" and
"restrained"—three of their favorite words—to the point of
being catatonic. Perhaps it is some manifestation of over-
weening guilt for being a Have in a world so drowning in
Have-Nots, but the rich never talk about money. Only her
friends know that Mrs. Pentersnippy's little madras Ber-
mudas, which she wears around the garden to prune the
azaleas, cost $55 at Abercrombie's. Only *they* know because
they own the same ones. But you certainly couldn't tell—
dear God, no—from looking at them, and of course no one
would dream of mentioning the price.

Gothic tales are recounted about the eccentricities of the
rich: J. Paul Getty's pay phone in the living room, H. L.
Hunt carrying his lunch to the office in a brown paper sack,
the Palm Beach retired millionaire who tyrannizes restaurants by collecting every nip of leftover food from the table
to take home. "The real sign of being rich," explains a
Washington Post article, "is making your salaried friend pay
the taxi fare because you don't have $2." Fixation on the
dollar is tawdry, my deahs, not to mention philistine. Disdain for money is one of the very best luxuries of being rich.

Manners, on the other hand, are of paramount value. And
that very elusive' lady called Good Taste. I myself do not
always know what is good taste and what is bad. Nor do I
frankly always care. In either case it's terribly hard to keep

it straight. My see-through blouse was fashionably tasteful last year, but gauche this. Picking up frogs' legs with your fingers used to be barbaric, now it's okay. Certain four-letter words teeter between chic and boorishness. The problem is that I don't always understand the rules, the nondefinable standards. Patricians do; they know Good Taste and Bad Taste from the cradle, from the tip of their curled pinkies to the very bottom of their manicured, buffed but definitely non-polished toenails.

Before our society (small *s*) was so fluid, it was easy to know who was Upper Crust. There was the list of "the 400" top families in New York and there was the Social Register or Blue Book in every major city. Inclusion had to do with wealth, position and how many generations one's family had been planted in the neighborhood. It was all very strict and sure. Actors, among other substrata, were *pro forma* excluded from the Register, and one's name could be removed —causing heinous, ruinous tongue-wagging—for doing something to disgrace oneself, such as having a messy divorce.

Today, in most cities, involvement in worthy civic events, like sponsoring the symphony orchestra, being what the society pages call a "doer," is requisite enough for the Social Register, regardless of the color of one's blood or the figures in one's checking account. (On the other hand, it appears that most families who have the time, money and connections to participate in the civic good life are wealthy WASPS.) Another way to get yourself In, at least in Los Angeles, is to be recommended by a listed friend and to pay a fee. And since the once uncrossable barriers between High Society and Show Biz have been lifted, well—there's simply no telling anymore who's the *crème de la crème* and who's riffraff.

One quality remains staunch: the commitment to tradition. The old guard swells tend not to move to new locales or new houses as frequently as the dizzily mobile middle class. They do not reupholster as often, buy and sell as many cars, change jobs or get caught up in current fads and fashions with five-second life spans. As their psyches are less joggled than ours by constant change, they are less apt to suffer from future shock. They are not as victimized by Madison Avenue and obsessive consumerism. Indeed, they are not the victims simply because they are the power.

Would you be surprised to know that The Beautiful People spend less money on their weddings than both the middle class and the working class? That a father who begins to save from the day of his daughter's birth (and perhaps has to hock something of value and borrow from the bank besides) in order to create the most memorable day of everybody's life—that he is very likely spending *more* than the gent who only has to scribble out a check, which doesn't even considerably alter the balance in his account?

The Wedding, for most Americans, is a psychologically loaded event, heavily weighted with fantasies of status, Making It in the community, and being—at least for a tiny time period—bigger than one really is. Daddy Thoroughbred is already a Brahmin; he adds not a single inch to his image by purchasing every nasturtium currently alive in the world. Mumsy is ho-hum used to swell parties—last night the Beri Beri Ball, today lunch at Le Haut Snob. The ritz is put on almost every day along with the cold cream.

Then, too, his daughter's wedding is perhaps the non-rich father's one chance in life to experience the luxury and affluence that the rich take for granted. The single occasion when he can unpress his nose from the glass and actually partake of the greatest of American dreams—extravagance, splurge, even waste. Most of us live with airy notions about what it would be like to be wealthy, how life would be sublime and trouble-free. But rich people, to quote *The Greening of America,* "know that not every day is filled with sports and glamour; they even know that the person who has everything might not even want all these things. The poor have no way of knowing this . . ." So they play out the dream in the only way accessible to them—The Wedding.

Speaking of that daughter, what does the formal wedding mean to her? To the average girl, it means everything. Absolutely everything. The society miss, on the other hand, is rather inured to buying zippy expensive clothing and having public attention paid her and going to spiffy shindigs, eight or ten of which will be simply *FAB* bashes preceding her own wedding. She has undoubtedly been to Dubrovnik and the Bahamas, not to mention 138 weddings of her classmates from Miss Finch's Finishing Farm. Because she's proud and secure with her heritage, she will even wear Granny's old wedding dress—Miss Average would rather go naked. Also, she gets to participate in another ritual which is not only more momentous to her but generally occurs several years before her wedding. The Debutante Cotillion—the formal introduction of young women into society—possesses all of the "princess" elements of the wedding. White gown, getting to play movie queen, moving from childhood to womanhood, reinforcing the continuation of tradition. For the mass of womankind, by contrast, The Wedding is their debut.

But a massive delusion is in operation. We have no real contact with how the aristocracy lives—we drive by their gigantic mansions and all we can glimpse are eighty-five windows and the silhouette of a pool. Little do we realize that the interior is peppered with peeling wicker rockers, an antiquated Steinway and Great-Granny's antimacassars, so we are left to our fantasies. When we plan that wedding of ours, we emulate what we believe to be the opulent style of upper-class life. Obsessed with the need to do it RIGHT, the way *they* would do it, we somehow confuse gaudy with classy, gilt with gold, quantity with quality. The truth is, of course, that patricians thrive on watercress tea sandwiches on Wonder Bread with the crusts cut off and would sooner fall on their swords than wear a single sequin.

Society folk, more than the rest of us, live according to rules of behavior. The undefined, intuited codes of good taste, or the spelled-out-to-the-nth doctrines of etiquette.

Laws for where to place the dessert fork (above the dinner plate with the handle on the left), ordinances for how to monogram the silver ("Three letters are standard and tend to look best. Two are permissible but seem somewhat inadequate," proclaims *Vogue*). As you might suspect, the statutes concerning the ceremonial rites of life make the Koran read like a Donald Duck comic, and their weddings, thus, are just ever so slightly less fixed than plays. There is a proper hour (four o'clock ceremony, reception five to eight is the most chic, and Saturday the smartest day); there is a breakdown of correct attire, depending on the place, day and time of day, that is so stern that a Los Angeles wedding consultant threatened to quit midstream of a big society Do where the groom wanted to wear a tuxedo. To hear her tell it, with righteous outrage: "*Naturally* a tuxedo isn't proper in the afternoon. I told him I wouldn't do the wedding if he insisted on wearing it. It's a terrible reflection on me if I allow that. Of course, he backed down." Then there are ten trillion details—as in any wedding—but among top-drawer-ites each of these picayune considerations is life-or-deathsville and has to be executed precisely according to Emily Post, or Amy Vanderbilt or whoever is the fashionable guru of the day.

I spent a morning in the company of Anita Farrington Earl, the aforementioned consultant, as she consulted with the tense mother of an upcoming bride. She works from her home in Palos Verdes Estates, a clifftop community on the ocean, south of L.A. Heavily populated with top corporate types (mostly aerospace executives until the recession decimated that industry) and homes that begin at $75,000, Palos Verdes is almost entirely Christian and about medium-high to medium-well-high on the social ladder. Mrs. Earl, I came to believe from my observations, considers herself to be the ritziest lady in town.

Blanche DuBois, I think to myself at the door, as she floats toward me in a floral semi-diaphanous hostess gown, yellow hair and purple eye shadow. But the voice changes that image, with a uniquely cultivated way of speaking that someone once labeled "Larchmont Lockjaw" because it emerges from a mouth that looks to be frozen into an unmoving smile and teeth that seem clenched together for dear life. It is a voice that is bred exclusively in the upper class and handed down from generation to generation.

Anita Farrington Earl believes in Etiquette the way some people believe in God. For her it provides structure, reassurance and answers to some of life's major questions. "But," she insists, "you can never really learn the codes adequately, no matter how many books you read. You have to be born to it." Mrs. Earl was. On the mimeographed promotion sheet that details her personal services as wedding coordinator, we get a brief bio—titled "QUALIFICATIONS" —as follows: "Undergraduate schooling in private schools in the East. Graduate of Skidmore College, B.S., Fine Arts. Descendent [sic] of Old American family dating back to pre-Revolutionary days. Listed in the New York Social Register and the California Register. . . . Thoroughly grounded in all aspects of Etiquette." Blood the color of the sky.

Her job consists of handling *everything* for a wedding from soup (except, as we shall see, there is no soup at a society wedding) to nuts (there may or may not be a scattering of macadamias). Pre-wedding counseling includes advice on bridal veil, trousseau, mothers' costumes, silver patterns, arrangements for out-of-town guests, the gift display, bridesmaids' luncheon, tea for viewing the gifts. And that's just a tiny part of it. She also arranges for the printed matter (invitations, menu cards, at-home cards, calling cards), the favors (rice, rose petals, boxes for the guests in which to take the cake home), food, liquor, flowers, photographer and anything else one could possibly think of, even the honeymoon. She goes to the ceremony and reception, making sure it all comes off without a single hitch, without the most minute digression from perfect form. She takes enormous pride in the fact that nothing unexpected ever occurs at an Anita Farrington Earl wedding.

This morning she is having one in a series of run-throughs with Mrs. Pillsbury, who refers to her husband as "Pill." The wedding is two weeks off, for three hundred people at a local church, followed by a reception on the grounds of a friend's estate. The girl is eighteen, her fiancé twenty-two, both students in a small college in northern California. There will be sixteen attendants and there have already been five harried months of preparation. Later on, after the woman leaves, Mrs. Earl will confide to me that this whole affair is, according to her standards, tacky. "We're doing things I don't approve of at all. A green and white tent instead of a white one, just to save a few hundred dollars. Really shocking . . ."

For now, they consort like Pentagon chieftains whose subject matter is no less than the future fate of the entire planet. "I want the ushers at the church an hour ahead of time with their boutonnieres in place," orders the general. "Don't forget—with cutaways they must wear gloves." The lieutenant takes frantic notes. "Now," Anita continues, "what about the receiving line? There are three correct ways. Amy Vanderbilt does it one way, but there are others too." She spells out the others.

On to the first dance, to occur immediately after the receiving line. A decree as to who starts, who then cuts in with whom, when and for how long. Ten minutes of floral discussion: has Mrs. P. ordered the corsage for the vocalist, for the guest-book girl, the bride's "going-away" corsage, flowers for the cake table and the base of the cake? Don't forget the underskirt for the cake table, don't forget the special cake for the groom's mother whose birthday is the same day, but when should it be served and should they use special candles and if so, what kind?

The throwing rice will be passed in silver bowls—don't forget to order the silver bowls. Remember to make up maps so the guests will know how to get from the church to the reception. Speaking of which, what about getting the ushers and bridesmaids out of the church first, because they have to be ready on the receiving line at the reception before all the guests arrive. The logistics would freak General Patton.

"Who pays for the out-of-town guests' hotel accommodations?" asks the befrazzled hostess. Mrs. Earl snips, "Why, you do, of course." Imagine not knowing that, how positively hoi polloi. Mrs. Pillsbury is put in her place with an icy gentility that makes it utterly clear who's the more *haute* of the two women. Mrs. P. continues sheepishly: Should the telegrams be read by the best man? When does the bride toss the bouquet, before or after she changes to leave? (For Gentile girls, it's before; after for Jewish. I have no idea why.) When does the bar open, after or before the receiving line? (After.) Is the guest book signed at the church or at the reception? Mrs. E. doles out orders: Hire a detective to guard the gift display. Make sure the parking service is bonded and insured. Find out how many reserved pews the groom's side requires. And, finally, rent the portable toilets. Mrs. Pillsbury leaves eventually, a bit bent under the weight of both the ceaseless details and her implied inadequacy, and Anita Farrington Earl regales me with wedding tales. Mostly about catastrophes which may not, to you, seem like much on the sliding scale of possible life catastrophes, but in her realm are indeed calamitous. A bridesmaid's bouquet missing, so that she has to pluck a flower from here and there to construct one; the bride's tipsy father leaving the marriage license in the rented limousine, which has already been dismissed; the disappearance of the ring bearer's pillow.

Or the stories of cheapness—the most plebeian horror of all: "The groom wasn't from a very good family and his friends weren't too much. One of the ushers stole two bottles of champagne and luckily I caught him as he was heading out the door. But what can you expect, really?" And those of unforgivable boorishness: a wedding where the bride and groom wanted to wear Mississippi plantation outfits, with the ushers garbed as gamblers, and everybody arriving in horse and buggy. "There are things I simply will not allow," she says, explaining why she quit the job. "I later heard it was big and showy . . . horrible." But what about the New Wedding? I inquire. "Nonsense," she assures me. "There are certain ceremonies of life that we observe with tradition. Without them we are barbarians." Period.

Another responsibility of the social consultant is publicity —making sure the engagement and wedding announcement, cum photograph, reaches prominence on the society pages of the local newspaper. Often a more substantial concern than the wedding itself (a party's just another soiree, but fame— well, my lambies), this is becoming increasingly problematic. Once upon a time the society pages were just that—a news-letter to let one Brahmin know what his friends were up to. From a quiet dinner *en famille* to a garden luncheon where elegant ladies held elegant chitchats in their elegant new bonnets, to a charity gala for the Albanian monsoon victims —every such happening was reported, obviously considered of fascination to *all* castes. (In fact, a sneaky means by which some *nouveau riche* peasants would attempt to worm their oily way up the social ladder was to hire press agents for the purpose of getting their names into the society columns.)

In smaller cities, or cities in which the population is not particularly transient, little has changed. Often the cover of the Sunday section, especially in the Midwest, is devoted to society brides, and more than one nervous squire has been known to attempt bribery. In San Francisco a social con-sultant reports: "Wedding announcements in the *Chronicle* are very essential to people. Sunday is for the key people, Saturday for non-society, when nobody reads the paper any-way." In a southern city last year a black middle-class girl, desperately wanting her engagement story in the paper, but knowing it would be impossible, sent in the data accom-panied by a picture of a white classmate cut out of her high school yearbook. The announcement was printed, accomplishing its purpose despite the ruse.

Remarkable, but predictable, changes have been occurring recently. Houston was growing so rapidly that both newspapers entirely abandoned wedding announcements over three years ago. Nowadays you have to pay, like a classified ad (a good-sized story can run $150), so *naturally* it's In to be Out. Nobody, but *nobody* who's anybody would BUY space. Betty Ewing, the society editor of the Houston *Chronicle,* says: "In an expanding city, the population is reflected in the number of weddings and engagements taking place, and here it just got overwhelming. We used to give big society weddings special coverage, not as an announcement but as a news story, but we don't even bother with that anymore." The *Los Angeles Times* now uses this material as filler.

The move, among many large papers, has been toward egalitarianism. Merit ranks higher—they claim—than pedigree. Charlotte Curtis, Family Style Editor of *The New York Times,* says, about choosing whose announcement is fit to print: "We feel strongly about kids who make it on their own. If your father is a garbage man and your husband's father is a street cleaner, but you and your fiancé are Phi Betes at Harvard and Radcliffe, you can be sure it'll get in." When pressed, she cheerfully admits that that tale will get in more readily and with more spatial prominence than if those same two Phi Betes have elite ancestors. "It's a more interesting news story this way," and Miss Curtis confesses she is concerned only with the news value, not in pleasing the old guard.

She has been known, in this spirit, to crash a wedding and call the story as she sees it. Thus, despite having been expelled by the ushers at George Plimpton's nuptials, she wrote up the announcement: "Mr. Plimpton was married here last night, not to Mrs. John F. Kennedy, Queen Elizabeth II, Jean Seberg, Ava Gardner, Jane Fonda, Princess Stanislas Radziwill or Candy Bergen, all of whom he has escorted at one time or another, but to Freddy Medora Espy, a wisp of a photographer's assistant." Under Miss Curtis' ideological banner, the *Times'* social stories can no longer be depended upon not to carry social satire ("It was not a happy day for the bride's mother. She did not attend the ceremony") or simply brazen truth, as when two gracious gazelles recently wed and the *Times* quoted the bride's mother as saying, "John Norwood is completely unacceptable to the family in every way."

The New York Times does as earnest a job of reporting wedding news as it does muggings and wars, it would appear. Contrasted to most papers, it has no questionnaire; the interested parties are just asked to write in, revealing all the dope. If it's a particularly noteworthy, newsy wedding, a five-woman team is sent out to interview the couple, their families and friends, to dig up juice, and about every two weeks an actual living reporter is dispatched to cover a fete. Approximately one in fifty notices finally appears in print.

"The majority of people in New York City read the wedding announcements," claims Miss Curtis. "That's why we print everything that we consider important about the participants, not just what they want us to say. A lot of society folk just want four paragraphs, not a story. They get furious at us for covering more than they had in mind. We do it anyway."

One matron whose blue blood boils over on this topic is Mrs. George Van Siclen, of the Tappin and Tew Agency in New York. As social consultants since 1930, T. & T. is one of the Top, Best, absolutely Cream of this field, their specialty being exquisite handwriting. (There is, in fact, a blond and extraordinarily thin young lady stationed alone in an office in a Pucci dress addressing wedding invitation envelopes in a classical Olde Englishe script. She was hired solely for this talent, and each envelope takes her ten minutes. They are simply pippy-poo.) Mrs. Van Siclen, yet another victim of Larchmont Lockjaw, almost loses her classical cool when we get onto the theme of the *Times'* recent policies. "What do you think the *Times* has turned into? There was a time we could guarantee a client we'd get an announcement in the paper. Now we can't. They've done away with chic, with social news. Now they're printing any old thing and it's terrible."

The lady is additionally upset about the undignified intrusion of the *Times* into locked genteel attics. "They demand to know outrageous things, like what the couple's families do for a living, and about previous marriages and divorces. Good families resent having to talk about these kinds of matters. You know, we used to think of the *Times* as a little local paper. It's just horrible that they've changed all that."

There is, certainly, a definable entity called a High Society wedding. Let us first talk about what it is not. It is not, under any circumstances, a regatta in which we will find doves, flambé, revolving pedestals or sequined clergymen. There will be no stomping, rollicking, yipping, no frenzied dancing, no weeping or heavy sweating. There will be no food.

Lest you be confused, a wedding such as Sharon Percy's to John D. Rockefeller IV, at which she wore a Mainbocher gown, and the 1800 guests were serenaded by the Chicago Symphony Orchestra, is not typical—although the cast of characters was certainly tip-top. Nor is the case of the two society sisters getting married at the hotsy Los Angeles Country Club one night following the other. The Friday night flowers cost $5000; Mummy insisted that not a day-old leaf remain, as the guest list was to be repeated face for face, so Saturday morning another $5000 worth of posies—brand-new—were installed.

Also atypical was the home wedding attended by ten people—"the biggest Gentile name in L.A.," claims the caterer—in which Belgian lace was imported to be specially made into tablecloths, each costing several hundred dollars,

the entire garden was replanted to form an aisle for the ceremony, and the whole quiet, tiny picnic cost more than a hotel
wedding for two hundred.

Just as irregular is the saga of Wendy Wanamaker, great-
granddaughter of the Philadelphia Wanamakers, who married the family horse trainer, so naturally a fiesta was hardly
in order. There is always that hairy possibility to contend
with in the *haut monde,* though the normal love match more
often resembles a corporate merger.

Characteristically, an upper-birth fiesta takes place in a
church. Episcopal, probably, but with the current breakdown
of previously unmovable lines, a thimbleful of Presbyterians
and Catholics have filtered into the ranks. No Jews, however.
(It is no coincidence that the words "Gentile" and "gentility"
bear the same root.)

The church will be decorously adorned with flowers and
the organ will play traditional wedding ditties. As the Episcopal church is rigorous about maintaining the basic form of
service ("We cannot make variations just on the whim of
the couple," insists the minister of New York's finest), you
will have heard these particular vows five hundred times.
The dress will be moderate and traditional (no extreme garb
allowed in church) and a smartly refined, tasteful air of reli-
giousness will prevail. Afterward you will make your way,
for the reception, to a gracious home or private club (the
Colony or Cosmopolitan in New York) or country club (the
Burlingame in San Francisco or Piping Rock on Long
Island). There you will crawl through a polite receiving
line, sip vintage champagne and dance to the cultivated
strains of Lester Lanin or Peter Duchin. You will do a special
form of dancing, a form you learned as a tot in dancing
school. It is an upbeat, bright two-step, a sort of "The Lady
Is a Tramp" beat, otherwise known as the Debutante Trot.
Peppy but subdued. "It's slightly faster than music for the
masses," explains bandleader Bill Harrington. In addition,
you will probably execute a couple of gracious Viennese

waltzes. Then you'll munch a bit of unctious wedding cake and be home precisely three hours later. You will not have drunk too much—getting sloshed is definitely *outré*—and the whole experience will be remembered in future years, by all concerned, as "Nice."

That is all there is to report about a society wedding. It is nice, which is perhaps a nice way of saying that it is dull, bloodless, diluted. Ethnic celebrations, we recognize, are always gustier than homogenized-milk American, but the pedigreed poodles are the most repressed of all. Good breeding has, it would seem, bred out all the passion and the primordial ecstasy associated with the wedding.

What, for example, about food? Why, when the conjugal rite is always, atavistically, connected to feasting—no matter what the economic station—do the masters and mistresses of savoir-faire dish up a lettuce leaf dabbed with Velveeta and call it "elegant simplicity"?

Isn't the psychology the same as not carrying cab fare, or driving a 1946 Packard? The thrust of the competitive, driving bourgeoisie is to outdo; the noblesse are obliged to "underdo." Furthermore, what separates the peasant from the patrician is hunger; what better way to illustrate one's complete detachment from the tawdriness of hunger (i.e., poverty) than by disregarding food. In Chaplin films the reminders of his destitute condition are immense objects of eating—giant sandwiches, oversized fruit. Then, when one achieves burgher prosperity, vast displays of food symbolize that solid state. The old rich merely disdain all such concerns.

The unyielding canons by which the gentry live are all rooted in propriety; exhibition of what would be considered "excessive" emotion is all right for the hordes who are, after all, somewhat lower on the evolutionary ladder. But as man becomes more civilized, he should surely develop more restraint. One simply does not sob openly at funerals or carouse at weddings.

Professionals who serve the rich perpetuate notions of

proper behavior with a stringency that borders on rigor mortis. They—the social consultants particularly—are haughtier, snobbier and much more elitist than even the loftiest of their clientele. Their standards of what's Right and what's Wrong (not morally, mind you, but tastewise—a force far stronger than Good and Evil) are totally clear-cut. And out of this vision emerges an interesting language. One dame talks about "People That Matter"; another breaks her categories down into "Nearly Everyone" and "No One"; Lester Lanin repeatedly refers to "The Top People," and Mrs. Earl speaks of folks who "don't come from much."

"Nearly Everyone," of course, refers to approximately eleven people in America.

To be sure, there is something anachronistic and naïve about the Upper Crust. So removed from the struggles of almost everybody else on the planet, their mode of life is completely out of sync. At its best it seems riotous: Gloria Upson, the society girl in *Auntie Mame,* relating the catastrophe of her whole life, the time she nearly lost the Ping-Pong tournament at the country club. At its worst it's shocking, obscene: the irrelevancy of the Debutante Cotillion, to be involved with "coming out" when the whole country frequently appears to be "going under."

Gertrude Doran is a well-known and notorious social coordinator in Los Angeles. A true innocent despite her sixty years, she gives the impression of having spent all of those years on a two-block expanse consisting of millionaires, polo ponies and family crests. Everything she says sounds borderline anti-Semitic ("I don't do many Jewish weddings. It isn't how much you spend, you know, it's the quality of the people"), but she is somehow more silly than offensive. Perhaps it's the innocence.

She gossips about other tradesmen: "Carl Levin [the big rentals czar in town] just is not my style. He doesn't have the background to deal with the type of people I work with." Because she gets so involved with the families and the household help, she gets to find out all—and tells me much more than I ever wanted to know about Mrs. Whatsis' skeletons. "A wedding last summer, Dr. ——, a perfect society wedding, exactly correct, both fine families. The boy was impotent and they were divorced three months later." Or the tale about the huge Bel Air pageant that she did, a $40,000 wedding, where the family refused to pay the sales tax on the flowers and she had to absorb it herself. (The thoroughbred nose wrinkles into a repulsed, how-did-that-dead-fish-get-in-here position.)

Members of the horsey set, who you would think could coordinate a basic thing like a coronation in their sleep, frequently employ somebody like Gertrude Doran even for intime little supper parties. It's not helplessness, and they are certainly not too busy. But they *are,* after all, used to servants, to the noble notion of having somebody else do the dregs. Then, Mrs. Doran believes, the elite are sometimes the teensiest bit insecure. "Frequently they need me just to smooth off the edges, to give them the confidence that everything is being done utterly to perfection."

Most consultants will, like Anita Farrington Earl, tackle everything. Eugene Ely, in Coral Gables, employs his very own eighty-two-year-old calligrapher and will return wedding gifts to the stores to avoid embarrassment for the bride. He charges a flat fee, he says, of $850, and takes no kickbacks from anybody. Jean Fay Webster, in San Francisco, whose service is called The Date Book and who began primarily as a clearinghouse for debutante parties so that no two would be scheduled for the same night, charges by the hour, doesn't get involved with bridal clothing, but will—for a small $50 fee—personally check the guests at the door. Gertrude Doran does everything short of dealing with impotent husbands. She owns her own gazebo and makes her own dainty little rice bags. Her fee, she says, is a mere 10 to 15 percent of the flower bill, although other coordinators will take 10 percent of the total, not to mention a kickback from the caterer, photographer and rentals man.

All social consultants possess a common personality quirk:

they are sulky, independent and continually threaten to walk out. Eugene Ely insists on starting the ceremony exactly on time and won't do a wedding unless there's continuous music; Gertrude has walked out when the groom or the groom's mother has butted in, sniffing, "It's none of their business." And all—but all—will pack their white, silk-lined tents and storm away into the night if a wedding anywhere near smells of uncouthity.

Nonetheless—in spite of the strict statutes—one sees some of the speediest, extremist swivels of lifestyle, some of our hippest hippies, among the offspring of the 400. Although the New Wedding is primarily a manifestation of middle-classism, the upper class has always had place for the eccentric, the oddball. Mrs. Pruneface may trudge to Bergdorf's in her ratty old fur, sure of herself and the fact that everybody knows who she is and what is her purchasing power. Mrs. Babbitt, more self-conscious with her position, daren't. It is therefore likely that she will freak out if her daughter declares that she wants to get married in tie-dyed overalls.

Patrician kids are not only less nervous about the rules but are lately appalled by the outdated performances of their elders. Once they reach college, they increasingly tend to identify themselves with values of the counter-culture, and, to quote *Future Shock*: "Today it is not so much one's class base as one's ties with a subcult that determine the individual's style of life. The working-class hippie and the hippie who dropped out of Exeter or Eton share a common style of life but no common class."

The Debutante Cotillion, the entire process of Coming Out, is in its death throes. Especially on the east coast. Within the last five years the official list of debutantes in the Boston area has declined from three hundred names to a paltry ninety-two; gone from sight are the classic Thanksgiving Eve Debutante Assembly, the St. Nicholas Cotillion, the Colony Debutante Ball, the Debut Ball and the South Shore Debutante Ball. In New York and Philadelphia times are also tough. A young Bryn Mawr freshman, from credentialed stock, who last year eschewed making her debut, says: "I would be mortified to go through that farce, all that snobby crap which is just another way of separating yourself from the great unwashed. It's absolutely irrelevant and immoral in today's world."

But even in nooks where the debut is still in swirling swing —San Francisco, for instance—the New Weddings are a big item. Jean Fay Webster explains it: "San Francisco society has a hold on its children until the age of eighteen—coming-out age—so they go along with the debut tradition. But by the time they're ready to get married, they're freer thinkers. So you see more and more so-called hippie weddings, on mountaintops or in glens, or at the beach. It's becoming *very* smart to serve organic food and white wine."

Some of what's behind the mode is definitely radical chicism. It's cute and IN to act poor and peasanty. One Atlanta society family threw a prenuptial "Tacky Party" in the barn of their country farm. All the kids wore faded jeans, drank sour mash and had the most adorable time ever. Do not, however, confuse "hippie" with "cheapie": many of these shindigs —like the one on a mountaintop outside San Francisco, where the guests *actually* had to leave the Bentleys at the bottom and climb, and all the food was vegetarian—well, they still cost plenty (the bride at this one had her little white peasant number designed by an *haute couturière* in France). A top caterer in San Francisco has had to add organic tasties to his meatball and breaded-shrimp repertoire, the demand is so great these days.

The New York Times' favorite wedding stories are of blue bloods gone hippie. A young descendant of Abner Doubleday (Union Army general who invented the sport of baseball) married a descendant of Commodore Perry (hero of the War of 1812)—two trees that, you will grant, could not possess more solidly embedded American roots—on the beach of the family's summer home in Massachusetts. She wore a gown of Canadian wool that she wove on a loom in her home and a floor-length shawl that she had also woven. The groom (who is also a relative of one of the original members of the Plymouth Colony) wore Levi's, high leather shoes and a leather vest. "Because the bridegroom dislikes catered food," the *Times* gleefully reports, "the bride and her mother cooked the wedding dinner of Ipswich Bay clam chowder, Maine lobster, roast beef and various breads."

Then there was the Connecticut garden gala of an Italian baron's son to a Greenwich debutante where they split for their honeymoon in a seventy-foot balloon, followed from the ground by a limousine.

Or the wedding of Ainslee Dinwiddie (my very favorite name), ex-Queen of the New Orleans Mardi Gras, aboard a seventy-six-foot reproduction of a nineteenth-century sloop, borrowed from Hudson River Sloop Restoration, Inc. How absolutely quaint and darling, how utterly original! And how our friends just *adore* hearing about it.

Frances Moffat, society editor of the *San Francisco Chronicle,* comments on who's having the New Wedding: "Frequently girls from good families who are simply tired of the old ritual." Often, too, it's the cleanest way out of a sticky wicket. There are so many religious and economic and social intermarriages these days—folks moving up and down the ladder, marrying out of their class—that a more informal wedding can prevent horrendous episodes. Where the two sets of parents come from different classes, would *never* see each other socially, and none of their friends can mix at all, well, *naturally* a terribly chichi wedding would be a nightmare for the klutzy side, who could never hope to fit in.

Gertrude Doran, staunch as always, says of the New Wedding: "The idea wouldn't bother you so much if the kids didn't come from such quality and they themselves weren't so WEIRD!!!"

But, often, what one finds is the grand generational compromise. The parents accede to an outdoor, simple ceremony with peculiar vows and funny clothes and the kids then come down off the mountaintop to a fashionably dreary reception at the club. Vintage champagne, an endive or two and three hundred Aryans from Darien smiling—not too excessively, mind you—through tightly pinched teeth.

12. The Odd Couples: Water Skis, Cemeteries and the Neon Nightmare

There are folks who, by some inexplicable behavioral quirk, some aberrant psychological force, do not get married the way everybody else does in America. People who shun the flowing white lace (with its monumental implications), the Swedish meatballs and the slinging of rice, whose sense of the majestic glorious tradition of THE WEDDING has been lobotomized, or translated into another language. In a country where the urge for Le Grand Wedding seems to be as timeless, as sweeping and as innately imbedded as the other heavy hungers, we find, nevertheless, a smattering of defiers.

They are not, let's make it perfectly clear, those involved in the New Wedding—kids whose values are anchored in the traditional but with desires for a less rigid, more intimate expression. They are also not, by profession, show bizniks—like the Fifth Dimension couple who ceremonied in a balloon hovering over Los Angeles while the band played their hit tune—where the wedding becomes an extension of their career shtik, an inspired press agent's dream. Although there is an unquestionable element of theatrics in the wedding of a salesgirl and a lion tamer set in the lion's den at the zoo (the five hundred guests paid an admission fee of 28¢ each and the beasts just yawned throughout), the motive was probably purer, having to do with the environment in which they pass their daily lives and which turns them on.

Water-skiing freaks in Miami did it on skis, with the reverend shouting the vows from the back of the boat (the ceremony had to be halted twice when the flower girl fell off her skis); a stewardess was married on Northeast Airlines Flight 52 from Miami to New York (they had met on the same flight three years before); an usher and a snack bar waitress at the Rodeo Drive-In Theater in Phoenix got married onstage between features; two equestrians wed on horseback in Syracuse, New York, with the minister and six attendants also mounted. (The bride's horse bolted after being hit in the face by a carload of confetti.)

Then there are those who dispense with plans, preparations, that intense portion of the ritual that—like the state of pregnancy—is often as emotionally essential and satisfying as the Big Day itself. They do it *fast,* in county courthouses, city halls, at a justice of the peace, or in Las Vegas. Not appearing to care about the environs, they rent a bridal gown or wear a T-shirt and chinos, maybe have a party afterward or maybe not, perhaps honeymoon, or not.

Are all of these defiers less romantic about marriage than most of our countrymen? Are they less cradled in familial responsibilities, less American in their fantasies and expectations of life's one perfect day? Or is it all ultimately the same, regardless of the surroundings? Is a wedding still a wedding, whether it takes place in St. Patrick's or atop a Ferris wheel?

As our culture has always made room for the quirky character—we accept him for what he is and just go on about our business—there is a tradition for the offbeat wedding that, while obviously not widespread, is worthy of consideration. Sometimes it cashes in on hot fads of the moment: the twosome that wed while whirling in hula hoops or the "walkathon" weddings of the 1930's (couples had to keep continually in motion, walking nonstop from contest arena to marriage license bureau back to arena where the minister walked backward while pronouncing the vows).

In the thirties, when it was common for movie theaters to hold contests and have live entertainment between features, an enterprising manager would stage a wedding. An inexpensive form of publicity, it drew crowds by the bushel. Later, when mass communication in the form of the television tube arrived on the scene, the TV sound stage became a popular conjugal pulpit. Lest you believe Tiny Tim was the first, recall a show of the early 1950's called "Bride and Groom," in which a deserving lucky couple was chosen daily to consecrate the sacraments before the unseen vast audience, then depart for their new life laden with toasters and waffle irons.

—In 1964 a couple was married in the Vineland, New Jersey, roller rink, on skates. The service was executed by the town mayor, also on skates, as were the four attendants. The couple had met there, two years prior, and he had later proposed in the same spot. Is that, or is that not, romantic?

—The bride wore a powder-blue gown over ski pants as she and her childhood sweetheart were spliced on Squaw Peak, in California, at a height of 8700 feet, in a raging snowstorm. Both wore skis.

—A manicurist in Louisville was married in her beauty shop.

—In Corpus Christi, Texas, a nineteen-year-old Go-Go dancer was married topless during the floor show, wearing a white veil and traditional white gown—*sans* front. The maid of honor, another dancer, wore topless blue.

—Two amateur sky divers jumped from a plane holding hands, followed by the priest who married them where they landed. The bride wore white leather jump boots, a white crash helmet and white satin overalls.

—A couple from Wichita exchanged vows in the dining car of the Santa Fe Scout.

—Two German acrobats were married 150 feet above the town square on a double trapeze.

—A man working for a scrap-metal company held his wedding in a junkyard.

—In San Francisco, a couple was married by a priest of Satan who asked the blessings of Lucifer and used, as an altar, a naked woman lying on a leopard skin on the mantel. The ceremony was conducted by candlelight—candles stuck in human skulls. The marriage was later declared illegal.

—Eileen Johnson and Robert Hornbeak held their nuptials in a plane circling over the Las Vegas airport. As the *L.A. Times* reported it: "Carrying on a traditional feud between Las Vegas and Reno, the 'Divorce Special' plane was waiting at the airport hoping the newly mated couple could be flown to a separation. They weren't."

Increasingly blossoming on the cuckoo scene is the nude wedding, the first publicized one occurring in 1934 in Chicago at the World's Fair Garden of Eden. The six attendants were bare, but the presiding bishop wore a goatskin. At a more recent naked nuptial in California, the pastor (whose friends call him Tony the Tiger) proclaimed: "You're married, as long as you dig it." More to the contemporary point, perhaps, was the wedding on Jones Beach, Long Island, where after the ceremony the couple consummated the event in front of the 150 guests. "They are trying to achieve a feeling of unity," the minister explained.

Folks get married on cable cars, in prison, on aerial tramways, by transatlantic telephone. But the location that seems to be sprouting in popularity is that of beneath the sea. If you crave an original, funny and kinky wedding and think that tying the knot, say, underwater in wet suits, flanked by a school of scaly gilled friends, will be a FIRST, you're wrong. In June, 1935, seventy-three-year-old John C. Benson married his blushing bride eight feet under in Puget Sound. The couple and the minister were connected to each other by telephone wires and, despite air pumps that jammed and leaky diving gear, the ceremony was gurglingly completed. A by-product, undoubtedly, of the scuba craze, one hears ever-increasing bubblings from the deep, like that of the briny bridal on the bottom of Higgins Lake in Michigan, the twosome garbed in white wet suits—hers covered with soggy lace—with vows exchanged by pointers and slates. A young girl, married underwater in Philadelphia to a navy submarine torpedoman, explained her unconventional choice: "I wanted dolphins on my engagement ring, because it's the symbol of the submarine service, but we couldn't find anything. Ralph felt bad and promised we'd have them at our wedding. One thing led to another and this is the way it wound up."

Odd couples seem to get married in settings that—unlike hotels or churches—have something to do with their real lives. And since, historically, the wedding is a public statement of private commitment, a declaration to the community, there seems to be a sense of relevance in the offbeat caper that is undeniable. If your life's passion is skiing, how sweet and pertinent to get married on a snowy mountaintop. If your life's work is to be a circus clown, and turning on the spectators with your magic is the loftiest moment, how appropriate to marry your lady clown in a grand, spectacular show with the whole world invited. Raggedy Robin and Raggedy Jane (the only female ever to graduate from Ringling Brothers' clown school) did just that. They held a three-hour public circus in a San Francisco church with bagpipers and belly dancers, a singing dog, dancing bears, trapezery, marching band, fire-eater, a female impersonator named Sylvester who sang "Over the Rainbow" and a Peruvian llama that preceded them down the aisle. "It was the only possible way we could envision a beautiful wedding," said Raggedy Robin to me, in describing their elaborate clown makeup and the lavishness of the show and the dazzling time had by all. As he saw it, he gave all the children a day to remember.

Let me tell you about Forest Lawn Cemetery in Los Angeles. What, you ask, does this subject have to do with weddings? Well, strangely enough, a lot. Forest Lawn is one of the true unnatural wonders of the earth and one of the great bizarre institutions of southern California. Besides being in the burial biz, it is profoundly immersed in the tourist biz and the wedding biz. In the early 1920's, the story goes, "a bride-to-be and her fiancé walked through the sunlit glades of Forest Lawn. Coming upon a charming old-world church in a setting of green lawns and tall trees, she exclaimed, 'Look!—a storybook dream come true!' Then and there they decided that this was where they wanted to be married." What the brochure describing this glorious epiphany leaves out is the interesting question of whether or not, when the couple spied the magical church, they were standing on somebody's grave and whether or not a funeral was going on in said church at the time.

Since this fortuitous discovery fifty years ago, more than fifty thousand weddings have taken place at Forest Lawn—either at the main arm in Glendale (just east of Los Angeles) or at the three branch "stores." As many as five or six ceremonies may take place a day, in the busy season, compared to twenty-five funerals a day, presumably in any season at all. "Weddings are not a thing that we make money on," quoted a spokesman for Forest Lawn in a *Los Angeles Times* article, the implication being that it's a public relations service provided so that satisfied bridal customers will remember Forest Lawn with fondness later on, if you know what I mean.

To comprehend the unfathomable notion of choosing to get married in a cemetery, you must understand the nature of Forest Lawn. It is unlike any other grave garden in the world. The founder, a Dr. Hubert Eaton, was a true God-fearing patriotic American with a moral credo for every aspect of human behavior. They are, as Jessica Mitford reports in *The American Way of Death*, "Perseverance Conquers All; A Place for Everything and Everything In Its Place; Anything That Is Worth Doing Is Worth Doing Well; and Let The Chips Fall Where They May." His credo regarding Forest Lawn began: "I believe in a happy

Eternal Life," and continued, "I shall endeavor to build Forest Lawn as different, as unlike other cemeteries as sunshine is unlike darkness, as Eternal Life is unlike death."

Well, okay, noble and schmaltzy enough, so far. I mean, after all, why should a burial ground be blackly gloomy and terrifying like those in the old horror movies? But then Eaton seems to have gone a bit off the celestial deep end when he extended his original concept into: "Forest Lawn shall become a place where lovers new and old shall love to stroll . . . where little churches invite, triumphant in the knowledge that from their pulpits only words of love can be spoken . . ." One wonders if he predicted the future, that Forest Lawn would come to be considered one of the top tourist spots in the Los Angeles area, the key stop on the bus tour that covers the Farmer's Market and the Universal Pictures studio. Schoolchildren are taken through Forest Lawn on outing frolics, and although picnicking is distinctly against the ordinances, one *does* glimpse little tads perched on the flat grave tablets nibbling their Twinkies and milk. Billboards line the main Hollywood thoroughfares—one, on busy La Cienega Boulevard, is a graceful white swan that, via optical trickery, moves across from left to right, while the message proclaims: MORTUARY, CEMETERY, EVERYTHING.

And the relentless commercials barraging local radio daily: rhapsodic testimonials from merry widows, from happy employees (the Boy Scout leader moonlighting as a mortician is my favorite) and from rest-assured folks participating in the Forest Lawn "Before-Need" program of pay-now-die-later. It's all treated with the kind of pizzazz of a stupendous new resort hotel in Acapulco. All it needs is a sauna and a kidney-shaped pool and we could come here for our vacation.

Forest Lawn is—yes, let's admit it—beautiful. If you didn't know what it is, what it contains, you would drive through the curving, hilly lanes and walk the sea-green meadow grasses believing yourself to be on some luxurious rolling

Kentucky estate. And the chaps at Forest Lawn have done everything possible to make you forget. Not a vertical tombstone exists to disturb the vista; they are all flat with the land and barely visible except when walking on them— thousands upon thousands (over two million in all). The grave sections are titled Slumberland, Rest Haven, Inspiration Slope, Lullabyland. Babyland is encircled by a heart-shaped drive.

Euphemism, of course, dominates: the "Court of Freedom" is, in fact, a quiet yard of graves, presided over by a statue of a soldier with a gun; the "Freedom Mausoleum," a quite incredible edifice populated by shining pink marble drawers, containing you-know-what, in separate cubicles with names like "Sanctuary of Humility" and "Sanctuary of Thanksgiving." Each cubicle has its own Miami Beach stained-glass window and a marble Bible and about fifty drawers. Then there are rooms with smaller drawers—either, one assumes, for smaller or poorer customers. And at the exit is a sign reading, "Know the peace of mind that the clean, dry, ventilated crypts provide."

Forest Lawn considers itself one of the finest art museums in America, with more than a thousand bronze and marble statues, and boasts that it is "the only place in the world where one can view all the major sculptural works of the greatest Renaissance artist, Michelangelo." No matter that they are copies and, as Mitford says, look "like the sort of thing one might win in a shooting gallery." Never mind that the "David" wears a fig leaf. Everything at Forest Lawn looks as if it were created or constructed just ten minutes before you arrived. That includes "The Crucifixion"— "America's largest religious painting—195 feet long and 45 feet high," and the monstrously oversized "Last Supper" stained-glass window. (Dr. Eaton, according to his official biographer, Adela Rogers St. John, was "a sucker for stained glass.")

This place is the embodiment of the California dream/reality where life—and, apparently, death—is one terrific jolly barbecue with plastic forks and franchised fried chicken and the outdoor stereo speaker system crooning Mantovani's rendition of "America the Beautiful." Only in California, where everything one owns is a toy and every place one goes must be a playground and neither the past nor the future has any relevance, only here could Forest Lawn thrive— the drive-in resting spot for all our happy surfers who have taken the Big Wave.

Only in California could such a graveyard gift shop exist, selling Forest Lawn salt and pepper shakers, platters decorated with Forest Lawn highlights, and a postcard with the message *already* printed: "Dear _____, Forest Lawn Memorial Park has proved an inspiring experience. . . . It was a visit we will long remember." All that is missing is the "Wish you were here."

One day I go to visit Mrs. Bobbe Bennett, the "Wedding Hostess," a saccharine, fairly spooky lady with a mountain of bleached platinum hair and very pale skin and the predictable black dress. Pretending bridedom, I ask a million questions which she answers in canned speech that flows so speedily I can hardly get it all down. "The basic cost is thirty-five dollars with five or six guests, plus the services of the hostess, or one hundred and fifty dollars for the deluxe; the organist is fifteen dollars, and that includes a uniformed attendant to clean the church and set up the flowers. We suggest a twenty-dollar minimum fee for the minister." (He is, incidentally, Methodist or Baptist; they cannot get a Catholic priest, and Jews are not exactly given the royal carpet at Forest Lawn.)

As you would with a swell hotel, you *must* use their florist—a sign, I am reminded, in front of the administration building reads, "After 5:30 P.M. order flowers from hostess in mortuary"—but there are loads of decoration choices. One pair of candelabra with seven tapers, trimmed with ivy and a white satin bow, is $7.50; bows for the pews are $1.50 each, or $3 if flanked with flowers. A special Forest Lawn bonus is six bows for $5.

The whole thing is, naturally, a terrific bargain as weddings go. Sort of like buying a haunted house. You can really get good value.

When pale Mrs. Bennett ends her routine, I ask her if I can see the wedding chapel. "Oh, yes, of course," she perks. "Unless there's a funeral service going on."

I had not, until this instant, considered the fact that citizens get married and put away all in the same churches at Forest Lawn, and it seems the weirdest notion of all. But then it's all so cute and lively and anything but what it is that ultimately it makes no difference at all. The Wee Kirk o' the Heather, for example, one of the four churches at the Glendale field (and carpeted wall-to-wall), is a commemoration to the love of Annie Laurie and Douglas of Finland and is, according to the brochure, "an ideal setting for lovers." A curious concept, it would seem, since what it's used for most is funerals.

Why do people want their weddings at a cemetery?

One apparent motive, a fairly common one, is that a parent or favorite relative is buried there and the family wishes to be close to him on this day. But surely that doesn't explain all. "Our couples have grown up with Forest Lawn," says Mrs. Bennett, which at first hearing sounds ridiculous, but on later thought seems more real. If you grow up in Los Angeles, and listen to your radio and drive a car, Forest Lawn is as much a part of your conditioned experience as the presence of the Pacific or movie stars or the smog. As the repetition of a single word over and over makes that word lose its meaning, so it is with Forest Lawn. It's not what it is, a graveyard; it's merely a California fixture, another recreation area. Still, I must confess to you, I do not *really* understand and doubt that I ever will. The masks are brilliant and pervasive, indeed. But ghostly vibrations are stronger than disguise, and what's essentially in the air here is—as it rightly should be—death.

One Saturday in the late afternoon I attend a wedding at the Church of the Recessional—poised atop Mount Forest Lawn, "with the vast city sprawling at its feet in a sea of twinkling lights or sunset haze. . . ." I am told that the girl chose this setting because she's British and the church reminds her of those in the countryside of her homeland. Makes sense, I think to myself, except that this adorable little English country chapel looks like a movie set, a two-dimensional flat, where there is no indoors. And when you're sitting inside, you're sure that there is no outdoors. One waits for the cameras to start rolling and Elizabeth Taylor and Spencer Tracy to spring forth from the fake front door. And you are sure this particular set was finished just before you arrived.

A rather lovely, peaceful courtyard surrounds the church. Muzak is evidently being piped in, but it is so eerily quiet that you're not sure but that it may be coming from the town below, or from your own head, or from God. Like every available inch of space at Forest Lawn, the medium is inevitably employed for the message. One plaque reproduces Kipling's "If"; another proclaims that "there is no charge for the use of Forest Lawn's churches. For weddings, however, there is an assistance charge to cover the cost of the necessary attendants, lights and cleaning. There is no such charge for funerals and christenings."

The wedding itself is a wedding: about 150 merrymakers, in very fancy formal doodads. The groom's side is Italian and the hairdos are splendiferous, as is the bride's lacy-layered gown-cum-train stretching to Pasadena. Pre-ceremony, a hidden soloist, a disembodied baritone voice that may or may not, one thinks, be emanating from the crypt, croons "Some Enchanted Evening." The rather impersonal service is short—ten minutes to be precise—but with a terrific smash ending. As the newlyweds kiss, a haunted house creak is heard overhead and a trapdoor springs open, assaulting them with a shower of torn paper. Not confetti, but big hunks of torn-up paper, like maybe yesterday's *Hollywood Citizen News*.

Just a wedding. Probably expecting something truly spectacular—a visitation from the beyond, maybe, or at the very least some major theatrics worthy of the Forest Lawn name —I find myself disappointed. Then, too, I seem to be the only witness who is aware of where we are. The only one who finds the whole concept imponderably grotesque.

"In settings of reassuring beauty," assures the promotional material, "funeral services are held, babies are christened, and marriage ceremonies are performed." It's all the same dream in California. Here, even death is easy and clean and sunny and—for God's sake—HAPPY. So, what the hell, why not a wedding at Forest Lawn? It comes with the territory.

Las Vegas is a place so tawdry, so evil and so unnatural to man that one would not want to do anything *real* there. I cannot envision cooking dinner in Las Vegas or taking my towels to the laundry or reading a book or having a tooth filled. Getting married in Vegas is a notion the awfulness of which I cannot begin to entertain.

But last year almost fifty thousand marriage licenses were issued in Las Vegas (a 3 percent climb over the year before) —100,000 lovers came here, to America's shlock city, to sanctify their bond. It's a town that thinks in these terms—in hard cash—so they estimate that weddings bring in $60 million a year. Peanuts compared to the crap tables and slots, but a hefty penny in any real world.

Nevada makes it very easy to spend your money simply by having different laws than the other states (though they already have the loosest divorce rulings, an attempt was made recently to change the waiting period from six weeks to one day), so getting married here takes ten minutes, the whole shebang. No blood test required, no waiting period. Proof of age (girls, eighteen; boys, twenty-one); that's it. You just hop over to the county courthouse—downtown near the low-end sleazy casinos—open, like everything in Vegas, twenty-four hours a day. Pay your six bucks for your license (on week-days, nine to five) or your sixteen bucks (weekends and odd hours). Hop to an office room in the back where somebody'll do the deed for $10 or $15, and in four minutes flat, you're wed.

Or if you want a little class, a little romance, saunter down the strip to one of the town's twenty-six "wedding chapels," like the Silver Bell (CALIF. CHECKS OK, PHOTO, FLORIST, DRESSING ROOMS, proclaims the flashing sign in front), wake up the proprietor (it's okay, he's open round the clock too) who'll phone and wake up the minister (he guarantees to be there, in black suit, within eight minutes).

Then, while you're digging out your $25 or so, depending on the elegance of the joint (plus $12 if you want a role of black-and-white photos, $5 for a tape recording, $3 for a plastic daffodil or $10 for a live orchid), the proprietor will be sizing you for rings ($15 for one, $25 for two, unless you want a special saying engraved inside, like "Forever Yours" or "Love Is a Many Splendored Thing." Most folks don't bother with those extras. Takes too long).

Before you can say "Frank Sinatra," you'll be back at the Thunderbird casino stuffing quarters into the old one-armed bandits, waiting for the Big Killing. Married.

It's our very own national Gomorrah, they say about Las Vegas. Carved out of the silent, difficult Mojave Desert and given perpetual life by the blood of suckers. The only sin in Vegas is being a loser, and then it's a slow, grinding death. After two days here you often find yourself driving out of town FAST, heading aimlessly into the stifling desert empti-ness, for relief. For reality. No dealers with dead eyes, no hookers, no junkies, ageless showgirls or losers gasping for one last breath on the fringes of the Vegas neon dream. Only lizards here, and rattlesnakes. Clean.

On the way out—and it takes all of twelve minutes to sweep the flat strip of Las Vegas Boulevard and be into the desert—you see everything, get the whole story. Gargantuan hotels, one practically atop another—Caesar's Palace, the Dunes, Frontier, Sands, Sahara—a Miami Beach of contiguous cement, all interchangeable, all beckoning you with seductive crooked finger toward the money magic that awaits within.

Farther on the strip gets seedier; hotels give way to shabby motels, used furniture marts, gas stations, cheap bar/restaurant/casinos and the wedding chapels. Some pose absurdly as quaint little New England white churches with spires and fake stained glass, others are just shanty houses, still others a section of a motel. Little Church of the West, Cupid's Wedding Chapel, Chapel of the Stars, Little Chapel of the Flowers, Desert Bells Wedding Chapel, Little Chapel Around the Corner, Chapel of the Roses. . . . The minuscule differences between them are irrelevant. One sign states: CHOICE OF THE STARS, IMMED. CEREMONIES, PHOTOS—FLOWERS—RINGS—RECORDINGS, and another brags: AMPLE PARKING, while the guy next door: MAJOR CREDIT CARDS ACCEPTED. Yet another, with evident concern for the values of the spirit, proclaims: SINCERE AND DIGNIFIED SINCE 1954. They are all, nevertheless, the same, and the cumulative effect of twenty-six—sleazy, plastic, broken-down, dedicated to the Las Vegas moral principles of FAST! EASY! CHEAP!—makes one feel the presence of decay. Surely not romance.

Leaving town, I stop at the Hitching Post, the last one on the strip. By comparison, every other chapel is St. Peter's Basilica. Despite the artificial wishing well by the front door, the vibes are inexplicably evil and I feel as if I am about to enter the motel in *Psycho*. The owner, thank heavens, is not Tony Perkins. He is, however, Bela Lugosi.

In an appropriate Transylvanian accent, he takes me on a tour of his bleak lair. Instead of a carpet aisle runner there is a white sheet—none too clean—folded in half. ("You go to church, you have white carpet," he declares curtly.) Plastic flowers that do not even attempt to look real, artificial electric candelabra, shabby graying curtains, no sunlight whatsoever. I ask about music and he plays for me an aged, scratchy record of "The Wedding March" which is far too slow and thus deadly flat. And then I ask if he takes checks or credit cards. "I don't take checks. Checks is like no money." What to wear? Does one need a veil? No indeed. "Nobody care what you wear. It's Las Vegas. Getting married no big deal in Las Vegas."

On the other hand, he offers a juicy bonus inducement: a card entitling newlyweds to a free pizza, beer and a roll of nickels at the Lucky Linda Casino.

Vegas is a town that should exist only at night, when the flashing neon hides the pores, when the gambling fever seems sexy and not so sordid. A town for night people—drifters, outcasts, lost souls. It's the end of the road, but the darkness can support delusions and it's okay, somehow. A roll of the dice may, after all, change everything. But during the day it's a totally different place, hideous and naked under an unyielding sun that burns away all hope.

On a scorching Saturday in May some nine hundred hopefuls come to town, mostly from other states, to get married. You stand outside the county courthouse and watch them file in and out, cramming the corridors, in an endless stream of traffic that never diminishes through the day and night. The action is as brisk as at the tables and the faces as varied.

—A motorcyclist in jeans, fringed suede vest, no shirt. His lady in hot pants and over-the-knee black boots.

—A middle-aged couple with eight friends and her two small children.

—Two young couples from San Diego who decided to

elope together. After both ceremonies are finished, one boy
turns to his companions, saying, "O.K., now you want to go
to Caesar's or the Sands?"

—A three-hundred-pound woman, with bouffant white
hair, and her nondescript boyfriend.

—A scrubbed boy in a ten-gallon hat and cowboy boots.
His girl sports a fancy white lace minidress, bleached, teased
and sprayed hair, and her parents snap Brownie pictures
without stop.

—A Mexican boy of eighteen and his Anglo bride of nineteen; he has an affidavit of consent from his father, but her
parents don't know they're eloping.

—A middle-aged black man in a dark suit and tie, with
a young white girl in purple jersey pants and a striped tank
top.

Seven out of ten people, by my informal survey, are chew-
ing gum.

There is no way to categorize the couples, just as there
is no way to generalize about who comes to Vegas itself.
It's a wee kaleidoscope of humanity, and there seem to be as
many reasons for doing it here as there are for doing it. But
everybody has a story; it is a real-life, no-kidding soap opera,
True Confessions. The first couple I speak with, outside the
courthouse where they have just been married, is from
Santa Ana, California. The boy is Mexican-American, twenty-
four; his nineteen-year-old wife is Anglo. They drove down
for the day with his mother, and the bride says the five-
minute ceremony was "beautiful to me, just as exciting as
in a church and more convenient." They will have, she says,
a church wedding and honeymoon in the future, but can't
afford either right now and couldn't wait to get married.
On a sharp second glance at her Empire dress, I notice that
she is pregnant.

Another couple, on their way from license room to wedding room, has been married fifteen years. They come to
Las Vegas periodically to gamble, and this is the fourth time

they've repeated the wedding procedure, in order "to renew our romance."

Roger, a boy of twenty, a fireman, and Faith, his eighteen-year-old girl, decided four weeks ago to get married and he was afraid to tell his parents. She has come equipped with her stepmother, father and sister, but they have found out that he is under age and must get his folks' consent. He has just made the call home but didn't have the courage to confess. Now she is furious, her family is overwrought, and he doesn't know what to do next.

An easily recognizable Hollywood starlet and her business-man boyfriend enter to get their license, will have a small ceremony in their suite at Caesar's Palace tonight, attended by some friends who have flown in for the weekend. It is her second marriage and his fourth and, he admits, "It would seem a little ridiculous to do the whole romantic number." Then, too, in Vegas they have a built-in honeymoon, can see all the shows and play blackjack. She says to me, "Vegas is the most exciting city in the world, don't you think?"

There's the sense that everybody has something to peddle in this burg. You want a hooker, easy; some cocaine, easier; a fast marriage, the easiest. I meet a couple—Jim and Dee— in front of the courthouse and decide to tag along as they look for a chapel and Dee—having quite suddenly gone senti-mental and decided she must wear white instead of her green pants suit—a gown. They are from Phoenix, Arizona, in their mid-twenties; he is a lab technician, she a secretary, both Methodist, both previously married and divorced. Neither has any family. At eleven o'clock last night they decided suddenly to get married and drove straight through the night to Vegas. They have been going together for two months. "Everybody gets married in church," according to Jim. "It's different to do it here." When I approach them he is bent over, taping homemade crayoned signs to his 1969 red Datsun that read: SHE GOT HIM TODAY, HE'LL GET HER TONIGHT; CANDY IS SWEET BUT SEX DON'T ROT YOUR TEETH; and

HONK IF YOU'RE HORNY. Sweet, jittery and touching, they have somehow picked up the Vegas tough uglies and make jokes about it's-all-a-big-crap-game and "I hear they do quick divorces here, too. Where do we go for that?" They laugh, I laugh. In another setting such witticisms might seem just a bit tasteless. Here it's part of the action.

On our chapel shopping tour the first stop is the Little Chapel of the Flowers, a small white house with a phony church spire, nestled between a Texaco station and the Yucca Motel. Like its competitors, it has two rooms, the anteroom-lobby where the plastic accoutrements are sold, and the chapel itself—wooden benches, two stained-glass somethings that may be masquerading as windows, which they clearly are not, a sparse sprinkling of artificial greenery and flowers (known in this part of the world as "perpetual plastic"). Comparison to funeral chapeldom would not be inappropriate. Music? "For your listening pleasure we have a high-fidelity lifetime recording," the owner answers, sounding like a brochure. From a curiosity that has been nagging all day, I ask her about Jewish weddings. "Rabbis won't come to the chapels," she explains. "We have a nondenominational minister who does many weddings here and it's taken very well by the Jewish people."

We move on to the next. The Chapel of the Stars has lavish displays of white plastic carnations and electric candelabra. The minister mentions God, or not, as you request; you can purchase a license covering with a white bow, a rose corsage (real, as opposed to perpetual), and a special courtesy provides a car to pick you up at your hotel, take you to the courthouse for your license, wait, then drive you back here for your wedding. No muss, no fuss. Thirty-five minutes.

Right next door, on the same premises as the Holiday Motel, is the world-famous Chapel of the Bells where, as the owner immediately tells us, Keely Smith was married. He also informs us that he once appeared on the "David Frost Show" and asserts that "this is the most famous chapel in the world," which I certainly would not think of refuting. "I don't want to say anything derogatory about the other chapels," he says, "but they're all dumps compared to the 'Bells,' " In fact, his place *is* sweller than the others we've visited. It has more vinyl couches and more plastic posies. "We'll make this a real red-letter day" is his loud zonker as we are almost to the car. Shrieking now, he climaxes with: *"You don't get any of your three-minute ceremonies here, just remember THAT!"*

Jim and Dee finally settle on the Little Church of the West, definitely the class operation in town. A dice-throw away from the Frontier casino but nonetheless snuggled into a little patch of fake New England grass. Looks like the spot where Great-aunt Sophie is buried, but rumor has it that Elvis Presley got married here. Next, a quick stop at the Stage Bridal Shop, where the sign reads: ASK US ABOUT ONE-HOUR TUXEDO AND BRIDAL GOWN RENTALS." We do, and the charges—$12.50 to $50 for a dress, $10 to $25 for a tux—suddenly seem prohibitive and foolishly romantic for a quickie Las Vegas crapshoot. With a shrug that conveys both oh-what-the-hell and disappointment, Dee opts to keep on the pants outfit she's been wearing since yesterday morning in Arizona.

Lovers tie the knot in Las Vegas with the same speedy indifference that they toss away thousands they can't afford at the tables. I serve as legal witness to several marriages this busy Saturday—most couples come to town alone and the chapels charge anywhere from $2 to $6 to furnish witnesses, so I am in popular demand as maid of honor to these utter strangers. As dreary as are the chapels, courthouse weddings are a notch bleaker. Not unlike the experience of going to the Motor Vehicle Bureau to renew your license. Cold, bureaucratic, listless.

One-third of Vegas weddings take place at the courthouse, and as a result of a recent law prohibiting justices of the peace from performing marriages (they were each raking in

$150,000 a year in fees), the job of Commissioner of Marriage was created, enabling the money to be kept in the Nevada coffers. Five deputies do the deeds, on three shifts—"the day shift, the swing shift and the graveyard shift," one explains, without irony. He himself works four ten-hour days, does ninety or a hundred quickies on a Saturday and insists he is romantic about weddings. "I've been married for thirty-eight years. It hasn't been all beautiful, mind you, but mostly it has."

The wedding I witness takes place in his office—a tiny cubbyhole populated only by a steel-gray desk with a box of rubber bands on it, a floor vase of white plastic lilies of the valley and one painting on the wall, a desert landscape, with a card scotch-taped underneath reading "Title: Landscape; Price: $10.00 plus tax." The couple is in their fifties, have been common-law married for years, now are "doing it right." One aches, of course, to know the whole saga, why after all this time they are prompted to legally cement themselves, and in this setting. But the ceremony is beginning. And then it is ending. The deputy drones relentlessly for three minutes in a bad southwestern twang (it is, let's be kind, his forty-eighth marriage spiel of the day, and he has four hours left on duty) and mispronounces their names. But a curious thing happens. The bride's hands tremble throughout, the groom's temples get damp, and they regard each other with the kind of starry-eyed adoration one sees in engagement ring ads. Or among children getting married in the divinely romantic church surroundings that fulfill their lifetime's fantasies. But *here?* In Low City?

Several moments later I follow another twosome across the street to the Courthouse Chapel. They do not even ask my name, although I will be their maid of honor. ("Terrific! You're saving us six bucks!") Theirs are Valerie and Eddie, and in many ways they are a typical Vegas couple or at least seem to possess many of the elements I've found repeated over and over this weekend. They are young (both twenty-

three), from out of state (Los Angeles) and appear to have
no family connections. They are very casually dressed. He is
a bartender, she a secretary in an insurance company; they
met a year ago in the singles complex in which they both
live, have now been living together for a month. Their
decision to get married was impetuous—made yesterday.

They play traditional boy-girl games. He: "She begged
me so much, I'm just doing this to get her off my back."
She: "It's true. I've been plotting to get him for a year."
Valerie is chubby, plain, and giggles inappropriately when
tense, which she clearly is. Eddie is handsome with blond
curly hair; he swaggers and is what used to be called "a
ladies' man." Urgently pretending cool with bravado remarks
like "I just don't want none of this ceremony crap. I want
to sign on the dotted line and hit the casino," he is clearly
a nervous wreck. Valerie says she never cared about having
a real wedding, and I get the distinct feeling she is delighted
—no, relieved—at just having caught this smooth halibut and
really *is* indifferent to the celebration. Walking to the chapel,
he keeps threatening to change his mind if this doesn't
happen FAST, and she giggles. They are incredibly touching, their vulnerability gleaming through all the pretense
and verbal silliness.

As in any delicious soap opera, there is a shocker. In this
case it is the revealed news that Eddie was previously married
—at the age of fifteen—and has a seven-year-old daughter.

The chapel is as we have come to expect. Sticky vinyl
couches in the waiting room, the armrests covered with
orange terry-cloth face towels. The minister doesn't even
have to be summoned; he is there, waiting, on call. He is a
sort of Texan and a little raunchy around the edges. He
works five or six other chapels, gets $10 for the gig and
believes in the Vegas Way of Wedding. "This way," he says,
"you get rid of the church, the marching down the aisles,
the veils. It's much easier all the way round." When the
girl behind the desk says, "All set?" to the quaking two-

some, the man of God interrupts: "Wait. Let her finish writing the check." Valerie pays, $27.95. No extras. No flowers, photos or tape of the service. Just the basic.

Valerie and Eddie make individual trips to the bathroom, preceded by jokes about looking for the escape window, and finally declare themselves All Set. On the way into the chapel, he turns toward all of us and says, gratuitously, from some deep well of personal panic: "Listen. I'll take another shot at it. Try it without the family this time, no kids. If it doesn't work, that's it for me."

Overhearing, Valerie grins, delivers to me—the stranger whose name she doesn't yet know—a tiny wink that conveys immediately, wordlessly, the female understanding that she will be pregnant in three months. And I feel, instantly and with arrogant certainty, as though I can see their entire future lives spread out before me, and I want to cry.

Nevertheless, the same sweet sentiment takes command of this dreary ceremony as at the courthouse. A tinny recording of "Because God Made Yoooooo Mine" filters through cloggy pipes, the minister drones about man's-most-ancient-and-meaningful-custom and the responsibility-of-meeting-each-other's-needs with the rambling disinterest of an auctioneer. And Valerie and Eddie look at each other—for the first time since I have met them—with all of the innocent and tender caring that has brought them to this point in life, and quite suddenly this becomes a lovely, solemn and romantic moment. As solemn and romantic as any wedding, anywhere. Even here in Las Vegas, Nevada, a world choking to death on plastic and greed. Even here.

13. Connubial Blintz

It was to be the most razzle-dazzle super-extravaganza of all time. Caesar's triumphal march into Rome would pale into a Main Street cub-scout parade by comparison. All the forces of the Fontainebleau Hotel in Miami Beach were commandeered into feverish action for weeks ahead, preparing the Grand Ballroom for the wedding of twenty-year-old Susan Grenald to Ronald Rothstein, a law student at the University of Miami. "This is exactly what I've wanted since I was a little girl," whispered the dewy-eyed blonde, surveying the specially built, twenty-seven-foot, pink-carpeted stairway down which she would float, trailed by thirty feet of white train and a squadron of concerned lovebirds. To the accompaniment of strings, she would first emerge from behind a curtain through a celestial white cloud—provided by a specially built white cloud machine—which would then envelop her in soft mist as she levitated to the altar. As her mother explained: "Susan will look like she's coming from heaven." Where, as we know, all good Jewish Princesses originate.

After the ceremony the three hundred guests would munch Oysters Rockefeller, a small mountain of Iranian caviar and filet of beef. When the bride sliced into the eight-tiered, six-foot-tall cake, two additional lovebirds would be released, to soar with ancient symbolism through the heavenly upper reaches of the ballroom. The couple would then depart for their eighty-three day round-the-world honeymoon, leaving Daddy to pay $25,000 worth of bills.

Mama, six months before, had tried to hire THE society wedding coordinator in the area, who refused the assignment. "What you need is a Broadway producer," he sniffed. As he tells it, she was elated: "Oh yeah? Where do I get one?" Most probably she *didn't* hire one, but the Fontainebleau public relations department, sensing the show to be a sure smash hit, gave it a title—as one would *any* Broadway spectacular. "Wedding Fantasia" was to be covered by a team from *Time* magazine, and although the reportage was not quite as planned, the event did indeed make nationwide headlines—the groom chickened out, making a panicky celestial exit the night before and leaving behind a hysterical bride and a carload of stuffed mushrooms to die an unnatural death in the Fontainebleau kitchen.

Such a burlesque has, of late, been tagged the *Goodbye, Columbus* wedding—in honor of the scene in the film where Brenda Patimkin's brother gets married in a lavish and jazzy hotel festival. It has become a shorthand for the kind of wedding celebration that characterizes middle- and upper-middle-class Jewish life in America, to wit: the twelve-hour fete in the gardens of a Beverly Hills mansion—the only daughter of a prominent Jewish psychiatrist—where a different meal was served every hour and two authentic gondolas (*cum* gondoliers) navigated guests back and forth in the swimming pool; the affair at a Westchester country club —a carpet manufacturer's offspring—where Papa had his mills cease their appointed tasks in order to produce a special rug, emblazoned with the words "Sandy and Norman," to cover the entire lobby; the real-life Joseph E. Levine production in New York's Plaza Hotel, in which his daughter wanted a synagogue wedding but Mrs. L. didn't, so—as a glorious compromise—the Terrace Room was transformed into a chapel. For a service that lasted one-half hour, they had made twelve plexiglass replicas of the Chagall windows—each six feet wide and twelve feet high.

All groupings in our country have had occasional sagas of

cloud machines, birds emerging from unexpected corners and an abundance of fried shrimp to provide heartburn for the entire Seventh Fleet. Among the Jews, however, this style of wedding is a Moral Imperative.

A Jewish wedding, to begin with, is embodied in three key elements: Food, Flowers and Noise. If a classic WASP nuptial is in some way judged by the flowingness and vintage of the champagne, the Jewish jamboree is measured by the amount, variety and quality of the eats. Historically, the food compulsion harkens back to the dinner table being the center of Jewish home life; now, to quote Los Angeles' Rabbi Will Kramer: "The essence of a successful Jewish wedding is that at the end there's as much food left over as there was at the beginning, and yet everybody goes home feeling sick. It means that you have stated to your guests that you are so prosperous and so generous that they could not eat you out of house and home."

Food, in a Jewish wedding, takes on such grandiose value as to become an Art Form. That is to say, sliced cucumbers are maneuvered and architected to look like whole scaly fish (black olive for the eye), chopped liver is shaped into luxury liners or hearts or roosters (pimiento for the comb), cream cheese is tortured into swans to accompany the lox which has been molded into a wedding bell. One family in a Chicago suburb had $800 worth of chopped herring sculpted into a replica of the bride and groom.

Food is an obvious necessity. Not the battleship quantity, perhaps, but what are we to say about the overdose of flowers at the Jewish wedding? Whereas President Nixon spent $700 for the posies at Julie's Plaza Hotel gala, Joseph E. Levine shelled out more than ten times that figure, ordering a different array, all in white, for every individual table. Mostly out of season, they had to be flown in from such exotic ports as South Africa. Mel Atlas, the hotel florist, has altered —to the tune of $9000—a massive hotel ballroom into a total garden by covering every inch of plaster with flora and greenery. The chuppa, historically a mere piece of fabric, is, in today's commercial scheme of things, a gardenia Garden of Eden.

I remember, in one of my clearest visions of my childhood, a monumentally exorbitant wedding (Cousin Myrna's) at the swell Delmonico Hotel in Manhattan. Among other fripperies, the walls were completely blanketed with flowered trellises; as the festivities waned and the last burping guests were staggering out, the vultures descended—Aunt Paulette, in her canary yellow brocade gown and angina condition, climbed hand over hand up the trellises, Uncle Sam's palm under her fanny for support, performing the *most* brutal rape of the aging flowers, alighting with at least $400 worth to take home.

Jews are no different than any other minority culture, in that the gigantic wedding is symbolic of having succeeded in the community, being a winner, shifting the scales from a long tradition of deprivation to comfortable solvency. If one can afford—I suppose the logic goes—to throw away thousands on something as prodigal and temporary as flowers (dying along with the last mambo), one must really be a mensh. Food is a permanent, a staff of life; never mind that we provide such an overabundance—the Cossacks may come tomorrow, who knows when we'll eat again? (I'm convinced *that* terror is built into the Jewish racial unconsciousness.) But flowers? Here today, gone tonight, and you can't even eat them, all you can do is look at them. What *real* and awesome extravagance. . . .

The wedding is one of the few occasions in life at which Jews feel justified in getting drunk, so it is unrestrainedly, relentlessly gay. The measure of the success of the Jewish wedding is in the joy of the guests: if Bertha, the spinster sourpuss of the family, got a little loaded, danced with all the men and whooped and hollered, *that's* a smashing wedding. And since the Jews have never cultivated the Oriental love for silence, or the American Gentile value for understatedness, the volume keynotes that success.

A bandleader in New York says: "At a Jewish wedding, if you play soft and pretty background music, the bride's father storms up and screams, 'What's the matter, didn't your men show up?' " Aunt Sadie wants to do the hora and Cousins Selma and Irving want to show off the cha-cha that won them the Champagne Hour last winter in Puerto Rico. Grandpa wears a hearing aid, so everybody has to shriek and he shrieks back. Messrs. Simon and Silver negotiate a business deal with building lust, and a cluster of over-forties harangue with the under-twenties about how marijuana leads to heroin. Then, of course, the band has a master of ceremonies, a stand-up comic who not only bellows forth a stream of running sexy jokes but also announces every wee event of the evening as if he was proclaiming THEWINNERANDHEAVY-WEIGHTCHAMPIONOFTHEWORLD: *"And now,* Morty and Judy have their first dance . . ." *"And now,* the maid of honor's sister dances with the groom's brother-in-law . . ." *"And now, ladies and gentlemen, the Baked Alaska. . . ."* To boot there is the ceaseless clatter of dishes and glasses and forks as the noshing-guzzling marathon plunges ahead into its sixth straight hour.

The reasons for the flamboyant Jewish wedding pageant are as complex as the motivations and values operative in all crevices of American Jewish life. Many are so deeply rooted in the past—like the idea that they're-coming-to-get-us-tomorrow-so-we-better-eat-hearty-tonight—that the fact of their irrelevancy today does not diminish their power. Jews function heavily, for example, on the concept of "shonda" —shame. The expression, "It's a shonda for the neighbors," tossed at me throughout my childhood years as criticism for all varieties of bad public behavior, is as firmly etched into my psyche as "Thou shalt not kill." What the neighbors will think of us—indeed, the assumption that they are *always* observing and judging us—molds our actions, and what on earth will they think if we do not provide our daughter with a proper wedding? That we're paupers, or cheapskates or—horror of horrors—Bad Parents.

The most dread accusation of all to a Jew, worse yet than being a failure in business, is to be a bad parent. In Jewish lore, what that means, specifically, is not providing your off-spring with the best of everything, the creamiest that money can buy. It's like the food obsessions: the historical depriva-tion of rights and privileges taken for granted by everybody else is so ingrained in the Jewish genes that only outlandish excess will wash the memory away. Thus bursts forth the new generation of Have, the Jewish Princess—she who is denied nothing, to whom every material luxury is not a luxury at all but a life's-breath necessity. Daddy must—as his proof to the world and himself that he has done right by little Shirley —furnish her with the most lavish send-off available to mod-ern man.

In the past, being concerned about one's neighbors had validity for the Jew. They were often his enemies, often to be rightly feared. Today the neighbor can be Jew or Gentile, friend or stranger, yet the anxiety of being judged and found wanting is still a prime mover. Jewish weddings have become so copiously overdone, so laughably jazzy, pre-cisely because of this: in order that the fabled "neighbors" shouldn't talk, yours has to be more *more* than his. There is simply no choice about whether or not to play the game at all. Your friends have given big blowouts, your business partner did it, and all the ladies in your wife's Mah-Jongg club. You must not only do it, but it invariably has to be a four—compared to the Feinbergs' three—ring circus. If Mrs. Feinberg had sixteen hot items on the smorgasbord, you must naturally have twenty-two. And there seems to be, to look at the evidence, no way to de-escalate, no way to select the roast chicken dinner when everybody you know has bought the prime ribs. Good God, wouldn't the telephone wires just be sizzling the next day with *that* news?

And what about the groom's family, what will *they* think about the kind of people their prince is marrying into? A simple algebraic equation governs: the richer *his* family, the more *you* have to spend. It is not an original thought that intramural competitiveness has burrowed deep into the heart of middle-class Jewishdom, but nowhere is it seen in quite such living color as in the universe of the wedding.

At the Hampshire Country Club in New York's Westchester County the average wedding costs $10,000, but they not infrequently soar to double that amount. (The producer of *Goodbye, Columbus* belongs to Hampshire and apparently patterned the wedding scene on all the shindigs he's witnessed there.) Pete D'Angelo, the club's manager, tells more riotous stories about nuptial ridiculousness than anyone I've met. "The competition is murderous," he explains. "At one wedding the whole ceiling of the ballroom was covered with silk fabric, to look like billowing clouds, and tiny bulbs were planted above, twinkling through like stars." At another he had to have all the linen dyed gold to match the bride's mother's gown, to the tune of $3000. Two hundred and fifty pineapple shells sprayed powder blue, a cake sculpted in the shape of a synagogue with an icing couple departing through the door, champagne fountains where the wastage is 25 percent—small but key (and highly visible) symbols of going your neighbor one better.

Pete recalls: "One man, a furrier, insisted that all the scotch be at least twenty-one years old; it cost us eighteen dollars a bottle and we charged him fifty. A month later his best friend's daughter got married and they had to do something to top *that* number, so they threw a breakfast for three hundred the morning after their gigantic wedding." The crisis often arises where three weddings occur on three Saturday nights in a row, with virtually the same guest list. Each menu and color scheme has to be completely different; each

woman demands that *her* party be showier than those of her
two pals.

The propelling force behind many weddings is the gifts.
Among less affluent Jews, where cash (as opposed to china
or toasters) is the expected token, the receipts of the day
can go far to set up the young couple's new life. So the
wedding becomes a sort of fund-raising drive, the big pay-
off for those skillions of affairs *you* attended and thousands
of greenolas *you* parted with over the years. A friend of
mine told me about his sister's nuptials, in which the
declared, specific goal was to make a profit; her father calcu-
lated that the average gift would be $25 a person so, accord-
ingly, he planned a bash for two hundred where the total
expenses would divide out to $17 a person—exactly. The
bride reimbursed him the cost of the spree and got to keep
the $1600 profit. Which is not bad for one day's work. . . .

(The gifts, I am told, also can determine the hierarchy of
seating at the dinner. The place cards are left blank until
the very last instant, when all the presents are in. Then—
by the same economic system that secured one a seat in
either the third row center orchestra or the last row of the
balcony—the bearer of the French crystal candelabra gets to
be at the choice table, while the Waring Blender giver is
exiled to Siberia.)

This sort of Jewish fiesta is the prime illustration of
the it's-all-for-the-parents syndrome. Of all the recently married couples I have interviewed, it is *only* the Jewish girls
from moneyed families who reported that they loathed their
weddings, never wanted such a Mardi Gras but felt overwhelming parental pressure (funny, Daddy thinks he's doing
it for *her*) and not only acceded, but abandoned total responsibility. Would David Merrick allow his fledgling assistant
to produce *Hello, Dolly!?* Certainly not. *This* production
is staged, controlled, shaped by that mythic figure, the Jewish
Mother. The sole function for her daughter is to go for

fittings, write thank-you notes and prevent her skin from breaking out before the big day; the groom is a phantom, and Daddy writes the checks. It is, perhaps, the classical acting out of established Jewish family roles. . . .

Small wonder the kids relinquish: the stakes are simply too high. Poker is jolly fun when it's nickels and dimes but another game entirely when the bets are pot limit. Once the wedding machinery is set into operation, the accumulated tensions over the months of planning become volcanic. Every decision becomes so fraught with weighty implications that one senses there is clearly something much heavier at stake, for the family, than just the load of money being spent and the fever to create a memorable barbecue. It seems to represent an affirmation, a validation of one's total life. Christians—the majority culture, the true Americans—do not, I believe, bear this need. The American Jew of immigrant or second-generation stock knows, on some level, the limitations of his options: he cannot be President, either of the country or of its most powerful enterprises. What *is* open to him is acquisition of the symbols and their display for the world. The ghetto black goes hungry to buy the Cadillac and the color t.v.—on American terms, his only validation. The Jew, obviously more privileged but still an outsider, and with the same needs, just exhibits more symbols—the hoopla wedding being among the most mighty.

It is for the parents, *their* affirmation, thus the guests (or are they witnesses, judges?) will be primarily Daddy's business associates, Mother's Hadassah clique or the family ancients who surface only for funerals and weddings. Leftover space will be filled in with a scattering of the couple's friends. The twosome complains, but only to a reporter; control has long ago been abdicated. Listen:

"My mother's very determined and strong-willed and she wants to do everything herself, she barely consults me at all. I resented it terribly at first, but when I realized what a big deal this wedding was becoming, I figured I couldn't handle it anyway. So I'll go through it sort of like I'm a guest."

Or: "We've just been bombarded since the minute we got engaged. Mother offered us the choice of a wedding or money, but in a very teary voice. For years she's been saying how much she regretted never having a big wedding herself, never walking down the aisle, so how could I refuse?"

Or: "This is a terrible time. We've been in a constant state of tension since the engagement. People are always pressuring you to pick out your furniture, find an apartment, register the gifts, and now we spend every single weekend introducing all our distant relatives to each other."

And: "I feel like a puppet. I have no say over anything that's happening. It stinks."

Like the Fontainebleau fiasco, couples not infrequently break up as a result of the escalating strains. One twosome, who eloped to Las Vegas midstream in the preparations for a Beverly Hills Hotel spectacular, talks about how their love story degenerated into a sequence of daily squabbles over the centerpieces, the napkins, whether the cigarettes should be plain or menthol, whether the herring should be in cream sauce or wine sauce. Now married four years, the girl recalls: "One night, three months before the wedding, we sat there with our parents arguing about should the tablecloths be pink or yellow. Jerry snarled at me, 'I can't stand pink. If the table-cloths are pink, I'm not going through with it.' And I thought, 'I can't marry this jackass. He hates pink.' At that moment I knew we'd better elope or we'd never get any-where near the altar." They did, that weekend. Three months later, never having told their parents, they went through with the hotel rodeo as planned. And everybody got exactly what he wanted.

When I asked her what this little charade cost, she chuckled. "It could have cured cancer."

The *Goodbye, Columbus* wedding does more than its share to support the industry. The average American reception (according to *Modern Bride*) costs $601.21 and the largest percentage of families spend between $1000 and $2000; while no available statistics break down these figures ethnically, the industry experts agree that the Jewish middle class spends at least ten times the nationwide norm.

The cost of the average diamond engagement ring (half a carat) is $328.85. Our Jewish Princess wouldn't be caught dead on the line for her unemployment check in less than two and a half carats. The national bride spends $164 on her bridal gown; Marjorie Morningstar tosses those pennies away on three sets of Pucci underwear. And whereas only one percent of American brides get married in hotels, approximately one-third—again according to estimation from the pros—of all Jewish couples tie the knot in these establishments. Most hotels calculate that at least 50 percent of their total banquet business comes from weddings (as opposed to conventions, sweet sixteens or bar mitzvahs) and, of that, anywhere from 60 to 85 percent are Jewish. Jews being the only religious group that is permitted to hold their ceremonies outside of the home or a house of worship—as long as the setting is spiritual, say the ordinances—*every* hotel ceremony is Jewish. As is virtually every sit-down dinner.

Although most Jewish girls still get married in synagogue, in large cities where the hotels have adequate banquet facilities an increasing number pick this particular "spiritual setting"—the most expensive and statusey of all. An elegant hotel, after all—the Beverly Hills, say, or the Regency in New York—offers a kind of nonreligious prestige that the neighborhood temple just can't match. Even the snazziest suburban sanctuary, often architected these days to resemble a Florida resort spa, often as concerned with the party business as the praying business, simply can't touch the crystal-chandeliered, balconied, gold-angels-with-violins magic of the Hotel Pierre ballroom in Manhattan. Then, again, it's the unstoppable escalation: the Goldfinger fireworks took place last month in the chic gardens of the Bel-Air Hotel, so how could you possibly send *your* daughter off at B'Nai Whatsis, an inescapably obvious step downward? Or, as one Philadelphia girl, wed in the fashionable Barclay Hotel, responded to my query of why she didn't get married in synagogue: "Ick, temple is so *Jewish!*"

Hotels that cater to the wedding trade range from the high-elite to the ever-spreading chain commercial establishments. All that's really needed to compete for a piece of the silver pie are a couple of rooms of varying sizes to accommodate the demands of the tiny, private affair or the super-soiree—and those falling somewhere between. The premise of the hotel wedding is at opposite poles from the wedding palace. At Leonard's the whole shebang comes in a package, a set price, and your only decision is the chicken-or-roast beef one; the hotel fiesta is geared for the matriarch who wants, *needs,* to maneuver EVERYTHING—absolutely everything. From the style of engraving on the personalized matchbooks, to the color of the spotlighting on the cake, to—and this is ultimately the costliest, weightiest choice—the quality and quantity of the liquor.

Each item is charged for separately. Scan a bill from the Plaza Hotel for a recent Jewish pageant for 220 guests, the total cost $10,013.07—and this doesn't include photography, music or any of the other non-hotel purchases. The dinner, châteaubriand at $23 per guest, came to over $5000—the major expense. But then there was $68.75 for Don Diego cigars passed "to the gentlemen with their café," "pink cathedral candles at $1.25 each, 4 per table" (for a total of $56), $100 for extra-fancy gold water glasses, and $30 to the washroom attendants.

(One of the key charges not included herein is that of the traveling hairdresser—only slightly less necessary to our Princess than the groom. He does the tresses of all the female cast the day before, then arrives with an entourage of assistants on W-day for makeup and more hair duty. A bride reports: "Georgio did my hair *again* right before the ceremony, then into a more casual style right after. Then anytime during the ceremony if he saw it getting out of hand he'd whisk me into the back room and fix it all up again. . . ." Many such brides, in fact, reserve their Georgios the same time they reserve the hotel.

It is on the booze that the hotel makes its fattest profit (65 percent as opposed to 30 percent on the food, says the banquet manager of the Beverly Hilton) and for which all accusations of hotel cheating—like bathtub gin being poured into the Beefeater bottles—are leveled. Most establishments charge either by the bottle ($10 to $25) or by the drink at $1.15 each. Now there are lots of ways to serve liquor, each one cutting or accelerating the costs, and hoisting or lowering your status. The top extravagance is to have rolling bars from beginning to end, meaning that drinks are always available and you don't have to shlep to the bar to get one. In fact, you don't even have to snap your fingers to summon service; it's right at your fingertips. The ice starts to melt in your just-barely-sipped Chivas Regal and soda ($18.50 a bottle, $.90 per quart of fizz) and lo and behold, there's the grinning garçon with a bubbly fresh one. And the liquid wastage goes on all night, added to by the flood of vintage champagne ($12.50 a bottle) with the food, and the cordials *après*. The rule of thumb for this kind of service is that each guest consumes one drink every fifteen minutes.

There are ways to economize—subtle to the outsider but sore-thumb visible to the cognoscenti. You can have a stationary bar, where one has to exert some effort to get a drink (the average consumed then drops to five or six per person over the course of the evening). Or you can cut off the hard booze right before dinner, from then on serving only champagne. Or—El Multo Cheapo—you can decide precisely how much you will spend and close down the drinking when that sum has been reached. In general, the guilt-edged Jewish ego will not permit any of these frugaling measures. You and I, if neophyte wedding-goers, would probably not notice the cutback; the eagle eye of the "neighbors" will, no doubt, and the mind boggles to consider how lightning fast that tidbit will spread—plaguelike—through the beauty shops and golf foursomes.

All of this paranoia and guilt derives not only from Jewish heritage, the Bad Parent terror and dread of the serpent-tongued neighbors. It is fed, watered, nursed and nurtured by that outstanding figure of hotel wedding life—the Banquet Manager.

Every hotel has one. He is to the Jewish regatta what the wedding consultant is to the *haut monde* Gentile; that is to say, he coordinates, oversees, advises and makes you feel your own tragic ineptitude. As you become more dependent on his experience, superior taste and aggressiveness, he becomes increasingly in charge of *your* party. His purpose is not so much a gratuitous ego/power trip as a quite deliberate means to a businessman's end—getting you to shell out as much money as possible. That is his job, after all. Not unlike funeral directors who are able, without big difficulty, to convince us that we are horrible humans for considering the burial of a loved one in a plain pine box, that somehow love means planting Aunt Nellie in mahogany. Vulnerability to the unspoken accusation is equally as operative for weddings as funerals—the crucial rites of passage. You may not be sending your Princessdaughter off to the great hereafter, but you *are* sending her off. How American that the commodity, the judging scale, is the dollar. A bad parent spends few, a good and noble parent spends the contents of Fort Knox. Or more.

There is not a banquet manager worth his smoked sturgeon who does not understand this psychology and exploit it. On a warm spring afternoon I made an appointment to consult with one of the managers at the Beverly Hills Hotel, the lovely and smart haven for show business types on expense accounts from New York and local royalty getting bar mitzvahed or married. Posing as a future bride auditioning hotels, I learned—instantly—the name of the banquet manager game: Intimidation.

This particular lady—very Teutonic, ultra chic—from the moment I entered her domain, appraised me blatantly, surely wanting me to squirm under the appraisal. With one lingering, piercing glance that traveled down my body as if she were reading a map of New Jersey looking for Weehawken, but in fact was computing labels and price tags of my pants suit, shoes, jewelry and underwear, she succeeded wordlessly in making me feel abysmally shabby. Tacky. Poor. Unworthy. And it only took twenty seconds. At that instant I would have done *anything* to reverse her judgment. "Are you on a budget?" is her first question, and I feel, by my "yes" answer, that she envisions me living in a subway station ladies' room. Obviously, I assume, no one who has ever taken up one moment of her time has ever been on a budget, has ever had the tiniest flash of a thought for the cost of her fete. One could, of course, respond: "Yes, I don't want to spend a nickel over four hundred thousand," but that would still not justify having a budget to begin with. Tacky. Tacky, tacky.

Plainly repelled by me, she rushes me through a tour of the Crystal Room and the Maisonette Room, all with the impatient and bored spirit of the *grande dame* showing her mansion to the new maid. She doesn't suspect I'm a reporter —it's not that; it is more some unspeakable, fatal blemish (having to do, I gather, with my insistence on asking what everything costs) that revolts her. I am in and out of the Beverly Hills Hotel in twenty minutes, certain that if I were to rush back and say, "Okay, I want to have my wedding here," I would be rejected.

Banquet managers come in different styles, ranging from oily obsequious to horsey WASP to Nazi. Whatever the approach, they all play Intimidation. And it absolutely works to perfection. Gerd Ries is in charge of banquet activities for New York's very nicest hostelry, the Regency. A small, quiet, utterly iffy-piffy establishment, only ten years old, you will rarely spy a movie star in the lobby. In fact, you will hardly ever see a famous face at the Regency, unless you happen to be able to recognize kings, presidents of countries or the top financial monarchs in the world.

With banquet provisions less extensive than the Plaza, St. Regis or the Pierre—the Regency Suite can accommodate only two hundred with no dancing—their wedding image is soaring among Jewish parvenues who require "Quiet Elegance"—that interesting WASP expression that used to be used in the ads as code for resorts that didn't allow Jews.

Mr. Ries is a terribly personable European who seems to be, although he isn't, wearing white gloves. His basic training was taken at the Plaza (banquet managers ping-pong between the classy joints: Moore at the Plaza used to be at the Waldorf and the Biltmore; Hanline at the Beverly Wilshire worked for the Bel-Air and Beverly Hills); he hates noisy frolics and rolling bars, permits only French service—each item is served individually, as opposed to bringing out the already piled plate *à la* dinner on an airplane—and all his waiters wear high-winged collars and gloves.

I am permitted to be present for his prenuptial conference with a thirty-year-old schoolteacher named Rita who is three months hence marrying a wealthy stockbroker from an our-crowdish family. It is obviously a heavy Jewish status number. She is, as a result, insecure and desperate. Ries is the super-elegant gourmet pro daddy. Although he could not be more soft-spoken, polite and genteel throughout the interview, it becomes more than clear that, by the nature of the game, he could easily sell her the Throgs Neck Bridge for her wedding cake.

It is to be a small affair, sixty guests ("several doctors and judges from Michael's family," she later boasts to me), with a buffet supper and dancing. The purpose of this meeting is to plan the menu. Watch the game in action. Rita has been suggesting dishes; Ries has, in response, been blanching, frowning, all but groaning audibly. "In order to keep up with the expectancies of the Regency and yours also," he commands, *"this* is the environment I think you should have." Whereupon he suggests two esoteric dishes that I have never heard of, and to judge by her terror, neither has she. Suddenly, in her rapidly zooming nervousness, she becomes *très* pretentious. "I love the flavor of Boeuf Bourguignon," says she, pronouncing "beef" as "boeuf," "but it's so terribly passé, so trite." He agrees, much to her relief, although he says "beef," which sends her plummeting once again. They fence, finally agree on a Carbonnade of Boeuf (or beef, as you will).

"With that," he insists, "spaetzle—little flour dumplings, Swiss, sautéed in butter." She is confused, doesn't know what a spaetzle is and now is definitely one-down. (Actually she has been one-down since she entered the fortress but is just beginning to feel the wounds.) When it happens, a few seconds later, that she mistakes Newburg sauce for cheese (it's red), he's utterly in command. "Salmon," he suggests. "Yes," she agrees enthusiastically. "With mayonnaise. I love that." "No," he sneers. "Rémoulade."

Ries: "I banned onions and roquefort from my buffets." She has just asked for roquefort dressing, naturally. "What about Salade Niçoise?" she begs, painfully needing *some* approval. Now, the question is, does she *really* want tuna fish salad at her wedding or is she desperately trying to regain her footage by exhibiting familiarity with *La Langue Française?* He agrees to tuna fish and she exhales for the first time in many minutes. Next the dessert. With great agitation she proclaims, about the ice cream: "Vanilla is so mundane." They run through the flavor catalog, finally deciding on a non-mundane chocolate and a highly original butter pecan.

But the real crisis of the day arises when Rita mentions that she has hired some uncle or other to do the flowers. Ries becomes pinched and—so quietly that one can barely hear the words—tells her she *must* use the Regency florist, it is a hotel ruling, and he will be severely criticized by management otherwise. (This is a general dictum among the finer inns throughout America.) Things get murderously tense for a long silent minute while Rita fearfully calculates how much more this will cost than Uncle Sidney's wholesale daisies. Guess who surrenders? Guess who wins the point? Guess who does Rita's flowers?

Rita's wedding, they estimate, will cost $3000, or $50 a person. And that is for a mere buffet ($10–$20 a head), not the sit-down dinner ($15–$25). What her tip will be, in cash, to Mr. Ries, for his abiding help and taste, is hard to know; a gargantuan picnic can easily bring the banquet manager $500 from a grateful parent.

There is apparently no way to judge or really control the skyrocketing costs of the hotel wedding. As the good father cannot tell his guests to cool it with the drinking, so can he not ask them to leave after the standard four hours—just because it will cost him up to $250 for the room for each additional hour, plus hundreds more for the musicians. In some hotels, like the Plaza, he must use not only their florist but one of the few photographers and bands that management finds acceptable. "We're jealous of our reputation," claims F. Bart Moore, the top-drawer, haughty banquet manager, "and everything concerned with the total effect concerns us." Moore claims he has more weddings than any hotel in the world—between eight hundred and a thousand a year—and though clearly he is supported (like all hotels) by the Jewish spree, he loathes ostentation and doesn't think too much of chicken soup either. "We at the Plaza like elegant simplicity." There it is again, the password. "We like to do things differently, to avoid the fruit cup and the noodle soup. We like to make a different sauce, a different garniture." Does he impose on his customers' taste? Is there any kind of bacchanal he wouldn't tolerate because of the Plaza's worship of elegant simplicity? "It is our obligation," he states as if delivering the commencement address at Princeton, "to recommend to our guests procedures that are acceptable today in our society, as far as wedding etiquette is concerned.

Nevertheless, if he rents the room, he can do what he wants with it."

What will happen, one asks the obvious question, when the Jewish wedding snowballs itself into science fiction? When every dove in America has congregated, been dyed pale lavender to match the tablecloths, the bridesmaids' frocks and the ice in the shrimp bowl, and has been encapsulated in a sixty-foot-high, rhinestoned cake that croons The Godfather Theme from its innards? Where do we go from there? Apparently, from all indications of the trend, we go to the super bar mitzvah.

"They're getting exactly as crazy as weddings," says the country club manager. "People do them for the same reasons. They lay all their drives for a circus on a thirteen-year-old who doesn't know what he wants and has no say in the matter anyway." There's the tale of the $60,000 bar mitzvah done in an African jungle theme with hundreds of fake stuffed giraffes and elephants, zebra tablecloths and jungle foliage planted amid the garden geraniums. Or the bash in a Long Island mansion, prepared by Mel Atlas: "It was supposed to be a Cinderella theme—what that has to do with a bar mitzvah, I have no idea, but that's what the family wanted. We built miniature castles and pumpkin coaches with rented, costumed footman to carry the kiddies from the driveway to the house. It was the most outrageous thing I ever saw."

The need for spectacle, the urge to produce an unforgettable, knock-'em-dead extravaganza, has resulted in Jewish musical comedy—the *Goodbye, Columbus* wedding. What makes jollier sagas the morning after than an adventure in gross excess? Venetian gondolas floating down a Jewish swimming pool? Hilarious. Princesses materializing from cloud puffs? A howl. Chagall windows? The best. Hollywood does it on a huge screen and we adore the flamboyance, get high on the overdose. Why not, then, in real life?

Well, perhaps the jaded banquetman says it: "What bothers me most is looking at the thousands of dead flowers piled up the next day, waiting for the garbage man. It's such a damn incredible, astonishing waste. Such a waste."

14. Consummation
in the Poconos

Your honeymoon is a once in a lifetime happening . . . a
premiere of the joys of ten thousand tomorrows. You are a
pair now . . . two young individualists choosing togetherness, choosing to set your sights on the same point. The
first highpoint will be your honeymoon, your first decision
will be where to spend it . . . the many faces of Penn Hills
are enough to keep the whole world in smiles . . . except
that the whole five hundred acre estate is for young marrieds Only . . . the lively, lovely ones. Essentially . . .
YOU. And more . . . Because Penn Hills is the Four Sea-
sons center of the Pocono mountainland. And it's beautiful. In fact it's so romantic that the sun and moon hold
hands and make never-endingness. We invite you to try a
little of our tenderness, mix it with a little of your own.
  —From the brochure for Penn Hills honeymoon
  hotel, Analomink, Pennsylvania

In that remote historical time when Marriage by Capture
was the norm, when the male brute dragged off some re-
luctant lady-fair into the night, it often followed that her
tribe would come in hot pursuit, making it necessary for
him to take his bride into hiding until the search was abandoned. They would remain in seclusion for about a month
(or "moon") until familial tempers cooled. During that time
they got to know each other and drank a lot of "mead," a
honey wine symbolically associated with sweetness and sen-
sual delight. Thus—The Honeymoon. Rumor has it that

Attila the Hun, shortly after his wedding, died of an overdose of mead.

The Honeymoon still flourishes as a vital part of the wedding ritual. *Bride's Magazine* claims that 98 percent of their readers take a honeymoon trip, and the figures rise every year. Whereas in 1958 it was estimated that $235 million was spent on honeymoon travel, the sum leaped 300 percent in ten years, to $994 million.

The average American newlywed couple honeymoons for 9.1 days, travels 1922 miles and spends $680 if they stay inside the United States or $1111 if they leave the country. In 1969 they purchased 1,351,764 pieces of luggage and they account for a whopping one-quarter of all the travel business in America. The publication that carries more hotel, resort and travel advertising than any other consumer magazine in this country is none other than *Modern Bride.*

The *raison d'être* for the honeymoon today is fundamentally similar to its ancient purpose—to provide a transition between one's past and future lives, a smooth path from leaving the child-nest to becoming one's own adult. Then, too, it is a means of prolonging the delirious high that surrounds the wedding festivities, a way of staving off the mundane realities of married day-to-dayness.

The primary reason for honeymooning traditionally has been to introduce the couple to sex. Virginity was a crucial commodity and the Wedding Night, clearly the major magic moment of life, the realization of all those years of ignorance and fantasy. I remember many teary teen-age scenes of my own, usually set in somebody's car, climaxed (as it were) with the cliché line of the 1950's: "No, no, no, Bobby"—or Charlie or Tommy—"I'm saving THAT for my wedding night." The myth, the promise was that the experience of first lovemaking —wedding night bliss—was to be attended by cymbals crashing, earth quaking, stars exploding. One was obliged to wait, to save IT, for that.

One might nowadays imagine the Wedding Night, if not

the honeymoon, to be obsolete; indeed, for citizens of the Woodstock Nation, it is. The honeymoon, to that segment of American youth, is probably an excuse to backpack through Switzerland or float down the Mississippi on a houseboat or snorkel in Barbados and is accompanied by the same quantity of sexual activity they've been having with one another for the months or years prior to their marriage. On the other hand, if you're one of the 50 percent of newlywed couples (according to the Institute of Sex Research in Bloomington, Indiana) who have *not* slept together before the wedding, the dramatic impact of the honeymoon looms very heavy indeed. It is these particular children to whom the resorts of Pennsylvania's Pocono Mountains—"The Number One Honeymoon Capital of the World"—are dedicated.

Today's average newlyweds tend to go to the same spots as their forebears (with the exception of Niagara Falls, which has succumbed to subhuman squalor): Bermuda, Nassau, the Virgin Islands, Miami Beach, Las Vegas, Hawaii. Plush, glamorous, exotic tropical nooks, remote both physically and spiritually from anything resembling their real lives. The Poconos, hardly exotic, must, however, have something else going for it—it captures the largest percentage (14.5) of the honeymoon trade, as opposed, for instance, to the 6.5 percent who last year visited the Bahamas.

It has, to begin with, twenty-eight resorts, many of which cater *exclusively* to honeymooners. Business has soared an astonishing 500 percent in the last ten years; last year 150,000 kids spent over $35 million in the area. It has, at least according to the Penn Hills brochure, "the wonderful nectar of fresh mountain air, the sweet fragrance of blossoming buds and the tingling of a cool spring-fed brook . . ." It has sunshine which "comes softly to dapple the kingdom of Honeymoon Haven. It brushes everything with glowing radiance. It will do the same to every moment that you spend with us." It has skiing, swimming, golf, riding, skating, boating, tennis and fishing. Most spectacularly, extravagantly, incredibly of all, the Poconos has Cove Haven, Land of Love, home of the Heart-Shaped Bathtub.

"We're selling one thing here and one thing only. Sex. Let's face it. Everything we do is built around the sexual angle. Right now we're testing round mirrors over the beds in eight units. We've had them in there almost five months and I haven't had one complaint. I definitely think we've got a winner there!"

I'm sitting—somewhat agog at this revelation—across a large, busily papered desk from Morris Wilkins, co-owner of Cove Haven, on Lake Wallenpaupack in Lakeville, Pennsylvania. A polite, mild-mannered, staid bachelor in his mid-forties, Morris was once a plumbing contractor in the mountains, working primarily for resort hotels. Thirteen years ago he and a local carpenter, Harold O'Brien, each borrowed $5000 and opened a small (fifty-room) honeymoon heaven. Last year Cove Haven grossed $5 million. They now have 150 cottages, are building another forty and installing a new dining room. While we chat, in fact, over several hours of a warm summer morning, Morris' secretaries in the outer office will book—through letters and telephone —twenty-six reservations, ranging ahead from six months to a year and a half.

The exterior of Cove Haven looks no different from many other middle-class mountain resorts in the eastern United States—indeed, much less grand than the historic New England hotels and infinitely less sumptuous than the zingy haunts of the Catskills. The grounds actually remind me of the summer camps of my childhood—square wooden cottages, dry scrub-brushed baseball diamond, the omnipresent "social hall," a small lake with an unpronounceable Indian name. I half expect the loudspeaker to announce at any moment that those campers who haven't written their letters home won't be allowed to buy candy from the canteen.

The only visible signals that this is a place more interesting than appears at first glance are the ground signs. You see, every sign at Cove Haven—from "No Smoking" to "Guest Cars Are Not Allowed Past This Gate" to "You Are Entering the Land of Love"—is bright red and heart-shaped.

So this is Cove Haven, Land of Love. I first heard of it, this apparent phenomenon of Americana, a few years ago when *Life* magazine ran a two-page color photo of an attractive young couple, immersed in a gigantic five-foot-deep, crimson-and-white-tiled tub in the form of a heart. In the midst, enveloped in bubbles, surrounded by floor-to-ceiling mirrors, crystal chandeliers, urns of perfume, oils, ointments, creams, soaps, and a remote-controllable camera on a tripod to permanently capture the whole remarkable tableau, sat the blissful twosome, necking. Is this to be taken seriously, I wondered at the time, ingenuously assuming that such grandiose gaudiness must be, at its core, a huge put-on.

But then *I* am standing in front of my very own oversized valentine of a bathtub, ushered in by Morris to my home for the next few days: "the luxurious Cove Harbour cottage —a masterpiece in design and elegance." Eight days, seven nights, $440, everything included except lunch, horseback riding and firewood.

Shall I describe the living accommodations?

If the exterior looks to be a rather undistinguished Girl Scout camp, the inside of a Cove Haven cottage resembles a nineteenth-century New Orleans whorehouse. A joke. A garish, grotesque, hilarious exaggeration. Surely a put-on. The front door opens onto a tiny living room—velvet couch in brothel red, thick carpet in red, red velvet drapes. A minuscule fireplace, color TV, refrigerator. The room is, really, just a balcony for the purpose of looking down to The Shrine below—the 12½-foot (12½-foot?) heart-shaped bed, covered in quilted white satin, canopied in lush purple velvet. This edifice, itself big enough to contain a small swimming pool, or a medium-sized orgy, is the focal center of the cottage, arrived at by walking down several steps. (Everything at Cove Haven is either sunken or raised—beds on platforms, bathtubs sunken. You step up to the toilet or down to the closet, down to the fireplace, up to the shower.)

Next to the bed a blue velvet "love lounge"; over the bed two ornate chandeliers, with dimmers controlled from where one lies. The drapes can also be electrically drawn and opened from this position. Need I mention that the lighting in this Garden of Earthly Delights is so subdued as to make it *practically* possible to trip over the mammoth sleeper?

The bathroom: giant, split-level, entirely carpeted in red velvet. To the right is a raised platform with toilet, stall shower and his and hers toilet paper dispensers. On the left, the aforementioned tub (down four steps). Gold chandeliers, twin heart-shaped sinks. Morris tells me the astonishing news that the most critical selling point for a honeymoon hotel is the bathtub—not even the bed, but the tub. It's sexier.

"We started with Roman baths [rectangular, sunken] but our newer units have the heart-shaped numbers. All our advertising is geared toward the bathtub. I think the popularity is because sexual relations are related in some way to cleanliness. And it's glamorous, like Hollywood 1930's movies. You know each one costs over three thousand dollars to build, but it's worth it. Couples call us for reservations and don't even care what kind of accommodations they get, as long as they get the big bath. Often they don't even think to ask anything about the bed!"

Not that he's indifferent about the bed situation, mind you. He started out with canopy double beds, moved speedily into king-size. Then to round, which are currently on their way out, then wall-to-wall (wall-to-wall?), now heart-shaped. At the moment he's researching the notion of waterbeds.

Glamorous, like the movies of the thirties, he says. Yes, there certainly is that Mae Westian florid hyperbole about the decor, that Hollywood ethos that claims Flashy is Beautiful, Vulgar is Opulent. And although my temporary love nest makes me giggle, it is, admittedly, sexy. Like a dirty joke can be sexy. Not subtle, or sensuous, or even low-down Tina Turner funky, but the most obvious and brazen kind of sexy.

The entire cottage, by the way, is lushly carpeted in reds and passionate purples—floors, walls and ceilings. Living room, closets, boudoir and the john. Wrap-around carpeting, Morris' personal innovation. Soundproof, get it?

> No expense has been spared to give you your spacious sunken living room, furnished in antique White French Provincial, dominated by an impressive Italian Renaissance log-burning fireplace and console TV.
> —Pocono Gardens brochure

Who comes to Cove Haven for a honeymoon? For whom is this extravaganza in heart-shaped Kitsch designed? Who is it that digs, or is it needs, such distortion in sexual hype? To find out, read the *Cove Caper,* the mimeographed "newspaper" published daily:

> Harry and Karen Endick live in Whiteboro, N.Y. He is an Assistant Manager and she is a Keypunch . . . Bob and Kay Kelly live in York, Pa. He is a Postal Clerk and she is a Postal Clerk. They both like sports . . . Joe and Barbara Sinclair live in Snowshoe, Pa. He is in Construction and she is a Beautician . . . Gary and Linda Fogarty live in Chicago, Illinois. He is a Pipe Insulator and she is a Typist . . . Ed and Ellen Meg Hubbell live in Milford, Conn. He is a Fireman and she is a Nurse. They met through a mutual friend at a discotheque. Both of them thought each other was a snob and couldn't care less about one another . . . Chris and Debby Moffett live in Wilmington, Delaware. He is a Telephone Switchman and she is a Jr. Discounting Clerk. Deb was a clerk in an A & P and he just got off active duty and visited the store (he used to work there.) He went to her booth and closed it so they could meet . . . Andy and Nancy Potoski live in Pittsburgh, Pa. He is a Corporate Trader and she is a Clerical.

They met on a blind date at a friend's house while showing slides of Vietnam . . .

One begins to draw a character sketch from scanning
several *Cove Capers*: North Adams, Mass.; Point Pleasant
Beach, N.J.; Syosset, Long Island; Warren, Michigan; Wil-
liamsport, Pa.; Windsor, Ontario. Small cities or medium-
sized towns in the East or near Midwest (I didn't find anybody listed who lived farther west than Detroit). Names like
Duffy, Pichnarcik, Santanello, Edwards, McGeary, Anderson
and Fredmonski. (Not a Levy in the whole shebang. They
go to the Catskills, claims Morris. Eighty percent of his
couples are Catholic, he says.) Car salesmen, clerk/typists,
machinists, butchers, waitresses, telephone operators, truck
drivers, soldiers, bookkeepers. Lots of Vietnam veterans, only
a smattering of college students. The girls tend to be nineteen, the boys average out to twenty-two.

The first couple that I speak with is having lunch in the
coffee shop—lunch being the only meal not programmed and
prepaid. Also serving as general store, this is where the kids
buy six-packs of Bud to keep in their cottage refrigerators
and postcards of bathtubs to send home. Nibbling on a
cheeseburger, I've been observing this particular twosome
since they entered a few moments before. They seem piti-
fully, vulnerably young, but perhaps that is only due to their
shyness, which suggests that they are not on a honeymoon
but a disastrous blind date. Painfully awkward with one
another and removed from the other couples in the room,
they hardly speak, only stare silently into their Cokes. All
the other couples behave the same way, so that this atmosphere of ostensible honeymoon ecstasy is torturously quiet,
uncomfortable. It is a room filled with youngsters who,
given their druthers, would probably make the fastest mile
dash in history—straight home to Mama.

They seem instantly relieved when I approach them with
friendliness, are delighted to share the story of their lives—in

truth are thrilled to be talking to *anybody*. Chuck, a laborer, is twenty-three; Cathy is a twenty-one-year-old secretary. They are from Indiana, Pennsylvania, population 13,000. Having gone together since the ninth grade, they were engaged for one year, have been married for two days. (Ninth grade? And such uneasy strangers together?)

Cathy is a nondescriptly pretty girl with unstylish, thin brown hair that she wears in a 1957 pageboy. (That night I spy her in the bar, all done up in a shellac wig with two thousand unmoving curls.) Chuck has a mustache but no sideburns, a hair style we used to call a "duck's ass," wears madras Bermuda shorts and red socks. Each is wearing, pinned to the sleeve, a red and white heart-shaped name tag.

Both Chuck and Cathy have always lived at home with their parents. After this week they will move into an apartment for which their only acquisitions, so far, have been two rugs, the bed and a color television set. They got married in Pittsburgh at a Presbyterian church and had a reception for two hundred (buffet, champagne punch and a band), for which his parents paid. It was held at the Eagles Club. Both feel it was "the most beautiful, wonderful wedding in the whole world."

Why did they choose Cove Haven? "My sister went to Stricklands [another resort in the area] and loved it," says Cathy. "The honeymoon is one of the biggest things you ever do in your life. It's something to always remember and you want a place that's luxurious and there are all these activities that you can't do at home. We came here because of the bathtubs and the beds and the horseback riding."

She reels off a rundown of the activities in which she and Chuck participated yesterday—the first day of their married life: 10 A.M. breakfast in bed. ("It was the first time either of us had ever had this. It was *so* exciting. I thought at first I was supposed to do the dishes!" she says, both of them relaxing, finally, into mild laughter.) Then to the gift shop to buy Poconos souvenirs; 12 o'clock to the rifle range with about ten other couples. Each couple is given six shells, three for him, three for her; 1 P.M. swimming, with two other couples, in the heart-shaped pool (as opposed to the indoor pool or the outdoor rectangular pool, or the lake); 3 P.M. bicycle riding; 6 P.M. dinner; 8 P.M. out on the lake in paddle boats; 9:30 dance in the Mermaid Room. And now, after that whirlwind day of organized jollies, does the dreamy-eyed couple *finally* retire to nuptial paradise in their 12½-foot playpen? No way. They make a beeline for the gym, where "we played the pinball machine until one A.M. It was fabulous!"

Whatever happened to young honeymooners spending every instant of every day in bed? The great American terror that everybody-is-having-more-sex-than-I-am certainly surfaces in honeymoon mythology, where one envisions a haggard but smirking twosome emerging, "spent," from their boudoir once in every twenty-four hours, merely to take in enough nourishment to keep up their strength for the renewed ardors ahead. Either that doesn't occur anymore or—like most of our predominant sexual fantasies—it never did. In any case, it certainly ain't happening at Cove Haven, where the pinball machine appears to see a lot more action than the mattress. You see, despite the apparent fact that kids *do* choose this particular love nest primarily for the symbolic sexual importance of the bed and bath, they spend little time romping around in either. With Chuck and Cathy, for instance, the odds are fifty-fifty that until last night they had never had sex with each other. Chances are also pretty good that she was a virgin.

I don't expect you to believe me. NOBODY's a virgin anymore, not even these very straight, very clean-cut, utterly respectable children of religious working-class parents. Even kids for whom, as several tell me, this is the first time they've *ever* been away from home, *ever* stayed overnight in a hotel. Still, what about the sexual revolution, and the back seat of the convertible?

Ask Charlie Poalillo, owner of Penn Hills. "We get the average, down-to-earth type individuals, typical American couples. I'd say it's probably true that they haven't slept together before, although the boy probably has *some* sexual experience." Could it be like the old days, from my dreary fifties' adolescence, where he would get it from the neighborhood nymphomaniac, while she preserved her chastity for the Big Night? Could it be true? Ask Barbara Kolosky, Morris' night secretary and—not coincidentally—a registered nurse. She frequently becomes the surrogate mother whom couples turn to in desperation. "It's their first time away from their families, and together, and often they're scared to death, need somebody besides each other to talk to. I'm on duty all night."

Barbara receives an average of one nightly call from the cottages between midnight and dawn and generally the problem is sexual. "Shall we call it a gross ineptitude of technique?" she asks with sympathy. Instances of hysteria, excessive bleeding, general terror. Sometimes girls have to be carted to the hospital for stitches. Full of gory, poignant anecdotes, Barbara tells me a pip of being called in by a gal who was chafed and raw, in horrible pain, and didn't understand why. It seems her new hubby was a cleanliness freak and for three days had been making her douche eight times a day, whether they were having intercourse or not. "Are we doing something wrong?" they asked her.

Often the kids are unable to reach out to anybody for help and Barbara will get a wee-hours request to check out. She immediately runs to their room, tells them she's a nurse, probes, soothes. "They almost always stay," she says. "They're just overwhelmed by all these brand-new, crucial experiences that they're having for the first time. They want somebody to tell them everything will be okay. That's just what I do."

Which also helps to explain why they like being totally surrounded—indeed engulfed—by other honeymooners. Looking over every shoulder, they feel an unspoken communion and solace with hundreds of other young souls, all in the same foundering boat. "You take two kids who get married," explains Morris sympathetically, "get in their car and drive, thinking they want to be alone. After two days they don't have a single thing to say to each other." When I comment on how frighteningly that bodes for the long winters of togetherness ahead, he answers cheerily: "Oh, when they get home it's a different situation. They go to jobs, she keeps house, they have babies, there are all those domestic things to talk about. But that's later. For now it's just a big letdown. What we do for them is critical. Seventy percent have had huge weddings; they've been big stars and all of a sudden they're by themselves. We don't allow a minute of letdown, we shove them right up again. I go down to the bar and get all the new couples together talking about their weddings. Even the people who pick them up at the airport are instructed to do that. You certainly don't want them to get depressed here!"

Too, at other resorts not devoted exclusively to newlyweds—Puerto Rico, say, or Miami Beach—honeymooners are conspicuous, often the object of chuckling attention; yet, at the same time, they are left utterly alone, under the mistaken notion that they prefer it that way. Isolated, thrust into an enforced intimacy that they are not ready to handle, they are frequently miserable and will rush back to spend the remainder of their honeymoon at Cove Haven.

Here they have constant and myriad programmed activities; if they so choose (and most do), they never have to be alone together except to sleep. There's a sexy atmosphere but still lots to do to keep them away from the dread bed. A daily schedule of horseback riding at eleven, volleyball at one, bowling at two-thirty, bingo at three—on and on until the wee hours—fills time and dispels the existential angst arising from total freedom. Although, on the surface, it seems that a couple is exercising free will ("Shall we do water skiing at two or play Ping-Pong?"), the subtle reality is that the basic choices are being made for them—just as for children in summer camp—by the Big Daddy benevolent management. And, of course, that is precisely what they want, what makes them feel secure. They are assigned a specific table in the dining room, served the same food as everybody around, told what to wear, what's right, how to have fun, how to make friends. It's just like home, really—lots of rules and lots of hand-holding. And lots of nice young couples, just like themselves.

> Every bride is a belle-of-the-bath in Honeymoon Haven's eye-widening baths. A sense of Roman splendor and nice naughtiness. You'll acquire a "Peaches and Cream" glow lying on the chaise longue under the ultra violet ray sun-lamp. To your bathing is added a little dash—a little daring.
>
> —Honeymoon Haven brochure

Lounging on blankets by the heart-shaped pool are two couples who met that morning on the speedboat ride. The girls are wearing modest two-piece bathing suits; the guys both wear Hawaiian-printed trunks and have bellies. Conversation is animated and of the oft-heard "My-wedding-was-bigger-than-your-wedding" variety.

"I had six bridesmaids, six ushers, two main ushers, two preachers, a flower girl, a ring bearer, a maid of honor and a matron of honor," says the eighteen-year-old file clerk from Richmond, Virginia. "We did somethin' nobody's ever done before in that church. We had a whole archway of flowers goin' down the aisle, and my flower girl went ahead of me, droppin' aqua and pink petals from her bouquet."

"Oh, we didn't go that far," confesses the undaunted beautician from Farmingdale, Long Island, "but we had a sit-down dinner for a hundred people and we bought our bridesmaids lingerie, real nice gifts. We paid good for them."

The four talk a great deal about money. They admit mutual, naïve surprise at discovering that drinks at the bar are not included in the basic package, and as a result they hardly drink ("maybe one a day, when they have the cocktail-hour special for eighty-five cents"). They articulate an insistence on getting "every damn penny's worth," thus also explaining the frenetic dash from one "free" activity to the next. And their minds are utterly blown by the unaccustomed luxury of having their beds made by somebody else.

"And THREE pools," says one awestruck groom, a foreman in a printing plant. Cagey Morris, with that intuitive sense of Who the Customer Is that marks the true genius salesman, keeps building pools—wherever he has a spare foot of land and an extra couple of bucks. He clearly understands that, to his young blue-collar clientele, a swimming pool is the big symbol of upper-class affluence and three pools is—WOW—what status! Lovely Lake Wallenpaupack goes barren while the cement and chlorine playpen packs 'em in.

I ask the quartet their feelings about the New Wedding, to which a blossoming portion of their generation is attracted. None had ever been to one or even really thought about it. "When I think of a weddin'," says the Virginia slim, "I think of somethin' that's just so heavenly and traditional. Hippie weddin's don't shock me, but they don't appeal to me."

"I think you have to be a special kind of person who likes nature a lot and likes doing your own thing and not caring what other people think," says the other bride.

"I believe in live and let live," grants one of the guys. "If somebody invited me to a wedding like that I'd go, but people expect a certain thing of you and I wouldn't ever have one myself." All nod agreement.

The scheduled activity for three o'clock that Tuesday afternoon is the Bride and Groom Game Party in the Mermaid Room (the wall decor therein consisting of portraits of famous brides of history—Martha Washington and Mrs. Jesse James, to name two—in their wedding regalia). It's presided over by Bernie Richmond, the archetypical "social director" to be found in every mountain resort west of the Alps. A true blend of Jack E. Leonard and Willy Loman, he's been trudging around the Poconos for twenty-one years. At Cove Haven, where Bernie's been Yiddishe Papa for the last eleven, he plays the piano, acts as comic M.C., pours champagne at dinner, runs the bingo game as well as the hubby bathing beauty contest, puts out *Cove Capers,* and is on duty six days and six nights a week. Although, he says, "the couples look exactly alike week after week, they never change from one year to the next," he's obviously a romantic old-timer who digs his work—to the seeming extent of having no outside life.

And he's certainly good at it—taking these silent, strained youngsters and teaching them how, at least for this moment, to have a good time, enjoy, relax, kill an hour. For the first game everybody (there are thirty-five or so couples present) stands in a big circle and passes a tray. Bernie tickles "Anchors Aweigh" on the upright, and when the music stops, whoever is holding the tray is out. Not the bounciest of diversions, I grant you, but it works. The atmosphere loosens, the children begin to chatter and twitter. Nothing *ever* raucous, perish the thought, but at least that terrible, grave stillness is gone for now. They next play a slightly suggestive game involving the holding of a balloon between one's legs and passing it to the person behind. One dumpling drops it, shrieks, "Oh, I lost my *thing!*" I gulp, terrified Bernie will respond precisely the way he does. *"I'll just bet you did!"* he bellows, and seventy married people absolutely fall apart in hilarity.

It's all a dirty joke. "Foxy" the photographer (he's called "Sneaky Pete" at Penn Hills) takes "candids" of the couples in cute positions in bed and in the tub, but they're really dressed. After dinner Bernie the host leaps onstage to announce the evening's festivities: "Okay, kids, get into something comfortable—like a bed—and come back at nine-thirty for the show." I'm the only one who flinches. The couples chortle with an embarrassed delight.

The show, this night, features one of the regulars, Dick Knight. Now, if you can imagine a comic who only works the Poconos—one rung above Appalachia on the ladder of mountain resort entertainment—and, at that, a different honeymoon nook each night of the week and, to boot, is introduced as "our very own Don Rickles," you can perhaps dig the essence of Dick Knight's talents. On the considerable other hand, the couples adore him.

The Cove Cave nightclub is, as one has come to expect, quiet. A lifeless rock band honks, nobody dances. At my table the three couples—decked out in Senior Prom finery, sipping 7-Up or long pink somethings with maraschino cherries—whisper infrequently to their mates or randomly stare at some unnamed point across the room. They rarely attempt contact with the others, and when some conversation does by chance occur, it is over almost immediately. No wonder there is a wildly excited, relief-filled roar of applause when Dick Knight takes over the focus. "*Now* we're off the hook," is the silent understanding. "Now somebody's here to entertain us, we can sit back and have a ball."

Morris says that Knight's "brilliance" is in knowing exactly what the couples like. Which is, evidently, wedding night gags and ethnic slurs. And that's the sole content of a routine that lasts for a straight hour and a half. Ten minutes of Puerto Rican jokes aimed at one boy in the audience, an air-conditioning repairman from Florida: "Hey, Santos. I saw you check in with your matched luggage—three shopping bags. . . ." "Hey, Santos, how does it feel sleeping only two in a room?" He has a trunkful of five-years-ago's Polish, Irish and you-name-it jokes which, in his barrage, may not gain in wit but do somehow become diluted in their offensiveness. Then, when his audience is primed, all hot-to-trot, really loving it, he socks the real juice of the evening to them, the honeymoon humor.

Sauntering around the tables, Knight picks the most vulnerable-looking kids to poke. "Hey, honey, I hear you got married Saturday. How come you didn't get here till Monday?" Howls of enthusiastic appreciation. "What do you do?" he asks one lad. "I'm a carpenter," he responds. "What do you know about that? Made anything lately?" The assemblage freaks out. Next he stops at a table where two of the guys are named Dick; don't even ask about the mileage he gets out of creaky "dick" jokes. . . .

His wedding night routines assume virginity, bespeak the "magic moment." Singling out a shy couple in the corner, he fastens a green spot on them, then launches into a seemingly impromptu bit: "Now we look in on the first night of Joe and Donna. She's been in the john for three hours, preparing herself for Joe. He's stretched out on their big double bed, in all of his splendor, preparing for his new wife. She comes out and says, 'Joe, we're married now. You don't have to do that anymore!' " (Masturbate, get it?) "He says, 'Donna, take that splendor off.' " This monologue rambles on and on and on, until Joe and Donna finally do the deed. That part, interestingly, is glossed over very fast and in no graphic detail whatsoever. Apparently Knight's "brilliance" intuits his audience's limits.

At the end of the show silence descends suddenly, bleakly. Some couples dance now, a very few make a move for their cottages, most just sit—oh, how to delay the long hours ahead. "They're terrified to go through that door," said the bartender (in an interview in *The New York Times*). "They watch it like it's the chopping block. I sit here and make drinks for them every night, but I don't ever get used to the apprehension they carry around with them." Whenever it is that they do finally leave the group sanctuary of the Cove Cave with this stranger, their mate, they will pass under yet another sign, this red, heart-shaped coyness proclaiming: "We Know Where You're Going."

On first thought, how bizarre this contradiction between the gross, snickering sexuality of Cove Haven and the panic-stricken innocence of its clientele, the decor's gaudiness and the drabness of its inhabitants. I can envision Mae West or Mamie Stover frolicking on a platformed purple playground, but surely not Susie and Johnnie from Wilkes-Barre. Yet, on prolonged second consideration, it seems to make peculiar sense. For all of their lives these kids have believed the classic American double message that sex is, on the one hand, dirty and on the other thunderclouds, lightning and starry-eyed fervor. Cove Haven plays out that dual fantasy every day in every way. The accoutrements at Cove Haven are sexual props, ways of making it all easier. These children would never in a million years leap together into the plain old porcelain tub at home, but the romantic valentine bath virtually beckons with siren powers. It's okay, that's what it's here for. Go ahead, enjoy.

Similarly, it's okay to have intercourse in this immense passion pit which bears no resemblance to any bed in the Real World. If we don't yet possess any of our own feelings of sensuality, Uncle Morris will provide the red velvet, heart-shaped substitutes. We may never have the nerve actually to take a peek in that round mirror looming over us, but it gives us a mighty charge knowing it's there. How can sex be bad in such gorgeous surroundings? And how can it be bad if all these nice kids—kids just like us—are also doing it?

The next morning Morris takes me on a lingering drive through the area to visit some of the other honeymoon resorts. En route, passing through the pretty, green and hilly—rather than dramatically mountainous—terrain, he tells me more of his philosophy of running Cove Haven. He never, for example, allows a couple to stay longer than one week. "After you're married seven days, you're not a newlywed, you're a vacationer, an old married couple. And that's bad for Cove Haven. You can't communicate with the brand-new marrieds. Honeymooners who got married yesterday want to be with other couples who just got married yesterday."

He's also adamant about not permitting parents on the

grounds. Sometimes they call up—generally it's the bride's mother—and pretend they're "just in the neighborhood, just passing by." It turns out they're 350 miles away but want to come up anyway, just to reassure themselves that everything's all right. He recalls one case of an engaged couple who wrote requesting reservations for themselves and both sets of parents, in adjoining cottages. And folks who take a vacation at a nearby hotel while the kids are honeymooning here, then casually pop in twice a day. When I ask whether a tiny part of his reasoning might be a dread that the folks will get a gander at the cha-cha inside the cottages, he admits it. He's right, of course.

Morris' most recent acquisition is Paradise Stream, about a half hour's drive from Cove Haven. Although it is six years old, he and partner O'Brien have had it for eight months only and, as befits their style, the changes have been splendiferous. Previously Paradise Stream was just another marble-cupided grotesquerie. Now, as we drive through the entrance, it is mid-construction of a new nightclub, double-decker dining room and—can you top this?—fifty units entitled "The Garden of Eden," each with its very own indoor kidney-shaped swimming pool! That's not to replace the ubiquitous sunken heart-shaped bathtub, fear not. It's but a glorious addition, in the never-ending search for mind-boggling glorious additions, situated somewhere between the fireplace and the bed, "not visible from outside the cottage, thus assuring your own private world of pleasure and enchantment," assures the brochure.

A small point of sociology is observed as we take our leave of Paradise Stream. The parking lot overflows with cars, all American, almost all brand-new. My eye fastens on a glistening orange baby with a rear bumper sticker: HONK IF YOU LOVE JESUS.

I am somehow amazed, on my Poconos tour this day, to find all the honeymoon spots virtually interchangeable. Okay, Penn Hills has a "No Parking, Dears Crossing" sign, a King and Queen Award for the most typical couple of the week, Cupid's Kissin' Bridge, and the pool is shaped like a wedding bell. The social hall at Pocono Gardens is called "The Grand Palazzo," the Summit Hotel has the "Cloud Nine Cocktail Lounge" and Birchwood boasts a bidet in every bathroom.

But the hidden message, the subtext behind every honeymoon nirvana nestled into Poconoland, is the same, and it goes something like this: This is it, kids, the peak in fantasy perfection. You'll never have sex in an atmosphere like this again, you'll never again be pampered and indulged this way, at any other moment, on any other vacation. It's all right here, the ultimate. One nineteen-year-old bride told me, as she was having a forest of big rollers installed by the Cove Haven hairdresser, that this week was her first—and last— chance for luxury and glitter "before life settles into that old rut." Nineteen years old and she knows, by God she expects, that in two months her life will have no further surprises, no more gorgeousness, no glamour, no adventure. She's had her Big Day in White, now she's having her bubbling heart-shaped bathtub, and that's it. That's all there is, there ain't no more. Real Life takes over next Monday.

15. The New Wedding or Power to the People

A rocky cliff overlooking the ocean in Big Sur, California, was the scene of the wedding of Ms. Myrna Schwartz of Beverly Hills to Mr. Foster DeWitt III, of Nob Hill in San Francisco. Ms. Schwartz, the daughter of renowned physician Dr. Harold Schwartz ("the brain surgeon of the stars," as he is popularly known), was, until her recent arrest for the attempted assassination of David Susskind, a student in business administration at Yale. Mr. DeWitt, otherwise known as "Eldridge," is a former student at Sarah Lawrence and the son of Foster Hubbard DeWitt II, president of United Oil, Steel, Motors, Steamship and Broadcasting Corporation of America.

The wedding, which took place at precisely 5:22 in the morning ("We want to commune with the sun, man—you know—birth, resurrection, the whole bit," articulated Mr. DeWitt), was what is today called a "New Wedding." The 369 guests made their way up the steep cliff-face by climbing hand over hand and using ropes and picks where particularly treacherous. The ceremony, performed by a defrocked priest, Father Patrick "Blow-em-up" O'Shea, had been created by the bride and groom and included readings from "The Anarchist Cookbook" (instructions for building a Molotov cocktail), "Schizophrenia and Capitalist Society," and the Marquis de Sade. Michael "Mao" MacGregor IV served as best man; Mrs. Irving Lipschitz, sister of the bride and president of the Scarsdale Radical Feminists, was matron of honor.

As the couple, clad in matching black leather jumpsuits, marched down the aisle, a contemporary musical group, The Dope Fiends, played "Theme from Hell's Angels Strike Again."

Ms. Schwartz and Mr. DeWitt are currently free on $500,000 bail and are awaiting trial for the hijacking of a TWA jet in protest of United States intervention in Monte Carlo.

Neither the bride's nor the groom's immediate family were present at the wedding.

This wedding, which may or may not ever have happened, certainly *could* have happened and surely would have been hailed by the media as the style that is sweeping the country. Rumor and *Time* magazine to the contrary, the New Wedding is hardly an epidemic on the American scene. Macrobiotic brown rice and seaweed are in no way on the verge of annihilating the pig in the blanket. But, just as a crystal-spangled extravaganza at the Huntington Town House reflects the values of the folks giving it, so the New Wedding is an emblem of the youth counter-culture.

Almost. But not quite.

Illustration: Bergdorf Goodman, an exclusive New York department store, devoted one of its front windows recently to a bride in an Indian crewel gown, wearing no shoes—the exactly correct costume for a New Wedding. It cost $500. Another emporium, Franklin Simon, has opened a bridal salon entitled "The Barefoot Bride."

Further illustration: the gala Hancock Park wedding, on Daddy's estate, of an oil scion (previously described), replete with the tossing of the I Ching, the best man reading astrological charts, and dancing of the hora.

Yet another: a very fashionable caterer of the Jewish horsey set in the suburbs of Chicago is publicizing his new service— elegant menus for the Hippie Wedding. The absolute divinest of vegetarian casseroles (eggplant and zucchini flown in from the ends of the earth), and the upper-crustiest of homemade organic bread. Since silver service would simply be déclassé for the mod squad, he boasts a pantry of imported French country crockery on which to serve the darling nibbles.

Radical chic in action? Another cutesy-poo idea for a party when we've "done" the mariachi bit and the omelet maker and the whole lambs roasted on the spit and the soul food? Certainly, but let's not be confused. The New Wedding, in its pure form, is a very real—if still infant—metaphor of change in this country. It speaks of a "greening of America," of a journey among certain pockets of youth away from fraudulence and toward a new humanism.

"Some of our ancient language simply doesn't express the meaning these kids want to express to each other when they take marriage vows," says the Reverend A. Myrvin DeLapp of Philadelphia. "Their great concern is for the honesty of the human relationship; the sense of personhood is to be honored and respected. They don't view the marriage as simply entering into a contract, nor the wedding as a performance. They want their marriage to have the fullest possible meaning, validity and integrity."

Distaste for the way one's elders do things is a classic youthful pattern. You see the failure of their dreams so you simply discard those dreams and replace them with the polar opposite. Theirs didn't work, ours will. The kids of the upwardly striving middle class, especially, have seen the hunger for The American Dream burning in their parents' eyes, have felt the heavy price they paid to reach it and, having reached it, its ultimate unsatisfactoriness. Even its destructiveness.

The New Wedding, like the counter-culture itself, is, in the main, a syndrome of children from the successful middle class. (One Boston minister reports most of his offbeat "cases" are kids from Ivy League schools who are in psychoanalysis.) The offspring of folks who have "made it" in our traditional American terms and in whose bosom bloodless revolution is tacitly permissible, and small rejections are understood not to rend the family fabric. The rebellion is against what the kids consider a dearth of values and values of the wrong kind. It is a rejection of plastic, of false emotion, of obsession with material things to validate who we are, of sterility, of hollow forms, of competitiveness, of white bread, of super-technology, of isolation. In theory, the New Wedding is spontaneous, without artifice and "personally relevant" (an expression that is used as often in this crowd as is "dearly beloved" in the black-tie set). Sometimes even in practice. It is often, this sort of pageant, moving and irresistible and indeed "personally relevant." Sometimes it is self-conscious and ludicrous. I have seen both.

There is a myth afoot in the land that youngsters of the new consciousness have no sense of romantic love, that their relationships mostly consist of leaping from bed to bed with the capricious speed of fleas hopping from one dog to another. "Doing your own thing," it is believed, implies living only for the moment, for the peak experience, eschewing concepts like "future" and "commitment" and "responsibility." Couples move in with each other easily, swiftly, moving out with the same ease, only to be replaced before the mattress is yet cool. Musical sheets. Those few who stay together surely do not do anything as mundane as getting married.

But, according to a Manhattan rabbi who has performed over five hundred weddings, all of them of the "new" species, every one of his couples has been living together previously, but still—to smash the mythology—opt for marriage. For all the reasons that people want to get married. "The new wedding is more a ceremony to confirm what a couple has found by living together rather than to make promises about what they hope will happen," says Rev. William Glenesk, the Brooklyn clergyman who joined Tiny Tim to Miss Vicki. A celebration of what is already there, a public reaffirmation of the commitment and continuity, rather than a beginning. "We don't believe that our wedding is going to be the most important event in our life together," quoted one bride in the *Los Angeles Times,* "and we don't believe that a wedding makes you a married couple."

Does it seem paradoxical then that the loveliest of the new weddings are extremely romantic, poignant in a way that the American matrimonial machinery has otherwise demolished? To the degree that today's traditional American weddings are fixated on a thousand concerns other than the relationship of two people, that the issue of should the chopped liver be beef or chicken transcends—no, obliterates—the issue of the vows, that is the degree of our dehumanization.

So the key word in the new wedding is "meaningful." "I had never been to a wedding that had any meaning at all until the past year or so," says one girl who has recently gotten married on a beach in Virginia. "When Tom and I planned our wedding, we talked about all the formal church and hotel affairs we'd been to—those of friends and relatives—and realized how empty they were. Phony, with all that etiquette junk and everything done for the parents who just wanted to show off for their friends. You never knew what the couple was like and you never cared. And there was no real joy at all. We knew we wanted to have something that would be more than just another drunken party, something uniquely ours."

What seems to be most "meaningful" to the new breed is the beauty of an outdoor setting. Beaches, hilltops, meadows, parks, in caves, on rocks. Free space. Serenity. (Anyway, few kids attend church in their daily lives, and nobody's been inside a synagogue since his bar mitzvah, so that environment would seem as false as a catering hall.) The *Goodbye, Columbus* revelers spend $5000 transforming the Plaza ballroom into a forest; these kids simply use the forest. And the setting naturally dictates the tone of the fete. One cannot quite summon up visions of haughty white-gloved waiters trooping through the sand dunes with silver trays of miniature quiche lorraine, or a trumpety band blasting out the strains of a bossa nova through the Grand Canyon. Or a bride in Piccione lace and satin greeting her chiffoned guests in a receiving line—on top of a rock. The setting indeed sets the tone and thus the new weddings are natural and informal.

So is the food. Wine or even milk has killed off Jack Daniels, and the vittles are so virtuous as to make one pant for a lead-filled ravioli. Organic everything is the order of the day. Goat cheese, homemade yogurt, soybean concoctions, stone-ground bread, health-food brownies. One would kill for a knish. "The hardest thing for me to get used to in these new weddings," says one minister in San Francisco, "is how lousy the food is. The kids may like all this organic stuff, and I'm sure it's good for you, but I just can't face honey on *everything*. As a matter of fact, everything they serve is just like what I eat when I have the flu!"

(At a wedding on a hilltop outside Denver, an array of various salads was created and we guests commanded to eat with our fingers, right from the huge communal bowls. The only liquid available was a tragic blend of wine and beer.)

The most graphic departure from the conventional American wedding scheme is that the new frontier has usurped control from their parents. Normally the event is unquestionably in Mother's hands, or perhaps really in the caterer's. Surely there is no space in a multimillion-dollar spectacle for self-expression and spontaneity, so the bride bows out under the tidal pressures of money and minutiae. That's the unspoken bargain between mama and daughter. But the conventional wedding is not "personally relevant," so it is said—at least not to the two people who are being married. And the new wedding is, in spirit, a statement about who the bride and groom are. Mother is but another guest.

Self-expression and spontaneity. Who ever heard of it at the Beverly Hills Hotel or the Houston Country Club or even on the grounds of Daddy's Connecticut estate with the tennis courts tented for the dancing? (Footnote: Weddings on Daddies' estates *do not* qualify as New Weddings, even though they are outdoors.) But the theme of this wedding as an expression of who the couple is permeates the day. Dress, for example, is of the anything-goes school, and men—as a FIRST in wedding history—are encouraged to groove, the rebel grooms looking easily as zingy as their brides. I attended one dune-top frolic where the boy, clad in the smashingest getup of white satin bell-bottoms, white boots and a balloon-sleeved silk shirt that didn't omit one color in the entire spectrum, received the awed gasps classically reserved for the bride. She, you see, was bedecked only in your ordinary white suede hooded monk's robe and was completely overshadowed.

A new wedding is an exercise in Do-It-Yourself. And not just for the bride, but also the guests, who are thought of as significant participants, instead of passive audience. One doesn't invite fringe people to this intimate day—none of Father's business accounts or Mother's bowling team will clutter *this* hilltop with indifference. Only true loved ones to share and care. And join in, not merely on the dance floor or in polishing off the prime ribs remnants, but in the essence of the wedding.

—A prominent New York psychiatrist's son married the girl he had been living with for three years and the wedding consisted of an encounter group where the twenty-odd guests all sat on the floor in a circle and shared anecdotes from their own relationship with the couple, as a gift in understanding. Much hugging and crying and primal kissing took place, and everybody remembers it as "a beautiful ceremony."

—At one wedding the bride and groom walked through the assemblage, handing out flowers to everybody, then passed their rings around while they and the rabbi sat on the grass and held a breezy chat (which turned out to be the only vows) about marriage and air pollution.

—On a beach in New Hampshire the minister encouraged the guests to express anything they felt about the bride and groom during the ceremony. The response was spontaneous, to be sure—one young woman burst forth with the news that she had always, until this moment, believed her dearest friend had made a terrible choice and that the groom was in fact a jerk, but that she was beginning to change her mind.

The notion of Do-It-Yourself (with a little help from your friends) begins from the beginning—with the invitations. Sometimes they are in the form of a scroll, sometimes a mobile, even a message written on hard-boiled eggs. They are generally original, hand-made and highly personal. "We have found ourselves in each other and want you to share the ceremony of commitment to our love," stated the hand-printed prelude to a classic new wedding held in Los Angeles' rustic Topanga Canyon. Linda, the bride, made her own white peasant dress and her groom's white pants festooned with yellow ribbons; she composed a song for the ceremony and together they wrote their vows; each of their friends contributed some organic tidbit to the feast (including a wheat-flour wedding cake), and folk dancing to the music of an Autoharp continued long into the night. "All the work that went into it," reminisces Linda, "was a true labor of love and we felt that the wedding expressed the feelings that all of us have for each other."

The new gifts are as far afield of the rococo silver samovar as the commune from a condominium. If they are not yet the manure spreaders advocated by the *Whole Earth Catalog*, they are at least as contemporary and utilitarian—like the delicate glass hashish pipe. And often they are handmade—quilts, candles, pottery, jewelry. A California group called the Los Altos Neighborhood Conservationists published a mimeographed sheet called "For a New Life, a New Life-Style Wedding Plans"—a sort of renegade Amy Vanderbilt adviser—with hints for gifts that include a wicker basket filled with biodegradable cleaning agents, or "soul gifts"—season concert tickets, gift certificate to a plant nursery, a course at a university. They recommend not giving the mechanical gadgetry that overkills our lives and makes every newlywed's kitchen resemble a Sears, Roebuck warehouse—the electric bread warmers, the fondue pots, those frills that alienate us in small but cumulative ways from our hands and the sources of our satisfactions. Instead, in this spirit of self-help, they suggest gifts of garden tools and seed packets, ice cream makers, a supply of various flours and pans for baking bread.

The conventional middle-class American wedding serves as a reconciliation—at least for one day—of disparate elements within the family. The two brothers who have loathed each other for twenty years because each insists the other screwed him in business bury their hatchets in the veal Parmesan; octogenarian great-aunts are invited to waltz by young lads who can't even remember the Korean War. Folks who in normal life have nothing much to say to one another today somehow find a commonality. And the inevitable, inexorable war of the generations is called to a temporary cease-fire on this meeting ground where for once everybody's needs seem to jibe.

But the New Wedding stretches the parental/offspring generation gap into a continental divide. When I was in college the most defiant gesture I could make, the apex of rebellion against my background, was to date a black boy (who was then called a Negro). Today, I am told, what with liberal guilt, that act is no longer guaranteed to send a white Mother to the Nembutal. The announcement, however, that you are abandoning her lifetime plans for The Wedding and having a barefoot gypsy fest on a Big Sur rock surely will. She does not, cannot, understand; you are stamping on her sand castle of dreams and, in truth, challenging everything in which she believes. You are also demolishing tradition, and that is frightening.

In *Fiddler on the Roof*, each of Tevye's three daughters defies the established nuptial customs—the first by marrying the boy she loves instead of the arranged match, the second by not asking her father's permission, the third by marrying a Gentile. "Because of our tradition," Tevye says, "everyone knows who he is and what God expects of him," and each time he is sorely threatened by the collapse of the rules by which he lives.

But his misery and that of the mother described above also emanate from the inescapable message that they have lost power over their children. The wedding is the rite of passage that symbolizes the end of their child's childhood and dependence. Unconsciously they prepare themselves for the inevitable, just as we unconsciously prepare ourselves for pain before an operation. But parents *do* see the wedding as their day, the final chapter that *they* are the authors of, and to disrupt these ingrained assumptions is to cause an earthquake of major proportions.

Usually the quake takes the form of Mama summoning up the old head-in-the-oven number, and if that doesn't work (as it generally doesn't anymore—the new species of youth does not seem to have guilt as its prime mover), Daddy threatens withdrawal of the purse. Then several things may happen: (1) as in the story of the New England society lass who announced that she and boyfriend intended to consummate the marriage in front of the assembled guests, Mother fainted, Daddy made the classic threat, lass reconsidered and got married in the Episcopal church in a $600 Priscilla frock, saving the lust for later; (2) the parents do not come to the wedding, so disgraced are they and so unthinkable is it for them to accept the horror; (3) a compromise is made, as in the Long Island two-ceremony wedding—the first in the woods, with flutes, Indian drums and original poetry, followed instantly by a standard service and reception within the gilded confines of Leonard's of Great Neck. Or the one in a Japanese restaurant in L.A. where the bride's psychiatrist (who was also a mail-order minister) performed the ceremony, and the ensuing reception feast of tongue and pastrami was served by mincing ladies in kimonos.

The most commonly seen denouement of the drama is that the folks relinquish, bitterly, and finally attend this peculiar happening over which they have had no dominion. I would like to tell you that they get caught up in the spirit, groove on the jubilation and freedom and ultimately understand and accept. Mostly, I am sorry to say, they do not. Mostly they hate every moment.

Not too long ago I attend a New Wedding in the woods of Malibu Canyon, just north of Los Angeles. The setting is lovely, utterly removed from any vestiges of city life, and the day is sunny, balmy. Virginia and Ken, the couple, are in their early twenties and have lived together for about a year; he is a film editor and she works in a plant store; they are both from L.A. and Jewish. Although Virginia's family knows that she has been living with Ken, they still expected her to have a veritable Barnum and Bailey spectacular at one of the local hotels, and a great rift followed her declaration of wedding intentions. But tempers eased and now both sets of parents are present, along with a dozen or so close relations and fifty of the couple's friends.

One has to park the car at the bottom of a rolling grassy hill and walk for about half a mile, the hill changing to woods, then back to hill. Lining the path and sitting poised in several trees are young friends playing soft rock tunes on flutes, guitars and harmonicas. The scene is idyllically beautiful and the aura of open friendliness and joy is pure, un-trammeled by the robot presence of banquet managers or the rigor mortis of etiquette edicts. I saunter up the hill, feeling the magic of the day, and almost immediately have my first confrontation of many with the generation chasm. It seems that behind me the bride's aunt Florence, wearing a pink brocade Hadassah gown, has caught the heel of her pink satin shoe in a tree root and now she wants to go home. I don't know whether I feel like laughing or sympathizing, so terror-stricken is she about this wedding, so incapable of bending to it, flowing with it, even seeing how inescapably pretty and sweet it is.

But then, nothing that occurs this day bears any familiarity for Aunt Florence. The bride does not march down an aisle, enveloped in trick lighting; she is standing on the hill when we arrive, wearing a long peasanty dress made of patchwork tablecloths, no shoes and a coronet of daffodils. Ken is splendid in orange-and-yellow-striped bell-bottoms and a fringed Apache vest and a matching daffodil headpiece. All the friends are dressed flamboyantly, exuberantly, as if for a fabulous costume revelry. Bare midriffs, leather shorts, gypsy wildnesses. The clothes of the counter-culture have become—as they say in the world of *Vogue*—"a fashion story."

The elders, of course, are in their spiffiest wedding finery—except for one or two chic matrons in peasant frocks from Beverly Hills boutiques, who are urgently "With It."

People are talking, drinking wine, joints are being passed with some discretion (I cannot tell whether the older generation detects, but certainly nobody hands one to Aunt Florence), and both sets of parents are trying, they are really trying—desperately, with smiles frozen like the masks of comedy. Soon a rabbi appears—one of the "hippie rabbis," as they are known around L.A., not because they themselves are hippies, mind you, but because they do this kind of wedding—and the joints are extinguished. (This cleric has insisted ahead of time that no pot smoking take place while he is on the premises; Rabbi Bruce Goldman in New York prefers the presence of marijuana to cigarettes or alcohol.)

At some point everybody casually sits down on the grass (chairs have been provided for Aunt Florence, et al.) in a circle around Ken and Virginia and the rabbi, and easy rapping just sort of flows into the "ceremony." A young girl carrying an infant (which she periodically nurses in front of everybody during the day) hands the child to somebody, picks up a guitar and sings a Joni Mitchell ballad in a clear soprano. The rabbi then recites some familiar lines from *The Prophet* that begin "Love one another but make not a bond of love . . ."

Virginia speaks a Carl Sandburg poem, looking lovingly into Ken's eyes: "But leave me a little love/A voice to speak to me in the day's end/A hand to touch me in the dark room/Breaking the long long loneliness." Now, so far everything is terribly romantic and touching and even the elders, poised stiffly in wooden chairs, their regal hairdos and garbs successfully defying the strong breeze to make them budge— even they are moved. After all, Ali and Ryan in *Love Story* read Elizabeth Barrett Browning to each other in their nuptials, so it must be sort of okay.

But then the recitation takes a turn away from the schmaltzy, a bizarre turn with Ken and Virginia together reciting the Fritz Perls "Gestalt Prayer": "I do my thing, and you do your thing./I am not in this world to live up to your expectations/And you are not in this world to live up to mine./ You are you and I am I, and if by chance we find each other, it's beautiful." (The last line, "If not, it can't be helped," was tactfully omitted from the reading.) The families start to twitch nervously and glance around at each other over their shoulders in unspoken *you-see-I-knew-it* looks of anger.

Then something incredible happens, something awful, the coalescence of everybody's terrors of how this debauchery would turn out. Okay, maybe all these hippies aren't screwing on the grass or going berserk on LSD or all those other things that these kids do, but suddenly this strange ceremony —not even a word of Hebrew, or a "for better or worse"— suddenly it gets POLITICAL. Virginia stands up and reads from Emma Goldman on Woman's Suffrage, all about "asserting herself as a personality and not as a sex commodity" and "refusing the right to anyone over her body" and "refusing to bear children, unless she wants them" and "refusing to be a servant to God, the State, society, the husband, the family . . ." And the kids shout *"Right on, sister,"* and the family drops dead.

In ancient Jewish lore, when a girl marries a Gentile, she is declared dead by the father and, in effect, is treated as such forever. Virginia—I see by the faces of the judges on the chairs, faces at once iced and terrified—has just been pronounced a corpse. When, at the end, the couple shatters the traditional glass, adding the hope that the noise will drive away the repressive forces in our society like Nixon and Agnew—well, hardly anybody even notices. They are all comatose.

The party following is jolly, with lots of group singing and folk dancing and the playing of games like Spin the Bottle and Pin the Tail on the Donkey, and an organic feast which includes fruit salad, homemade breads, the invariable honey-in-the-comb. The only incongruous note is the presence of a whole roast suckling pig, which reclines dead-center in the mélange of food—like a gigantic middle finger pointed upward.

The pig is just one more stab to the older generation, who has not yet recovered from Emma Goldman, and their rage and confusion suffuses the otherwise joyful ambiance. I am saddened by the real depths of the breach—they cannot step down off their chairs and the kids cannot understand or lessen their pain. As a final event, Ken and Virginia open the gifts—a gesture hopefully meant to involve both planets —but even there the barriers prevail. One present is a garish cut-crystal something—a bowl, or a decanter, or a lamp, it's hard to tell which—and the next is a membership in Zero Population Growth.

Mother tries hard throughout the day but finally falls apart, goes limp. I go over to her as she is sipping some rose-petal soup and it is as if she is in shock. "This has nothing to do with anything I've come to associate with a wedding," she mourns. "I don't know what to do here and to tell you the truth, I don't really believe they're even married."

(What the lady doesn't realize, of course, is that the New Wedding is nothing if not a direct throwback to the past, to the style in which *everybody* got married before the entrance of the church and the caterer. All weddings took place outdoors, were cooperative ventures with the whole tribe or village sharing in the experience, the feast and gifts and decorations hand-wrought. The rebel youth, it appears, in their rejection of their parents' vision of The Good Life, have instinctively turned back to pure folklore, to a sense of the communal and a way that seems to them richer, more natural.)

In most American weddings today the content of the ceremony is shunted into oblivion by the other concerns. The clergyman distantly invokes the impersonal verbiage over a couple he barely knows, and the guests click off 95 percent of their brains much in the same way that we sing "The Star-Spangled Banner" at baseball games. And they pass those moments fantasizing the roast chicken or concentrating on Cousin Selene's new leopard coat, and before you know it (a smart clergyman knows not to tax his audience's patience by prolonging his spiel), it's over and one can get on with the real business of the wedding.

The heart of the New Wedding, on the other hand, is the ceremony. The couple's own unique expression of commitment and consecration, the statement they wish to make before their friends and family about themselves, each other and their lives. And with the same spirit that they usurped the reins from their parents, they take them away from the clergyman whose role they see as catalyst, not absolute monarch.

"Most weddings have little to do with marriage and that is kind of sad," says Rabbi Bruce Goldman. "One can go, for example, from one Jewish wedding to another, listen to the ceremony and never learn anything during the entire event about who the two people are entering marriage; their hopes, aspirations, fears and hesitations, their moods, or who they are, where they have been and where they are going." Rabbi Goldman, a young Afro-haired, bearded cleric who looks more like the student radical than most of his customers, feels that the building of a wedding ceremony helps the couple to understand and confront more deeply all the elements of their relationship. "People who write their own vows are thinking more about each other than what they're going to get as gifts," he says.

With individuality the touchstone, the ceremonies can be anything. But anything. Reading from sources as varied as the Bible, Tennyson, Goethe or Eldridge Cleaver; vows that are totally original, or no vows at all. At one wedding on a suburban lawn in Great Neck, New York, as reported by Rabbi Goldman, two former SDS members said, in unison, the following: "We have only two things to say. One is that we decided against including in the ceremony any kind of speech about what our lives or our marriage are supposed to be about—the way we live should show that. The other is that in the ceremony the man buys his wife. We believe in the liberation of women."

Sometimes the clergyman just sits on the ground and raps with the couple and after a while says, "You are now married." I witnessed two kids turn to each other adoringly and repeat the Boy Scout oath, reaching a grand emotional climax with the "thrifty, brave, clean and reverent" part. Occasionally the "personal relevancy" is so intimate as to sound like an excerpt from *The Sensuous Woman*.

Frequently these days the messages are political. In one ceremony the following was heard: "I, George, take thee, Agnes, to be my wife, to work for the liberation of all peoples." In another, the "chuppa" was a black and red flag —the symbol of revolution and anarchy.

Whatever the script created, most kids of the new world prefer that God be mentioned as little as possible.

The music, too, is who knows what. I have heard everything from Rodgers and Hart to *Hair,* from the Rolling Stones to the "Indian Love Call," crooned to one another by a couple who were not exactly MacDonald and Eddy. As the Vatican has banned the secular "Here Comes the Bride" and Mendelssohn's pagan "Wedding March," Purcell's "Trumpet Voluntary" has become the new hit tune in Catholic nuptial masses.

If the New Wedding defines the newlyweds' vision of marriage, then one thing becomes clear: these kids have as lofty expectations, as much hope and optimism about their futures, as anybody getting married in America. But they also bear a new sense of adult reality, a sense that married life is not quite what the bridal magazines are hawking. Vows frequently stress deep friendship and self-growth rather than roses and perfect union. And foreverness is dead: "till death us do part" invariably replaced by less permanent portents, like "so long as I am able" or "as long as our love endures" or "as long as we dig it." One couple announced mid-ceremony that they would keep their own names and she would not ask for alimony if they got divorced.

(Are these goings-on legal, one is often asked? The notion is, I suppose, that we've heard the standard litany so many times it must be necessary in order to sanctify the marriage. In fact, the only requirement of law for a wedding—that is, after the license and blood test, etc.—is that the couple announce their intent, a recognized official publicly affirm that intent and the witnesses sign the papers. Everything else that we've come to associate with the wedding ritual is essentially whipped cream.)

The new clergyman is as offbeat as the rites he encourages—or sometimes insists upon. He dispenses with the ecclesiastical rhetoric on which he was weaned and talks from the pulpit as if he were talking on the phone. Rev. Cecil Williams in San Francisco wears a dashiki to weddings, Bruce Goldman a blue jeans suit. (Goldman, too, has said that weddings held in synagogue turn him off.) Rev. Al Carmines in Manhattan has been quoted as saying that the wedding of a pregnant girl is "joyous" and Rev. B. D. Napier, at Stanford University, says: "I became increasingly uneasy with a wedding ceremony that doesn't speak to us now. The company assembled needs to be reminded that this ceremony takes place in a world of trouble."

Perhaps the oddest crazy quilt of styles belongs to Rabbi Will Kramer, who could be Zero Mostel's bearded double and officiates at virtually all of the new nuptials in Los Angeles. At his ceremonies he wears long robes and a prayer shawl and his voice is awesome, booming, Talmudic. But what comes out of his mouth is jarringly peppered with Hip, like, "I feel good vibes from you, Johnnie"—which he then translates into Yiddish for the older audience, coming on like a nervous Catskills comic. Then, as we sit in his home, flanked by a vast collection of biblical artifacts, he tells me that he believes marriages should be arranged like in the old days and that he will not perform a marriage between Jew and Gentile unless the children will be raised Jewish. But, as I am leaving, his parting sentiment echoes in my head: "Weddings are a high. Anything I can do to help people kick loneliness for friendship turns me on." And I pound the side of my skull with my palm, to shake out the confusion as if it were seawater.

If this handful of unorthodox, renegade clergymen scattered throughout the country doesn't share Dr. Kramer's apparent identity schisms, they *are* nonetheless in transition, trying to respond to the changing needs of their flocks. Most, these days, no longer perform traditional weddings—but then, as their "irreverent" styles have become widely celebrated (or notorious), most are not asked very often these days.

Undoubtedly, more New Weddings would take place—or at least more deviations from the established formal structures—if religion was more flexible. Most churches, however, are governed by rigid dogma from which individual clerics cannot swerve and for which reform comes so agonizingly slowly that by the time the battle is declared over the soldiers have long since deserted. But the overwhelming majority of American kids, we know from statistics, *want* to be married in church or to have a sacramental service, even in a hotel. So the old ways carry on and even the changes are too little, too late.

I have spoken with many clergymen of all faiths on this subject, and a singular voice seems to emerge, incorporating the same sentiments: the traditional wedding is good, appropriate, a fortress against the breakdown of family life; in uniformity there is strength, in rebellion chaos; to create one's own vows is to castrate the church; the liturgy as it stands insures dignity and solemnity, any departures save those few instituted by the church itself imply blasphemy. (Every church is revising the liturgy, but only in terms of modernizing the language.)

None of the theologians consulted by random choice had ever been to a New Wedding and none had ever even been asked to make a major alteration in his service.

The Episcopal Church has the most stringent edicts of all. "We have a form of service we *must* use at a wedding," says the Reverend Terence Finlay, of St. Bartholomew's in Manhattan. "We cannot change the ceremony to suit the whims of either ourselves or the people getting married. Also we

must use acceptable religious music, and only an organ."
The church has made microscopic changes, namely in the
addition of a shortened service that eliminates the "dreadful
day of judgment" line. "But we've had no requests to use
it," says the Reverend, "although people know it exists. We
still use the old one, which we've had since 1928." (At which
time, incidentally, "obey" was deleted from the text.)

Other limbs of Protestantism are more lenient, as they
do not fall under the ruling thumb of a bishop—as do the
Episcopal and also Catholic clergy. Methodists, Congrega-
tionalists, Baptists and Unitarians are more or less free to
make their own individual decisions. The Presbyterians, as
explained to me by Dr. David Read at the Madison Avenue
Presbyterian Church in New York, hover somewhere in
between. "I have the authority to devise an entirely new
marriage service, but I could be reproved if somebody com-
plained to the presbytery [the higher-ups]. We have a definite
doctrine of what comprises a Christian marriage, and my job
is to represent the view of the church in the ceremony. So
even if the couple wants to create everything they will say
as vows, I'm not going to rewrite what *I* say. It's their service,
naturally, but it's also a service of the church."

The most radical changes have been in the Catholic Church
where, since 1970, religious intermarriages can be performed
at a Nuptial Mass, by both the Catholic priest and the
minister of the other faith. Then, too, the non-Catholic no
longer has to make formal promise to raise his children
Catholic. For the ceremony, four choices of vows now exist
and thirty different scriptural readings. The declaration of
consent by the bride and groom becomes central, instead of
the priest's interrogation, and fidelity is now for the first
time an obligation of the husband as well as his wife. The
music for a Nuptial Mass offers a range of options, particularly since the banning of Wagner and Mendelssohn.
Much sacred music has been composed for guitar since the

1960's—and one New York City priest reports hearing a
medley of Beatles tunes played by guitar and organ—at
another church, naturally.

For Reform and Conservative Jews, the wedding service
is entirely a matter of custom. There is no hierarchy of
power, no Big Daddy to hand-slap for transgression, no ceremony written out which must be followed to the letter.
Tradition dictates the key features—sipping of wine, Hebrew
benedictions, the breaking of the glass. Among Orthodox
Jews, a New Wedding is, of course, as likely as a B.L.T. on
toast.

The fastest-growing church in America is one called the
Metropolitan Community Church, in existence only since
1968 but already with branches in thirty-four cities. While
the major organized religions often seem to be embedded
in dusty structures, frequently impeding growthful personal
or social trust rather than mirroring or aiding it, this new
church, ministering to all Christian denominations, reflects
another swelling social tide taking place today—the movement toward liberation and equality. Metropolitan Community Church is run for and by homosexuals.

Our society has always treated homosexuals as pariahs,
moral spiders, some loathsome form of subhuman species;
their degradation is built in to the rubric of our psyches
and our laws. When Troy Perry, a young Pentecostal minister
in Florida, was expelled from the church for divorcing his
wife of ten years and admitting he was gay ("Ministers believe you can't be gay and a Christian too," he says), he came
to Los Angeles, placed an ad in the local homophile newspaper for a church service to be held in his home, to which
twelve dubious individuals came and contributed a total of
$4.18. He now commands a huge church building in Los
Angeles, ten thousand members throughout the country, and
says, "We would be even bigger if we could find enough

gay ministers." (All of M.C.C.'s pastors were once establishment clerics—the Reverend Sandmire in San Francisco was a Mormon, the Chicago minister a High Anglican—and secret homosexuals.)

The function of this church is that of the gay liberation movement: to instill pride and eliminate guilt, to lead homosexuals out from the closet and into the mainstream, to engender political change. In this new spirit of openness Perry and his fellow ministers have been performing an ever-increasing number of marriage ceremonies between homosexuals.

In most states there are no laws against two people of the same sex marrying. But emotions are frequently stronger than legality, and public feeling has thus far prevented all attempts of gay couples to marry in the eyes of the state. Where they have tested—that is, gone to City Hall and applied for a license—they have been rejected on the grounds of "tradition." In Kentucky, where the laws against sodomy have been invoked as prevention, a couple who had been refused a license went to the state Supreme Court and was again turned down.

As it is not legally recognized, and since none of the practical purposes for marriage apply—no children, no protection of property, no tax benefits (although the Reverend Perry says gay couples have been getting away with filing joint returns, "since the computer is not yet set up to differentiate between a straight and a gay tax form")—why do it? Why, in this day when lots of folks who *could* get married are choosing to live together instead, go through the motions of a mock wedding ceremony?

The answers are as complex as for any heterosexual twosome. For the Reverend Perry, a militant activist, it's political: "I want to be able to do anything that any other citizen of the United States can do, whether it's work for the government, or serve in the army or get married." But most of his flock, including several with whom I've spoken, verbalize hungers for stability and respectability that clearly outweigh abstract concerns.

"The words 'we're married' take away some of the stigma of homosexuality, the belief that we're just promiscuous cruisers. At least with other gay people they do." Bob, who has spoken, is fingering an ornately carved gold wedding band, the twin of which is worn by Hank, sitting across the room. We are in their small apartment in Venice, California —a beach town noted for its huge homosexual as well as hippie population. They were married two weeks ago by the Reverend Perry in, what becomes increasingly clear to me as we talk, an urgent move to hold their affair together, a last-stand barricade against the temptations and nihilistic patterns of the gay life.

Bob and Hank—young, exceedingly attractive and never unaware of that attractiveness in themselves and in each other—confirm every stereotype I had ever held, and discarded several years ago, about the lifestyle of the homosexual. Their candor portrays—as true for them—that tragic cliché of gay relationships as being short-lived, tempestuous, promiscuous, superficial. In their particular corner of that world, an affair that lasts a month is cause for flag-waving; most of their friends are unattached and "have" a remarkable average of ten different guys a week, wherein sex is fleeting, instantaneous and singularly obsessive. The center of life is the gay bar, its *raison d'être* solely for making sexual connections, and its proliferation through Venice making it harder to avoid sex than to find it. "The guys in there don't care if you say you're in love with someone else," bemoans Hank, "even if they see the ring on your finger. They say, 'Oh, come on, it's just for the moment,' and you think, 'Why not, it's just for the moment.' After all, you don't have kids, no plans for the future, nothing to really tie you down or give you a sense of permanency."

So the ring becomes a chastity belt—enforced faithfulness

when internal fortitude isn't enough. Like taping one's mouth with Band-Aids when on a diet. The way these two men see it, the temptations of the flesh are more feverish than the ephemeral concept of fidelity. Having split up many times in the two years they have been together—in wrenching bloodbaths, always related to promiscuity or paranoid jealousy thereof—they have gotten married "to help keep it together more, to feel more secure with each other" and as a constant reminder of why one shouldn't devour that chocolate cake sitting right over there, beckoning.

When I recount this story to Pat and Jan, two women in their late twenties who are about to get married in a few weeks, they are slightly contemptuous—with that people-like-that-give-us-a-bad-name annoyance. They, by contrast, lead a quiet social life in which most of their friends are other gay couples who have been together for a while, are faithful to one another and do not go to bars. Their explanation of why gay female involvements seem to be more stable than male is the classic double standard: gay men have the same libertine orientation toward promiscuity as straight men, while women are more reticent.

Pat and Jan are churchgoers, active members of M.C.C., and their wanting to be married stems from a desire to have their love blessed in the eyes of God. They are having a small, informal wedding, just twelve friends, and neither of their families is being told. Jan's parents do not know she is gay, and although Pat's mother does, being present at her daughter's wedding would finish her. (Both of these women and Hank and Bob were heterosexual until their mid-twenties; two have been married heterosexually, and Bob has two children.)

Right after I meet with Pat and Jan, I attend a wedding of two women in the church sanctuary. It is a hot Saturday afternoon and the huge church is decorated simply with scatterings of flowers and satin bows on the pews. Besides myself, there are only four guests in the cavernous room, two female couples both in the old-fashioned lesbian role-playing tradition: one member is "feminine," the other is a "butch" in men's garb, distorting her "masculinity" into caricature.

As the ceremony begins, the minister (the Reverend Perry's assistant) enters in a long black robe, and from the side, appearing with customary groom's anonymity, two men enter, middle-aged, broad and swaggering. One wears a white cutaway, the other is in matching yellow, and I am baffled about who they are. The best man? An usher? It is several minutes before I realize that they are both, in fact, women and that the person in white is the "groom." (Terminology is thorny here. If the roles were not so exaggeratedly defined by the women themselves, I suppose I would refer to both as "bride." Perhaps I should anyway. A semantic dilemma.)

The processional starts. A lady in long yellow chiffon, carrying a bouquet of carnations, steps stiffly up the aisle, trying futilely to remain with the organ's beat. She is also trying to hold back the dam of tears that has just exploded and that will build to flood line by the end of the ten-minute service. She is the "bride's" mother.

Following her in parade are a teen-ager—the bride's sister—and an aunt, both in flowing, graceful yellow gowns. It is obviously a very formal, very traditional wedding. Except for the uncontrolled mother, the faces are unreadable.

Then the organ strikes up "Here Comes the Bride." And down the aisle, on the arm of an elderly husky man in a tuxedo, floats an uncommonly beautiful, tiny angel in white lace, long train, veil. She cannot be one minute over seventeen and could easily be the star of *Bikini Beach Party* or the winner of the Miss High School America contest. She is—astoundingly, bizarrely—the embodiment of the perfect fantasy American bride. Radiant, in love, as glowingly happy as any bride in America today. As she passes me, I suddenly realize that the man on whose arm she is leaning—the father about to give her away—is also a woman.

The wedding ceremony is the standard one from the *Book of Common Prayer,* with three alterations: "Do you, 'Jane,' take 'Mary' to be your wedded spouse" (instead of "husband" or "wife"); "I pronounce you married" (instead of "man and wife") and "so long as you both shall live" is replaced by "as long as there's love."

As the newlyweds kiss with tenderness, Mama breaks into great heart-lurching sobs. What terrible burden of failure is she carrying, one wonders, what repulsion, what blinding inability to comprehend the choice her offspring has made, what a travesty is this day of all of her lifelong hopes and dreams? I find myself more involved with the mother in her pain than with the couple, wishing that I could somehow explain to her what I cannot fully understand myself.

It is not, I think, the notion of homosexual marriage that shocks or offends or even mystifies me particularly. It is the Gothic visual quality of the scene, the role playing—tragic and unnecessary aping of the "straight" world while defacing one's own identity—the need to play "The Bigstrong Man" and "The Little Woman" that saddens and appalls just as it saddens these days when enacted *in extremis* by men and women.

The bedrock of society shifts slowly, imperceptibly. But it does shift. What the homosexual wedding and the New Wedding express in common is the budding claim for Self, for dignity and autonomy, for alternatives and for change. Some lovers are dispensing with the marriage institution entirely and drawing up short-term renewable contracts, specifying who will do what and what are the arrangements in case of "divorce." Others, finding fulfillment in numbers, are entering group marriages ("Do you, Martha and Irving and Emily and Benjamin and Rosemary and Avery, take . . ."). And who can tell what is waiting in the wings?

The one constant, in all of this, is our undying hunger for the wedding ritual, with all of its apparently crucial qualities and ingredients. Even the New Wedding in its insistence—sometimes poignant, sometimes strident—on "personal relevance" is beginning already to fall into the predictable, repetitive mold of its conventional cousins and to become Kitsch: ho-hum, another sunrise ceremony in a cow pasture, yet another crunchy granola soufflé, yawn, those same old weary passages from *The Prophet* that we've heard at the last three weddings. In ten years will every white leather photo album entitled "My Wedding" close with the New Cliché—Susie and Jimmy, framed in a heart, lovingly passing a joint to one another? Will we have to reserve cow pastures six months in advance? And are the different drummers ultimately just banging out the same old beat?

That, as they say, remains to be seen.

Bibliography

BOOKS

Bowman, Henry Adelbert, *Marriage for Moderns*. New York, McGraw-Hill, 1965.

Braddock, Joseph, *The Bridal Bed*. New York, The John Day Company, 1961.

Bright, Diane, *The Wedding Planner*. Los Angeles, Nash, 1970.

Editors of *The Bride's Magazine, The Bride's Book of Etiquette*. New York, Grosset & Dunlap, 1967.

Emrich, Duncan, ed., *The Folklore of Weddings and Marriage*. New York, American Heritage Press, 1970.

Fielding, William J., *Strange Customs of Courtship and Marriage*. Garden City, N.Y., Garden City Books, 1960.

Goodsell, Willy Stine, Ph.D., *A History of Marriage and the Family*. New York, The Macmillan Co., 1939.

Hanson, Kitty, *For Richer, For Poorer*. New York, Abelard-Schuman, 1967.

Howard, George Elliott, Ph.D., *A History of Matrimonial Institutions*, Vol. I. Chicago, University of Chicago Press, 1904.

Mead, Margaret, *And Keep Your Powder Dry*: An Anthropologist Looks at America. New York, William Morrow, 1942.

Mitford, Jessica, *The American Way of Death*. New York, Simon & Schuster, 1963.

Proxmire, Ellen, Boggs, Barbara, and Poston, Gretchen, *The Wonderful Weddings Workbook*. Washington, D.C., Robert B. Luce, Inc., 1971.

Reich, Charles A., *The Greening of America*. New York, Random House, 1970.

Roszak, Theodore, *The Making of a Counter Culture*. Garden City, N.Y., Anchor Books, 1969.

Routtenberg, Lilly S., and Seldin, Ruth R., *The Jewish Wedding Book*. New York, Schocken Books, 1968.

Toffler, Alvin, *Future Shock*. New York, Random House, 1970.

Urlin, Ethel, and Hargreave, Lucy, *A Short History of Marriage*. Philadelphia, David McKay, 1914.

Westermarck, Edward, *A Short History of Marriage*. New York, Humanities Press, 1968.

Wood, Edward J., *The Wedding Day in All Ages and Countries*. Franklin Square, N.Y., Harper & Brothers, Publishers, 1869.

Zborowski, Mark, and Herzog, Elizabeth, *Life Is with People*. New York, Schocken Books, 1962.

MAGAZINE ARTICLES

Battelle, Phyllis, "The Sky-High Cost of Hotel Weddings." *McCall's*, June, 1969.

Davidson, Bill, "Nothing's Too Good for My Daughter!" *Saturday Evening Post*, August 13, 1966.

Diamondstein, Barbaralee, "Here Come the Brides!" *Good Housekeeping*, June, 1971.

Hawes, E., "Lady Who Marries the Best People." *McCall's*, June, 1969.

Howard, Robert West, "Slave Wench to Wife: 10,000 Years of the Wedding." *Jewelers' Circular Keystone*, May, 1968.

Malcolm, J., "On and Off the Avenue." *The New Yorker*, July 3, 1971.

McDonald, John, "Diamonds for the Masses." *Fortune*, December, 1964.

Mechen, T., "Where Have All the Orange Blossoms Gone?" *Mademoiselle*, January, 1971.

Moran, Nancy, "The Bride Goes Barefoot: Styles of The New Wedding." *New York Magazine*, September 9, 1970.

Pace, Peregrine, "The Wedding Rocket." *Cook*, June 10, 1969.

Schoenstein, Ralph, "On Your Mark . . . Get Set . . . *Marry!*" *Cosmopolitan*, November, 1970.

Simons, M., and Kaytor, M., "Luci's White House Wedding." *Cook*, August 9, 1966.

Stolley, Richard B., "The Day All the Daughters Left Home." *Life*, October 22, 1971.

(unsigned) "Able Bess's Spectacular." *Time*, December 8, 1967.

(unsigned) "Behind the Main Event." *Life*, June 18, 1971.

(unsigned) "Change, Yes——Upheaval, No." *Life*, January 8, 1971.

(unsigned) "Diamonds: The Grit behind the Glitter." *Forbes,* February 1, 1970.

(unsigned) "Flight from Fluff." *Time,* March 20, 1972.

(unsigned) "The Free-form Wedding Game." *Life,* September 26, 1969.

(unsigned) "Getting Married." *Gentlemen's Quarterly,* April, 1971.

(unsigned) "Many Hands Slice the Wedding Cake." *Business Week,* June 2, 1962.

(unsigned) "New Brides Ring Out the Old Traditions." *Business Week,* June 19, 1971.

(unsigned) "Percy-Rockefeller Weddings." *Life,* April 14, 1967.

(unsigned) "Queen of the Aisle." *Time,* December 23, 1968.

(unsigned) "Sign of the Times." *Time,* August 24, 1970.

NEWSPAPER ARTICLE

Fosburgh, Lacey, "New Fashions in Honeymoons: Hip, Super Hip, and Super Square." *The New York Times,* June 13, 1971.

Index